Brussels
Bruges & Antwerp

WHAT'S NEW | WHAT'S ON | WHAT'S BEST

www.timeout.com/brussels

Contents

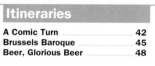

Don't Miss

Itineraries

Published by Time Out Guides Ltd
Universal House
251 Tottenham Court Road
London W1T 7AB
Tel: + 44 (0)20 7813 3000
Fax: + 44 (0)20 7813 6001
Email: guides@timeout.com
www.timeout.com

Managing Director Peter Fiennes
Editorial Director Ruth Jarvis
Business Manager Daniel Allen
Editorial Manager Holly Pick
Assistant Management Accountant Ija Krasnikova

Time Out Guides is a wholly owned subsidiary of Time Out Group Ltd.

© Time Out Group Ltd
Director & Founder Tony Elliott
Chief Executive Officer David King
Group Financial Director Paul Rakkar
Group General Manager/Director Nichola Coulthard
Time Out Communications Ltd MD David Pepper
Time Out International Ltd MD Cathy Runciman
Time Out Magazine Ltd Publisher/Managing Director Mark Elliott
Group Commercial Director Graeme Tottle
Group IT Director Simon Chappell

Time Out and the Time Out logo are trademarks of Time Out Group Ltd.

This edition first published in Great Britain in 2010 by Ebury Publishing
A Random House Group Company
Company information can be found on www.randomhouse.co.uk
Random House UK Limited Reg. No. 954009
10 9 8 7 6 5 4 3 2 1

Distributed in the US and Latin America by Publishers Group West (1-510-809-3700)
Distributed in Canada by Publishers Group Canada (1-800-747-8147)

For further distribution details, see www.timeout.com

ISBN: 978-1-84670-153-5

A CIP catalogue record for this book is available from the British Library.

Printed and bound in Germany by Appl.

The Random House Group Limited supports The Forest Stewardship Council (FSC), the
leading international forest certification organisation. All our titles that are printed on
Greenpeace approved FSC certified paper carry the FSC logo. Our paper procurement
policy can be found at www.rbooks.co.uk/environment.

Time Out carbon-offsets all its flights with Trees for Cities (www.treesforcities.org).

Brussels Shortlist

The **Time Out Brussels Shortlist** is one of a new series of guides that draws on Time Out's background as a magazine publisher to keep you current with what's going on in town. As well as Brussels' key sights and the best of its eating, drinking and leisure options, the guide picks out the most exciting venues to have recently opened and gives a full calendar of annual events. It also includes features on the important news, trends and openings, all compiled by locally based editors and writers. Whether you're visiting for the first time, or you're a regular, you'll find the *Time Out Brussels Shortlist* contains all you need to know, in a portable and easy-to-use format.

The guide divides central Brussels into five areas, each of which contains listings for Sights & Museums, Eating & Drinking, Shopping, Nightlife and Arts & Leisure, with maps pinpointing all their locations. At the front of the book are chapters rounding up these scenes city-wide, and giving a shortlist of our overall picks in a variety of categories. We include itineraries for days out, plus essentials such as transport information and hotels.

Our listings give phone numbers as dialled within Belgium. The area code for Brussels is 02. You need to include this code even when dialling from within the city. From outside Belgium, dial your country's international access code followed by the Belgian country code (32), 2 for Brussels (dropping the initial '0') and the number given in this guide.

We have noted price categories by using one to four € signs (€-€€€€), representing budget, moderate, expensive and luxury. Major credit cards are accepted unless otherwise stated. We have also indicated when a venue is NEW.

All our listings are double-checked, but places do sometimes close or change their hours or prices, so it's wise to call a venue before visiting. While every effort has been made to ensure accuracy, the publishers cannot accept responsibility for any errors that this guide may contain.

Venues are marked on the maps using symbols numbered according to their order within the chapter and colour-coded according to the type of venue they represent:

❶ Sights & Museums
❶ Eating & Drinking
❶ Shopping
❶ Nightlife
❶ Arts & Leisure

Map key

Major sight or landmark	⬛
Railway station	⬛
Park	⬛
Hospital/university	⬛
Pedestrian Area	⬜
Dual carriageway	▬▬
Main road	═══
Airport	✈
Church	✚
Metro station	Ⓜ
Tram line	‧‧‧‧‧
Metro line	▬▬
Area	IXELLES

Time Out **Brussels** Shortlist

EDITORIAL
Editor Gary Hills
Deputy Editor Elizabeth Winding
Copy Editors Hugh Graham,
Emma Howarth, Patrick Welch
Proofreader Mandy Martinez

DESIGN
Art Director Scott Moore
Art Editor Pinelope Kourmouzoglou
Senior Designer Kei Ishimaru
Group Commercial Designer
Jodi Sher

Picture Editor Jael Marschner
Acting Deputy Picture Editor
Liz Leahy
Picture Desk Assistant/Researcher
Ben Rowe

ADVERTISING
New Business & Commercial Director
Mark Phillips

International Advertising Manager
Kasimir Berger
International Sales Executive
Charlie Sokol

MARKETING
Sales & Marketing Director,
North America & Latin America
Lisa Levinson
Senior Publishing Brand Manager
Luthfa Begum
Group Commercial Art Director
Anthony Huggins
Marketing Co-ordinator Alana Benton

PRODUCTION
Group Production Manager
Brendan McKeown
Production Controller Katie Mulhern

CONTRIBUTORS
This guide was researched and written by Gary Hills. The editor would like to thank all the contributors to the *Time Out Brussels, Antwerp, Ghent & Bruges* city guide.

PHOTOGRAPHY
Photography by pages 7, 41,49, 86, 89, 134 Jonathan Perugia; pages 9, 12, 26, 28, 31, 65, 93, 101, 105,111, 115, 116, 120, 138, 140, 143, 144, 147, 151, 154, 156, 160 (bottom left),165, 172 Matthew Lea; pages 15, 18, 21, 24, 25, 42, 43, 48, 51, 52, 58, 61, 62,66, 71, 74, 79, 82, 90, 95, 98, 103, 112, 123, 129, 137, 169, 173 Oliver Knight; page 32 Greg Van Oz; page 33 OPT - Jean-Luc Flemal; page 37 Gaston Batistini, Labo River; page 38 OPT-Joseph Jeanmart; page 39 Daan Roose; page 50 Brasserie Cantillon; page 125 Paul Louis; page 133 Nicolas Borel, Atelier de Portzamparc 2009; page 160 (top) Musea Brugge; page 160 (bottom right) Jan Darhet/Toerisme Brugge; page 163 Toerisme Gent; page 175 Frederic Ducout.

The following images were provided by the featured establishments/artists: pages 51, 170, 176, 179, 180.

Cover photography: Buildings on La Grand Place. Credit: Photolibrary.com

MAPS
JS Graphics (john@jsgraphics.co.uk).

About **Time Out**

Founded in 1968, Time Out has expanded from humble London beginnings into the leading resource for those wanting to know what's happening in the world's greatest cities. As well as our influential what's-on weeklies in London, New York and Chicago, we publish nearly 30 other listings magazines in cities as varied as Beijing and Mumbai. The magazines established Time Out's trademark style: sharp writing, informed reviewing and bang up-to-date inside knowledge of every scene.

Time Out made the natural leap into travel guides in the 1980s with the City Guide series, which now extends to over 50 destinations around the world. Written and researched by expert local writers and generously illustrated with original photography, the full-size guides cover a larger area than our Shortlist guides and include many more venue reviews, along with additional background features and a full set of maps.

Throughout this rapid growth, the company has remained proudly independent, still owned by Tony Elliott four decades after he started Time Out London as a single fold-out sheet of A5 paper. This independence extends to the editorial content of all our publications, this Shortlist included. No establishment has been featured because it has advertised, and no payment has influenced any of our reviews. And, for our critics, there's definitely no such thing as a free lunch: all restaurants and bars are visited and reviewed anonymously, and Time Out always picks up the bill.
For more about the company, see www.timeout.com.

Don't Miss

Get the local experience

Over 50 of the world's top destinations available.

Grand'Place p52

Sights & Museums

High heel-twisting cobbles notwithstanding, the city's compact city centre is a delight to navigate on foot – and for further-flung jaunts, the public transport system of métro, rail, buses and trams is inexpensive and efficient.

Although it has its fair share of famous sights and grand museums, from the magnificent Grand'Place and masterpiece-filled Musées Royaux des Beaux-Arts to the famous Mannekin-Pis, unabashed by the throng of snap-happy visitors that pauses to watch him pee, the city also has unexpected sights to stumble across. Look up and you might spot an exquisite art nouveau façade; turn a corner and you could be confronted by a vast mural of a cartoon cowboy.

And if you thought of Brussels as grey and bureaucratic, head for its small but vibrant African area, the Matongé (see box p111). It may be the shortest of strolls from the offices and high rise blocks of the EU Quarter, but it's another world: here, grocers hawk chillis, manioc and dried fish, hairdressers do a roaring trade in extensions and gossip, and eateries serve up tasty mafé stews and marinated tilapia.

New developments

In recent years, the highest-profile addition to the city's sights has been the Musée Magritte (see box p86). It opened in summer 2009 in a grandly neo-classical building on place Royale, after months of work – during which the building was swathed in a giant, suitably surreal trompe l'oeil tarpaulin, inspired by Magritte's *L'Empire*

des Lumières. The museum has proved immensely popular, though to get a sense of the surrealist's unexpectedly ordinary lifestyle, you can't beat a visit to the modest suburban house in which he lived and worked, now a small museum (see p136).

On the outskirts of the city, meanwhile, work on the ambitious and much-needed reinvention of the Musée Royal de l'Afrique Centale (see box p104) is finally underway, after lengthy and delicate negotiations. The work isn't scheduled for completion until 2020, but the museum plans to stay open throughout.

In the same month that the Musée Magritte opened, another Belgian artistic icon was honoured with a major new museum just outside Brussels, in the university town of Louvain-la-Neuve. Georges Prosper Remi – better known as Hergé – was, of course, the creator of Tintin. Housed in a playful, ultra-modern building, the Musée Hergé is a must-visit for any fan of Tintin, Snowy and co.

Exploring the city

This book is divided by area, into a series of visitor-friendly concentrations of sights, shops, restaurants and bars.

At the heart of the city is the Lower Town. It takes in a tangle of medieval streets, a multitude of shops, bars and restaurants, the gay quarter, and sights as varied as the national opera house (Théâtre de la Monnaie; see p70) and the cheeky Mannekin-Pis statue (see box p58). Its epicentre is, of course, the Grand'Place (see p52), with its stately stone guildhalls, grandly Gothic town hall and crowds of camera-toting sightseers.

Belgium's love affair with the comic strip or *bande dessinée* is much in evidence in Lower Town, too. Classic characters loom large over the streets in a series of murals (see pp42-44), while the Centre Belge de la Bande Dessinée (see p52) showcases all the greats, in an old department store designed by the great art nouveau architect Victor Horta.

East of Lower Town – and ten minutes' walk uphill from the Grand'Place – is Upper Town, with the dignified rue Royale as its spine and the elegant, 18th-century Parc de Bruxelles at its centre. This was the stamping ground of the rich and powerful, whose legacy remains in the shape of royal palaces, grand squares and a wealth of magnificent museums.

The new Musée Magritte (see box p86) is the talk of the town, but the old-timers still have plenty to offer. You can wander amid paintings by Rubens, Van Dyck and Magritte at the Musées Royaux des Beaux-Arts (see p83), or head for an international array of modern masters: Francis Bacon, Dan Flavin, Claes Oldenburg et al. Here, too, is the Palais des Beaux-Arts (see p92) arts centre, whose popular moniker, Bozar, gives a good indication of its friendly, inclusive approach.

If the Upper Town has plenty of large-scale wonders – the cathedral (see p82), say, or King Léopold II's colossal, overblown Palais de Justice (see p87) – it also has its smaller gems, from the chichi little shops around the place du Grand Sablon to the Musée du Cinéma (see p92), whose screening room shows everything from spaghetti westerns to long-forgotten silent films.

East of Upper Town lies the EU Quarter. The high-rise offices and EU institutions may not appeal, but the district does have its attractions. Parc Léopold offers an overview of the area, and is home to the dinosaur-tastic Institut Royal des Sciences Naturelles (see p98) and the strange, violent paintings of the Musée Wiertz (see p100). From the park, it's the shortest of strolls to restaurant- and bar-flanked place Jourdain; at its centre, the neon sign of the celebrated Maison Antoine *friterie* (www.maisonantoine.be) exerts a siren song, dispensing fragrant cones of golden frites.

Although the construction of the EU Quarter caused the demise of numerous beautiful streets and townhouses (see box p101), the lovely parc du Cinquantenaire (see p95) survived. Its centrepiece triumphal arch was the handiwork of King Léopold II, known as the *koning-bouwer* or *roi-bâtisseur* (builder-king) thanks to his mania for construction projects; he left a less happy legacy in the Congo, which paid a heavy price for his grand schemes (see box p104).

A short stroll from the park is the beautiful, art nouveau Maison de Cauchie (see p99), with its sumptuously gilded art nouveau façade; once home to painter and architect Paul Cauchie, it's now a museum.

Bordering the EU Quarter is Ixelles, bisected by the broad avenue Louise. On the avenue's northern stretch, swish designer boutiques vie for shoppers' platinum cards and affections; at its southernmost end lies the leafy, lovely Bois de la Cambre – the perfect antidote to a morning at the shops.

Elsewhere, Ixelles is remarkable for its great variety. Its sweep encompasses rows of dignified townhouses, two tranquil ponds (the Etangs d'Ixelles), some delightfully idiosyncratic bars and restaurants, and a handful of interesting museums. Here, too, is the predominantly African Matongé quarter (see box p111) – a vibrant slice of urban life.

To the south of Ixelles, meanwhile, St-Gilles is a mix of down-at-heel streets and smart art nouveau houses and mansions, built in its 19th century heyday.

Musées Royaux des Beaux-Arts p83

Among them are architect Victor Horta's former home, the Musée Horta (see p126) and the grand Hôtel Hannon, which now houses the Espace Photographique Contretype (see p125).

The city's outlying areas, classed in this guide as Beyond the Centre, are not to be overlooked either. To the north, the green and pleasant Laeken boasts royal connections and a pleasingly eccentric array of attractions; below it, Schaerbeek and St-Josse are home to some stellar cultural venues, including Les Halles de Schaerbeek, Le Botanique and the swinging Jazz Station (for all, see p132). The old industrial areas to the west of the city centre, meanwhile, also have the odd tourist attraction, from Anderlech's historic brewery (see p135) to the unexpectedly small, suburban house where Magritte lived and worked (see p136).

Getting around

The centre of town, although uneven, is easy to navigate, with many traffic-free streets around the Grand'Place; the only real slog is the walk up to the Upper Town. Be cautious crossing roads, though: Belgian drivers favour a fast and furious approach, although a new speed limit within the inner ring road (see box p63) should improve matters. ARAU (02 219 33 45, www.arau.org), run by a not-for-profit local residents' group, organises themed walks.

If you can acquit yourself on a bicycle on busy roads, consider the city's urban cycling scheme, Villo!. For more on the scheme, and on cycling in the city, see p185.

If you don't feel confident on two wheels, Brussels' cheap, integrated public transport system (see p183) is made up of métro, rail, buses and trams.

SHORTLIST

Best new museums
- Musée Hergé (see p133)
- Musée Magritte (see p86)

Best for cartoon buffs
- Centre Belge de la Bande Dessinée (see p52)
- Lower Town murals (see pp42-44)
- Musée Hergé (see p133)

Best for architecture
- Galeries de St Hubert (see p64)
- Fondation pour l'Architecture (see p110)
- The Grand'Place (see p52)
- Maison de Cauchie (see p99)
- Musée Horta (see p126)

Best for art-lovers
- Musée Communal d'Ixelles (see p110)
- Musée Magritte (see p86)
- Musées Royaux des Beaux-Arts (see p83)

Unusual attractions
- Atomium (see p129)
- Bruparck (see p130)
- Musée BELvue (see p83)
- Musée du Cacao et du Chocolat (see p53)
- Musée Wiertz (see p100)

Best Baroque
- Eglise Notre-Dame du Finistère (see p53)
- The Grand'Place (see p52)
- Maison de Bellone (see p46)
- Notre-Dame du Bon Secours (see p53)

Best cultural polymaths
- Flagey (see p124)
- Palais des Beaux-Arts – Bozar (see p94)

World Class

Perfect places to stay, eat and explore.

Eating & Drinking

In 2010, Belgian restaurants were awarded a total of 114 Michelin stars – more per capita than France. Impressive as this is, you don't need to fork out Michelin-rated money to eat well in this little country – or in Brussels, with its 2,000 restaurants. Most of them have been around for years: if a new establishment arrives and doesn't come up to scratch, it soon closes. Brussels diners know what they like, and are not prepared to compromise on their expectations. The financial downturn seems to have had little impact on the dining scene, as cafés and restaurants remain packed out, at lunchtime as well as in the evening.

Drinking, meanwhile, is a key part of Belgian culture, just as ingrained with time, honour and smoke as the Gothic stones of the Grand'Place itself. At the centre of this culture is beer. Not just any old beer, but some 600 varieties in almost as many colours and flavours, brewed by everyone from Trappist monks to major multinational concerns.

Your choice of venues is as varied as the tipples on offer, running from no-frills pubs and late-night drinking dens to sophisticated style bars, where cocktail-sipping and flirting are more the order of the day.

New directions

As Breugel's vivid paintings and the banqueting scenes depicted in old Flemish tapestries testify, eating has always been a national pastime. Although Belgian-style cuisine still reigns supreme in

Whatever your carbon footprint, we can reduce it

For over a decade we've been leading the way in carbon offsetting and carbon management.

In that time we've purchased carbon credits from over 200 projects spread across 6 continents. We work with over 300 major commercial clients and thousands of small and medium sized businesses, which rely upon our market-leading quality assurance programme, our experience and absolute commitment to deliver the right solution for each client.

Why not give us a call?

T: London (020) 7833 6000

www.CarbonNeutral.com

Brussels, global influences are making their presence felt: you can feast on lemongrass-spiked red curry at Thai eatery Le Deuxième Element (see p113), dine on top-notch Indian cuisine in La Porte des Indes (see p114) or peruse the genre-defying menu at Bonsoir Clara (see p72), where dishes might include tuna with ginger and liquorice or goose liver crumble with rhubarb and glazed violets.

Seasonal ingredients and lighter styles of cooking are also becoming more of a focus. At the top end of the scale is the acclaimed Bon-Bon (93 rue des Carmelites, 02 346 66 15, www.bon-bon.be, closed Mon, Sun), in the outlying Uccle district. Here, chef Christophe Hardiquest's menus are a thrillingly moveable feast, changing from day to day according to market availability and in line with the seasons.

For more everyday prices, try the little Au Bain Marie (see p100) in the EU Quarter, open weekday lunchtimes only. The kitchen prides itself on its meatless, friteless menu, serving up great wedges of freshly made quiches, home-made pastas and verdant salads. Meanwhile, Exki (www.exki.be) has seen such a take-up of its inventive sandwiches, pastas and salads that it now has outposts all over town. This is fresh, ethical fast food at its best, with no sell-by dates; any leftovers are given to homeless charities at the end of each day.

A new organic restaurant that has made its mark is Soul (see p91), in the Upper Town, whose menu eschews additives, refined sugar, butter and cream in favour of nutritious, often organic ingredients.

Old favourites

In more traditional establishments such as Au Stekerlapatte (see p80), La Roue d'Or (see p63) or L'Esprit

SHORTLIST

Best for superior seafood
- La Quincaillerie (see p114)
- Restaurant Vincent (see p63)
- Sea Grill (see p64)

Most daring decor
- Cose Cosi (see p113)

Best for solid sustenance
- Au Stekerlapatte (see p80)
- Le Pré Salé (see p75)

Best for culinary sophisticates
- Bonsoir Clara (see p72)
- Comme chez Soi (see p59)
- Jaloa (see p73)

Best bargains
- Bosquet 58 (see p126)
- Le Cap Sablon (see p88)
- Aux Mille et Une Nuits (see p128)

Best for early-morning eats
- A la Clef d'Or (see p80)

Best for late-night refuelling
- Le Falstaff (see p59)
- La Grande Porte (see p80)

Best for beer-lovers
- A la Bécasse (see p56)
- Chez Moeder Lambic Fontainas (see p59)
- Délirium Café (see p59)

Best jukebox
- Goupil le Fol (see p60)

Best for laid-back cool
- Au Daringman (see p72)
- Fontainas (see p60)
- L'Horloge du Sud (see p114)

Best for night owls
- L'Atelier (see p110)
- L'Archiduc (see p77)
- Le Coq (p72)

Le Cirio p59

de Sel Brasserie (see p100), solid and sustaining meaty dishes are the mainstay. Among them are the ubiquitous steak-frites and *andouillette* – a massive sausage packed full of seasoned, springy innards. *Filet américain*, meanwhile, is raw, minced and spiced-up beef. The soft, pink patty of meat may look a little like cat food, but is surprisingly tasty. In hunting season, you might find venison, boar and wild hare from the forests of the Ardennes on the menu too.

Fussy presentation is generally frowned upon. Take *anguilles au vert*, a thick soupy affair in which chunks of eel lie suspended in a startling green sauce. A much safer bet, found on every trad Belgian menu, is *waterzooi*. Made with fish or chicken, this stew from Ghent is enriched with egg yolk and cream.

Seafood is a real strength: tiny shrimps (*crevettes grises*), sole and crab fresh from the North Sea, along with mussels and oysters from Zeeland. There are countless seafood restaurants to choose from, ranging from the timeless Restaurant Vincent (see p63) to

locals' favourite Jacques (see p73), or the übër-luxe, Michelin-starred Sea Grill (see p64).

But you don't need to spend a fortune to sample sparklingly fresh seafood. On place Ste-Catherine, Jeannot's seafood stall sells six kinds of raw *huîtres* (oysters) and *moules* (mussels), washed down with muscadet wine. Across from the Bourse, the more working-class Chez Jef & Fils van has been serving *escargots* (not the snails we know from France, but rubbery North Sea whelks) to regulars and passers-by for several generations.

Indeed, street food is big in Brussels. Paper cones of piping-hot frites are dispensed from little stalls dotted across the city – the best being Maison Antoine on place Jourdan. The chips are double-fried in beef dripping, and served with a bewildering array of sauces.

Those with a sweeter tooth can snack on the famous waffle, or *gaufre chaud*. The plain *gaufre de Liège*, sugary sweet but smaller, is popular, while the Brussels version is more full-on, with toppings such as cream and strawberries.

Forking out

Brussels is not particularly cheap when it comes to eating out, nor do all of its restaurants offer a set menu. The best bargains can generally be found at lunchtime, when you can order the plat du jour, often with a free glass of wine or a coffee thrown in.

Still, the price of spirits and wine is more reasonable than in other cities, and can help balance out the bill. Bills also come with service included, so there is no obligation to tip. Most diners leave a little extra; in smarter restaurants, a healthier contribution is expected.

Beer and bars

Beer is king in Brussels, with a heady array of brews and of bars in which to quaff them. As a starting point, it may be helpful to distinguish between *blonde* and *brune* (light or dark) types – and keep an eye on the alcohol content, generally marked on the menu.

If beer isn't your thing, try a *genever* (also known as *genièvre*, *junever* or *peket*), consumed neat or in a cocktail. Dutch in origin, this gin-like spirit is made from malt and juniper berries and is available in two basic types, *oude* and *jonge*. Add different flavourings and maturing processes into the equation and you end up with hundreds of varieties. Délirium Café (see p59) stocks around 500. Consuming them as a chaser with beer is known as a *kopstoot* (headbutt) – you have been warned.

Opening hours are gloriously lax in Brussels, and drinking until midnight almost anywhere in town is easy; past 1am, you'll need to be in the centre, where dawn is not an uncommon closing time. Smoking in restaurants is banned, but the regulations for bars are more flexible. Depending on their layout, and whether or not they serve food, bars can be all-smoking, have a designated smoking area or ban their customers from lighting up at all. If in doubt, check the door or window for the telltale little red circle.

Downtown drinking begins at the Grand'Place, which is lined with imposing, terraced guildhouse pubs where aproned waiters serve hulking portions of food. Prices are higher here, but not budget-bustingly so. Around it fans a large network of bar-studded streets.

South-westward snakes rue du Marché au Charbon, the spine of the gay quarter and Brussels' best bar-hop, sporting such treasures as the hip Fontainas (see p60) and buzzing Au Soleil (see p64). Follow the street to place Fontainas to reach Chez Moeder Lambic Fontainas (see p59), a sleek new arrival with a truly stellar array of draught beers.

Across boulevard Anspach, St-Géry is home to a clutch of stylish cafés and bars – including polished old-timer L'Archiduc (see p77), with its doorbell entry and decadently late opening hours.

Elsewhere, bars tend to reflect the area they serve. Sablon's are as glitzy as the neighbouring Marolles' are scuzzy. Ixelles' are a mixture of African (along rue de Longue Vie), trendy (around place St-Boniface), student-oriented (near Ixelles cemetery) and snobbish (avenue Louise). More modern establishments on the Ixelles-St-Gilles corridor are sure to have been trendified, while those in the heart of St-Gilles have a villagey feel; there's no fuss or flounce at locals' hangouts such as the Brasserie de l'Union (see p127). The pubs of the EU Quarter, meanwhile, provide expats with a drinking and networking facility.

FIND THE
Time Out
TOP SELECTION HERE!

SHOP  BRUSSELS

10,000 SHOPS, RESTAURANTS, BARS... ARE ON

WWW.SHOPINBRUSSELS.BE

provided by *Atrium*

Shopping

Although shopping doesn't loom large on the agenda for most visitors, trawling the city's quirkier boutiques can be tremendous fun. Brussels' little specialist shops offer everything from second-hand clothes and vinyl to antiques, bric-a-brac, homeware and comics – not to mention beer and chocolate. For an excellent overview of the city's shopping districts and highlights, check out www.shopinbrussels.be.

In 2010, the powers-that-be launched a late shopping night in the city centre, on Thursday. Shops are drip-dripping their way into the scheme, some dipping their toes, others going the whole mile. With strong unions and a strong desire for dinner, it's hard to tell how it will develop; check www.afterwork shopping.be for updates. Note that most shops are shut on Sundays and bank holidays, and smaller ones also close on Mondays.

Independent designers abound in the capital, but fashionistas should also consider a day trip to Antwerp (see pp138-155). The hometown of the renowned Antwerp Six group of designers, including Dries Van Noten and Ann Demeulemeester, is a mere 40 minutes away by train.

Around Grand'Place

Pedestrianised rue Neuve, Brussels' main shopping drag, is a rather soulless succession of chain stores, while most of the shops around the Grand'Place are squarely aimed at passing tourists, with chocolate, lace and suchlike.

You don't have to venture far to find richer pickings, however. North-east of Grand'Place are the

Bags packed, milk cancelled, house raised on stilts.

You've packed the suntan lotion, the snorkel set, the stay-pressed shirts. Just one more thing left to do – your bit for climate change. In some of the world's poorest countries, changing weather patterns are destroying lives.

You can help people to deal with the extreme effects of climate change. Raising houses in flood-prone regions is just one life-saving solution.

Climate change costs lives.
Give £5 and let's sort it *Here & Now*

www.oxfam.org.uk/climate-change

Be Humankind Oxfam

DON'T MISS

elegant, glass-roofed Galeries St-Hubert, opened in 1847 and the most famous of the city's covered shopping arcades. Divided into the Galerie du Roi, de la Reine and du Prince, they accommodate expensive, traditional boutiques selling lambskin gloves, hats, bags and the like.

To the south-east of Grand'Place, meanwhile, is rue des Eperonniers, with its quirky old-fashioned gift shops, while to the south-west, rue du Midi has camera and art shops. Boulevards Anspach and Maurice Lemmonier are dotted with comic shops, second-hand book and record stores and an assortment of dusty but quirky little businesses. In between, rue des Pierres and rue du Marché au Charbon are home to a mix of vintage clothes shops and streetwear boutiques.

Offbeat chic

West of boulevard Anspach lies St-Géry – the epicentre of cool when it comes to fashion and design. The unstoppable rise of rue Antoine Dansaert began in the mid 1980s, when the fashion-forward Stijl (see p77) opened; now, Dansaert and its surrounding streets are home to all manner of hip boutiques. Standouts include Annemie Verbeke's chic knits, the fab footwear at Hatshoe and Christophe Coppens' wonderful hats (for all, see p76) – worn by the likes of Rihanna and Beth Ditto.

Running from the southern end of Dansaert, rue des Chartreux is a bastion of independent traders and fashion boutiques. There's an appealing community feel, a sprinkling of tea shops and some fine vintage attire and bric-a-brac to peruse at the likes of Gabriele Vintage (see p76), new arrival Brocéliande (no.44, mobile 0477 353 607) and Boutique Lucien Cravat (no.24, 02 647 04 54).

SHORTLIST

Best for market-browsing
- Antiques market, place du Grand Sablon (see p24)
- Flea market, place Jeu de Balle (see p80)

Best comic-book emporium
- Brüsel (see p66)

Best for vintage finds
- Gabriele Vintage (see p76)
- Idiz Bogam (see p76)
- Look 50 (see p118)
- Modes (see p80)

Best of Belgian
- Annemie Verbeke (see p76)
- La Boutique Tintin (see p64)
- Martin Margiela (see p77)
- Rue Blanche (see p76)

Best for cutting-edge fashionistas
- Mapp (see p76)
- Own Shop (see p77)
- Stijl (see p77)

Best accessories
- Annick Tapernoux (see p76)
- Christa Reniers (see p76)
- Christophe Coppens (see p76)
- Delvaux (see p91)

Best for bookworms
- Filigranes (see p102)
- Fnac (see p67)

Best for sweet tooths
- AM Sweet (see p75)
- Dandoy (see p67)
- Pierre Marcolini (see p91)
- Wittamer (see p91)

Best for children
- Grasshopper (see p67)
- Kat en Muis (see p76)
- Serneels (see p121)

Antiques and boutiques

Sablon is the place to go for antiques. Pricey establishments can be found along rue Lebeau, rue des Minimes and **place du Grand Sablon**, where an antiques market is held every weekend. More affordable – and exotic – antiques shops are found down below on rues Blaes and Haute, in the Marolles neighbourhood; on rue Blaes, browse the different dealers' stalls at Les Memoires de Jacqmotte, then sift through the vintage clobber at Modes (for both, see p81). In the centre is place du Jeu de Balle, site of a daily flea market (see p80); seriously dedicated bargain-hunters turn up as early as 6am.

Heading down into Ixelles, avenue Louise and boulevard de Waterloo are where serious sums are splashed in the likes of Chanel, Gucci, Cartier, Cacharel and Bulgari – just a sprinkling of the big names dotted along these two wide, tree-lined streets.

Avenue de la Toison d'Or (the name given to the southern side of boulevard de Waterloo) is more mid-range, featuring the likes of Massimo Dutti and Petit Bateau. The three galeries leading off it, de la Toison d'Or, Porte Louise and Espace Louise, offer a mix of high-street and designer labels.

Halfway along avenue Louise, running west, is rue du Bailli. Along here, and radiating into the surrounding streets, gift shops and clothing boutiques are interspersed with chic cafés and restaurants, which converge around place du Châtelain. Shoe shops abound.

Delectable comestibles

It would take a will of iron to come to Brussels and not buy chocolate. Two of the finest establishments stand on place du Grand Sablon: the grandest dame of them all, Wittamer, and the chic Pierre Marcolini (for both, see p91).

For biscuits, try AM Sweet (see p75), which also has a charming café, or drop by Dandoy (see p67). Founded in 1829 and aptly located on rue au Beurre, the latter is best known for its melt-in-the-mouth *speculoos* (spicy, cinnamon-spiked ginger biscuits).

Dandoy

Music Village p27

Nightlife

It may not have the scope of the likes of New York or London, or the edginess of Berlin, but Brussels' nightlife is in fine fettle.

Closing time in the city's myriad bars may be gloriously late, but it's worth tearing yourself away from the beer pumps to sample the club scene. It's a mix of sleek, cocktail-fuelled hangouts and eclectic experimental nights, with one or two larger-scale clubs and a liberal sprinkling of underground parties and one-nighters to keep things interesting.

In terms of live music, there's plenty of variety too. A new wave of home-grown talents such as Absynthe Minded and the Vogues are touted to follow in the footsteps of Soulwax, Belgium's biggest success story to date, while plenty of international names also make a stop-off at Brussels' characterful venues. Whether you're into jazz, rock, world music, nu-folk, post-punk, pop, indie, electronica or all of the above, chances are you'll find a gig to fit the bill.

Club culture

Considering how compact Brussels is, the club scene is surprisingly varied and can be both heady and very hedonistic. Some venues have been around for years; others open and close with alarming regularity.

Chief among the long-standing stalwarts is the famous Fuse (see p81), launched in 1994. Expect two floors of pumping techno, peerless resident DJs (Pierre, Deg and Peter Van Hoesen) and globally-renowned guest DJs (the likes of Jeff Mills, Laurent Garnier and Derrick May)

Fuse p81

taking to the decks. Fuse also hosts La Démence (*see right*), the monthly gay super-club.

If you'd prefer a more intimate soirée, head for the small but perfectly formed Bazaar (see p81), Dali's Bar (see p69) or Marquee (see p92); for eclectic electro sounds and more space to dance, try Beursschouwburg Café (see p77) or Recyclart (see p81).

Various full-on one-nighters such as Catclub (www.catclub.be) and Libertine/Supersport (see p136) pad out the regular club calendar, along with a whole host of more loosely planned, unpredictable underground parties. Blink and you might miss something decent, but keep your eyes out for flyers in bars and record shops around town and also in venues like Le Soixante (see p69) and you'll be surprised at how much is going on. An up-to-date online resource for insider information on club nights and parties large and small is www.noctis.com.

Out and proud

The hub of Brussels' gay scene remains the area around the Bourse in Lower Town – and, in particular, bar-lined Marché au Charbon. An evening's bar-hopping could take in the likes of the hip L'Homo Erectus (see p69), frenetic goodtimes bar, Boy's Boudoir (see p69), or laid-back, long-standing favourite Le Belgica (see p68). Closing times are late, but the flip side is that many bars shut up shop Monday to Wednesday, so you might want to plan your trip accordingly.

It's in clubbing rather than hip bars that this city really excels, though – and a little forward planning pays dividends. The monthly parties thrown by La Démence (see p81) are the stuff of legend – or perhaps fantasy – with thousands of revellers from across Europe hitting the dancefloor or getting acquainted in the darkroom. Otherwise, Sunday's tea dance at Smouss Café (see p69) is a good bet, and scene stalwart the Box (see p77) doesn't seem to need any sleep, as it's open every night of the week.

Pump up the volume

Long known for its jazz affiliations, Brussels has expanded its musical horizons in recent years. Among the hippest hangouts are the multi-talented likes of Le Botanique (see p132) and Café Central (see p77), whose programmes mix gigs, DJ sets and one-off events with enviable aplomb, spanning folk, rock, electronica, indie and plenty more besides. Flemish cultural centre Beursschouwburg (see p77) takes a similarly offbeat approach, while Recyclart (see p81), a former railway station in Lower Town, is big on electronica.

Old-timer Ancienne Belgique (see p68) remains a fine spot at which to mosh, thanks to a massive refurbishment, while Magasin 4 (see p136) went one step further, moving into bigger and better premises in 2010 but retaining its anarchic, anything-goes spirit.

Jazz is, as ever, a huge presence on the city's musical agenda – and never more so than during May's Jazz Marathon (see p35) or the huge Skoda Jazz Festival (see p40). For the rest of the year, venues range from the diminutive, dapper likes of L'Archiduc (see p77) to Jazz Station (see p132), Music Village (see p69) and Sounds Jazz Club (see p122).

World-music aficionados fare well here, too, with African beats around the Matongé quarter (look out for posters), Flemish folk and flamenco at La Tentation (see p75) and one of Europe's biggest world music festivals, Couleur Café (www.couleurcafe.be), held in June at the sprawling, former industrial Tour et Taxis complex (see p136) in Molenbeek.

SHORTLIST

Best for hardcore clubbing
- Catclub (see left)
- Factory (see p69)
- Fuse (see p81)

Best for drinking and flirting
- Bazaar (see p81)
- Marquee (see p92)
- MP3 Disco Bar (see p78)
- Le Soixante (see p69)

Best all-rounders
- Beursschouwburg (see p77)
- Le Botanique (see p132)
- Café Central (see p77)
- Recyclart (see p81)

Best offbeat gems
- Grain d'Orge (see p121)
- Madame Moustache et son Freakshow (see p78)
- La Soupape (see p122)
- VK Club (see p136)

Best gay gatherings
- La Démence (see p81)
- Sunday Tea Dance at Smouss Café (see p69)

One-night wonders
- Catclub (see left)
- Libertine/Supersport (see p136)

Great gig venues
- Ancienne Belgique (see p68)
- Cirque Royale (see p92)
- Le Botanique (see p132)
- Halles de Schaerbeek (see p132)
- Magasin 4 (see p136)

Best jazz haunts
- L'Archiduc (see p77)
- Jazz Station (see p132)
- Music Village (see p69)
- Sounds Jazz Club (see p122)

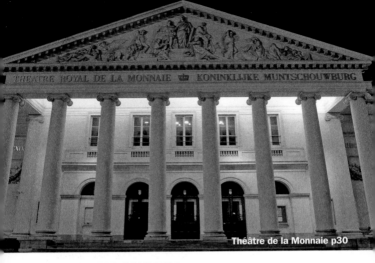

Théâtre de la Monnaie p30

Arts & Leisure

In Belgium, the performing arts are seen as an essential part of the nation's cultural life. As such, performances are often government-subsidised to allow everyone to afford them, whether it's strictly classical fare or fluffy revue. Top end tickets can still be expensive, though, particularly for opera, but aren't bad compared to elsewhere in Europe.

The big challenge facing Brussels' cultural scene remains the French-Flemish language divide. The city's official bilingual status means that spoken word theatre is organised along strict language lines – particularly in the bigger subsidised production houses, which rely on money from their regional governments.

With its international and all-inclusive programming, the vibrant Kunsten Festival des Arts (see box p35) is an inspiring exception to the rule, while the city's contemporary dance scene, being free of the spoken word, is among the best in the world.

Cinephiles will also fare well here, with an impressive array of independent cinemas, hotly-anticipated film festivals and cinematic events.

Film

With plenty of original language offerings, reasonably priced tickets, and seasonal events galore, Brussels is brilliant for film buffs.

The state-of-the-art Kinepolis (see p130) and UGC cinema (see p124) screen big-budget releases in some style, especially at weekends. Meanwhile, smaller cinemas around town show a heady mix of arthouse flicks and repertory films, from the swish Arenberg Galeries (see p70) to the eccentric Nova (3 rue d'Arenberg (02 511 24 77, www.nova-cinema.com) or much-loved, delightfully down-at-heel Styx (see p124).

Best of all, perhaps, is the Musée du Cinema (see p92), with a line-up chock-full of cinematic gems – this could be your big chance to see Greta Garbo in *Anna Karenina*, or catch a '60s Japanese Godzilla flick. The silent film screenings, with piano accompaniment, are not to be missed.

Now held at the multi-talented Flagey (see p124) cultural centre in Ixelles, the Brussels International Film Festival (see p35) showcases rising talents alongside prestigious European names over eight days in June.

Other treats include animation festival Anima (see p32), which celebrates its thirtieth anniversary in 2011; amid a tightly-packed programme, look out for sneak previews of big US and Japanese releases along with film-making masterclasses, hands-on workshops aimed at children and talks from an assortment of special guests.

Meanwhile, horror flick fans flock to the gory Brussels International Festival of Fantastic Film (see p33), which takes in late-night screenings of some seriously weird cinema, along with a zombie parade through town, a body painting contest and the eagerly-anticipated vampire's ball. Bring your fangs and tux.

From July to September, the Ecran Total season at the Arenberg Galeries shows retrospectives and new films from around the globe, while drive-in movies (see p36) are screened in the EU Quarter's lovely Parc du Cinquantenaire on selected summer evenings.

SHORTLIST

Best for arthouse aficionados
- Actors Studio (see p69)
- Nova (see left)
- Styx (see p124)
- Vendôme (see p124)

Offbeat films and oddities
- Brussels International Festival of Fantastic Film (see p33)
- Musée du Cinema (see p92)

Don't-miss cinematic events
- Anima (see p32)
- Brussels International Film Festival (see p35)
- Drive-in movies, Parc du Cinquantenaire (see p36)

Best for cutting-edge dance
- Chapelle des Brigittines (see p30)
- Halles de Schaerbeek (see p132)
- Kaaitheaterstudio's (see p78)

Best cultural hubs
- Beursschouwburg (see p77)
- Flagey (see p124)
- Halles de Schaerbeek (see p132)
- Palais des Beaux-Arts (see p94)

Best for classical music buffs
- Ars Musica (see p33)
- Conservatoire Royal de Bruxelles (see p92)
- Palais des Beaux-Arts (see p94)

Best bargains
- Half-price theatre tickets from Arsène 50 (see p31)
- Free concerts at the Eglise des Sts Jean et Etienne aux Minimes (see p92)

DON'T MISS

Dance

Belgium shines when it comes to modern dance. Anna Teresa De Keersmaeker, director of the Rosas company (www.rosas.be), Wim Vandekeybus of Ultima Vez (www. ultimavez.com) and Alain Platel and his boldly physical collective, Les Ballets C de la B (www.les balletscdela.be), are among its global success stories; the influential Charleroi/Danses (www.charleroi-danses.be) is another company to look out for.

In recent years, Sidi Larbi Cherkaoui, a young, Belgian-born choreographer of Moroccan descent, has collaborated with everyone from London-born kathak and contemporary dance virtuoso Akram Khan and flamenco dancer Maria Pagés to a group of Shaolin monks, to great acclaim. His new dance company, Eastman, is in residence at Antwerp's Toneelhuis theatre (www.toneelhuis.be).

Perhaps the most atmospheric of Brussels' dance venues is the 17th-century Chapelle des Brigittines (1 petite rue des Brigittines, 02 506 43 00, www.brigittines.be), a stripped-down decommissioned church in Lower Town that also hosts a summer dance festival.

The Halles de Schaerbeek (see p132) also afford a splendid and versatile showcase for visiting dance companies, while the esoteric performances at the intimate Kaaitheaterstudio's (see p78) are a delight. It's also worth checking the schedule at the mighty Palais des Beaux-Arts, better known as Bozar (see p94), which includes everything from African to Indian dance.

For classical ballet, look out for visiting international companies, and for performances by the Royal Ballet of Flanders (www.konink lijkballetvanvlaanderen.be).

Classical music & opera

Refreshingly, classical music is a genuinely egalitarian part of the city's cultural scene, attracting a wide audience wearing everything from jeans and trainers to frocks and fox furs. The splendid, 19th-century national opera house, Théâtre de la Monnaie (see p70), sets the tone with a vibrant, unstuffy programme that mixes new works with genuinely innovative stagings of the classics; it also attracts some big-name stars and directors.

Heading up the National Orchestra, Austrian-born Walter Weller has introduced a series of cycles by Schubert, Beethoven and Mahler at the prestigious Bozar (see p94); other important venues include Flagey (see p124) and the Conservatoire Royal de Bruxelles (see p92).

Churches, theatres and cultural centres dotted around the city also host concerts and events. The Chapelle Royale (see p92) is a little gem, while the Eglise des Sts Jean et Etienne aux Minimes (see p92) is home to the Minimes choir and orchestra, who perform Bach's cantatas; the church also hosts a series of free lunchtime concerts each summer. Details on all concerts can be found every Thursday in *The Bulletin*, or at tourist information offices.

The Festival of Flanders and Festival of Wallonia (for both, see p35) are key dates on the musical calendar, with extensive programmes. Contemporary classical music fans should also check out the annual Ars Musica festival (see p33).

Another major event is the Concours Musical International Reine Elisabeth de Belgique (see p33), a prestigious annual competition for young musicians,

Nova p29

composers and singers. The focus alternates from year to year between violin, piano and voice and the final concert is held at Bozar; the others take place at the Conservatoire Royal de Bruxelles. If you can't get tickets for the final, don't despair; it's shown on Belgian TV, and online at www.cmireb.be.

Theatre

Two of Belgium's most generous arts subsidies go to the Koninklijke Vlaamse Schouwburg (Royal Flemish Theatre; see p78) and the Théâtre National (see p70). Both are resolutely representative of their language communities, and there's little crossover between them.

For the more adventurous theatregoer, smaller venues such as the long-running Théâtre 140 (see p132) lead the pack, while political posturing takes place at the tiny Théâtre de Poche (see p124). Beursschouwburg (see p77) has some avant-garde, boundary-blurring offerings, while local and international theatre companies jostle for space on the stage at Kaaitheater (see p78), with plenty

of English-language performances.

Meanwhile, the diminutive Théâtre du Toone (see p70) offers a very different experience, with its world-class marionette productions of the likes of *Hamlet* and *Faust* – in Bruxellois dialect, mind – and a rather nice bar in which to imbibe a post-performance pint or two.

The best listings can be found in *The Bulletin* on Thursdays and in *Le Soir* on Wednesdays. Tickets are inexpensive, and most venues offer concessions. It's safest to call in advance but you can also buy tickets through online booking services such as www.fnac.be and www.ticketclic.be.

Bear in mind, too, that most theatres offload their unsold tickets with Arsène 50 (www.arsene50.be), which sells them at half price plus a €1 booking fee.

Note that venues are mostly closed in the summer, when arts festivals (see pp32-40) take over the city. The one truly international event is the wonderful Kunsten Festival des Arts (see box p35) in May, which boldly leaps into the artistic unknown, often yielding rich rewards in the process.

Calendar

Jazz Marathon p35

Special events and festivals of every stripe and scale take place in Brussels, Antwerp and Bruges, running from dignified classical music shindigs to edgy film festivals, offbeat arts gatherings and age-old rituals: Belgians delight in tradition and folklore, so don't be surprised if you stumble across an unexplained procession of giant mannequins or a marching band – just join in the fun.

One spectacular event in Bruges is the Procession of the Holy Blood (www.holyblood.org); dates vary from year to year, as it's held on Ascension Thursday. Lavish biblical floats, booming brass bands and costume-clad horsemen take to the streets, watched by thousands of visitors.

For further details on seasonal events, contact the relevant tourist information offices (see p188).

January

Ongoing Ice Skating (see Dec); Marché de Noël (see Dec); Bruges Christmas Market (see Nov)

Mid-late January **Belgian Gay & Lesbian Film Festival**
Various venues, Brussels
www.fglb.org
Founded in 1986, the festival is in fine fettle. As well as screenings, expect exhibitions, debates, an opening party and a European gala evening.

March

Early Mar **Anima**
Flagey, Brussels, see p124
www.animatv.be
This international festival brings a feast of shorts, films, features and all things animated to the city, along with retrospectives, masterclasses, children's workshops and guest speakers.

Early Mar-early Apr **Ars Musica**
Various venues across Belgium
www.arsmusica.be
A splendid celebration of new composers and contemporary classical music, with a particular eye for up-and-coming talent.

Mid Mar **Brussels International Festival of Fantastic Film**
Tour et Taxis, Molenbeek, Brussels
www.bifff.org
The BIFFF is a two-week horror and sci-fi shindig, with over 150 films from around the world. There's a Vampire's Ball, too; entrance in costume only.

Mid Mar **Cinema Novo**
Various venues, Bruges
www.cinemanovo.be
Founded in 1983, this ten-day festival screens films from Africa, Asia and Latin America.

April

Ongoing Ars Musica (see Mar)

Late Apr-mid May **Meifoor**
Around 't Zand, Bruges, see p156
A month long funfair, held at 't Zand and the adjoining park.

May

Early May-mid June **Concours Musical International Reine Elisabeth de Belgique**
The Conservatoire Royal de Bruxelles (see p92) and Bozar (see p94), Brussels
www.concours-reine-elisabeth.be
A prestigious competition for young professional musicians and singers.

Early May **Choco-Laté**
Museum of Bruges
www.choco-late.be
Four days of tastings, walks and talks of a chocolatey nature; note that some years the festival moves to Maastricht.

May **Kunsten Festival des Arts**
Various venues, Brussels
www.kfda.be

Unusually, this three week festival crosses Brussels' French–Flemish linguistic divide, taking in theatre, dance, music and more.

May **Zinneke**
Various venues, Brussels
www.zinneke.org
A huge biennial carnival-style parade.

Mid May **Dring Dring Bike Festival**
Parc du Cinquantenaire, Brussels, see p95
www.bikeexperience.be
A friendly, week-long cycling festival, with bike hire, tours and workshops.

Mid May **Lesbian & Gay Pride**
Various venues, Brussels
www.thepride.be
Thousands of revellers throng the city streets for Brussels' buzzing, three-day Pride; dressing-up, a grand parade, DJs and debates are all part of the fun.

Mid May **Les Nuits Botanique**
Le Botanique, Brussels, see p132
www.myspace.com/nuitsbotanique

Ommegang p36

1000s of
things to do...

**TIME OUT GUIDES
WRITTEN BY
LOCAL EXPERTS**
visit timeout.com/shop

International indie bands rock the various rooms, marquees and gardens at the Botanique cultural centre.

Late May **Jazz Marathon**
Various venues, Brussels
www.brusselsjazzmarathon.be
Three days of free jazz performances put a swing in the city's step. The 2010 event attracted over 300,000 fans.

Last Sun in May **Brussels 20km**
Parc du Cinquantenaire, Brussels, see p95
http://20km.chronorace.be
Some 20,000 runners enter this long-established race, which starts and finishes at the Parc du Cinquantenaire.

June

Ongoing Concours Musical International Reine Elisabeth de Belgique (see May)

June **Brussels International Film Festival**
Various venues, Brussels
www.fffb.be
The city's film festival features various themes, with Belgian films shown alongside shorts and European/US mainstream and arthouse pictures.

Mid June **Battle of Waterloo**
Waterloo Visitors' Centre, Braine l'Alleud
www.1815.be
A large-scale, visually stunning re-enactment of the battle takes place every five years in this Brussels suburb; the next is set for 2015.

June-Sept **Festival of Wallonia**
Various venues in Brussels & Wallonia
www.festivaldewallonie.be
Belgian and international orchestras play all over francophone Belgium, in venues ranging from small churches to major concert halls.

June-Oct **Festival of Flanders**
Various venues in Flanders
www.festival.be

Festival fever at KFDA

Brings the Flemish and French together.

The wackily named Kunsten festivaldesarts (see p33) has method in its madness. Known simply as the KFDA, it started up in 1992 when festival director Frie Leysen decided to launch a performing arts festival to cross the language divide in Brussels. Thus the name, Kunsten Festival in Dutch and Festival des Arts in French – all melded together in a melting pot of a moniker.

Leysen succeeded: to this day, the KFDA remains the only major arts festival in Belgium where the two language communities truly work together. Now under the leadership of Christophe Slagmuylder, the KFDA co-produces around 30 international projects each year, including theatre, dance and visual art. For three weeks each May, Brussels is taken over by the festival, regarded as one of the most innovative and progressive in Europe.

Two British companies have been festival favourites over the years: Sheffield's brilliantly experimental Forced Entertainment and Brighton-based Lone Twin, who in 2010 presented their internationally acclaimed Catastrophe Trilogy.

As an audience member, you'll have a ball. On average, tickets are around €15, and a festival pass (€130) will afford you entry to the entire programme. And the fun doesn't end when the curtain comes down, with DJs playing in the festival hub at the Beursschouwburg (see p77).

This classical music behemoth comprises eight separate festivals, with different themes in the big Flemish cities.

Late June **Antwerp Pride**
Various venues, Antwerp
www.antwerppride.com
Four days of parties, singalongs, sports events, city tours, exhibitions and more, promoting Antwerp's gay and lesbian-friendly credentials.

Last Tue in June **Ommegang**
Grand'Place, Brussels, see p52
www.ommegang.be
A spectacular parade of locals dressed up as nobles, jesters and peasants march from Sablon to the Grand'Place, commemorating the arrival of Charles V, the new emperor of the Spanish Netherlands, 500 years ago. It ends with a horse parade, stilt-fighting and jousting in the Grand'Place.

July

Ongoing Festival of Wallonia
(see June); Festival of Flanders
(see June)

Early July **Brosella Jazz & Folk Festival**
Théâtre de Verdure, Parc d'Osseghem, Laeken, Brussels
www.brosella.be
A free, three-day, outdoor festival of folk and jazz. Take a picnic along for the Sunday afternoon.

Early July **Cactus Festival**
Minnewater Park, Bruges
www.cactusfestival.be
This small, single-stage music festival attracts wonderfully varied artists, from Balkan Beat Box to Elvis Costello.

First Thur in July **Ommegang**
Grand'Place, Brussels, see p52

July-Sept **Drive-in movies**
Esplanade du Cinquantenaire, Brussels see p95
www.driveinmovies.be
At 10.30pm on Friday and Saturday evenings in July and 10pm in August,

the Parc du Cinquantenaire turns into a drive-in cinema, with first-rate sound.

July-Aug **Zomer van Antwerpen**
Various venues, Antwerp
www.zva.be
Summer in Antwerp brings an eight-week extravaganza of circus workshops, concerts, open-air film and theatre, at locations across the city.

Mid July-mid Aug **Foire du Midi**
Boulevard du Midi, Lower Town, Brussels
www.foiredumidi.be
Each year the largest travelling funfair in Europe sets up along a stretch of Brussels' inner ring road. Families enjoy the rides until early evening, when a more adult crowd arrives.

21 July **National Day**
Various venues across Belgium
National Day is taken seriously in Belgium – particularly in Brussels. The royals are out in force and there's a big military parade. The rest of the day settles down into family-friendly fairs, neighbourhood celebrations and late-night fireworks.

August

Ongoing Festival of Wallonia (see June); Festival of Flanders (see June); Drive-in movies (see July); Zomer van Antwerpen (see July); Foire du Midi (see July)

9 Aug **Meyboom (Planting of the Maytree)**
Rue des Sables & rue du Marais, Lower Town, Brussels
www.meyboom.be
This ancient ceremony dates back to 1308, and relates to fighting off rebels from Louvain and giving thanks to Saint Laurent, whose symbol is the fabled tree. It's also an excuse to dress up, parade around the city with the tree, plant it, then party into the night.

Mid Aug **Benenwerk**
Various venues, Bruges
www.benenwerk.be

Tapis des Fleurs p39

Christmas cheer

Markets and mulled wine.

Marché de Noël p40

Christmas in Belgium seems to get bigger every year, with festive markets in Brussels, Bruges and Antwerp the main draw for yuletide visitors.

Since the decision was made in 2001 to move Brussels' market out of the Grand'Place (it had become an overcrowded danger zone), it has extended along the streets to Ste-Catherine, covering almost two kilometres. In 2009, around 3.5 million people trod the festive path, passing 220 market stalls selling everything from garish candles to reindeer hats.

It still all starts on the Grand'Place, though – a stunning natural theatre set for Christmas. Electricity company Electrabel is currently sponsoring the deal, which means the square is imaginatively illuminated with spots and lasers. In 2009, an electric-blue tree formed the centre point of a laser show picking out the Baroque relief of the square. A scaffolding gateway leads you from the square to the market proper, which begins at the back of the Bourse and follows a festively lit trail across boulevard Anspach and onward to Ste-Catherine. Each market stall is a little wooden-roofed hut (some with illuminated sheep), selling mainly arts and crafts or food and drink, all of them having a pan-European flavour, tying Brussels in neatly with the utopian single-market dream.

By the time you reach place Ste-Catherine and the quays beyond, not only are you decently warmed up, but you're at the heart of the festivities. The quaint stalls continue, punctuated every now and again by merry-go-rounds, the largest travelling big-wheel in Europe (with 18,000 lights) and, of course, a skating rink. Set up for the whole month, it's overlooked by a Liberace-style mirror ball, throwing pinpoints on the old gabled houses. It's here that the crowds gather and settle; in the beer tents, at the food stands and in the surrounding restaurants and bars, as they watch their kids or mates glide along. The festive atmosphere is thick and warm, as is the mulled wine, both doing a good job of helping keep out the bitter cold.

Its name translates as 'legwork' – and there's plenty of that, with free lessons in foxtrot, salsa, tango and lindy hop.

Mid Aug **Jazz Middelheim**
Park Den Brandt, Antwerp
www.jazzmiddelheim.be
Expect big headliners – the legendary like of Cassandra Wilson or the mighty Toots Thielemans.

Mid Aug **Reiefeest (Festival on the Canals)**
Various venues, Bruges
www.reiefeest.be
This dazzling sound and light show features hundreds of performers and celebrates the city's history. It's held once every three years; the next is 2011.

Mid Aug **Tapis des Fleurs**
Grand'Place, Brussels, see p52
www.flowercarpet.be
The square is covered by an elaborate floral carpet (tapis), made up of a million cut begonia heads. The balcony of the Hôtel de Ville affords an aerial view.

Mid-end Aug **Brussels Summer Festival**
Various venues, Brussels
www.bsf.be

Ten days of rock, pop and world music in venues across town from superclubs to smaller bars, there are also outdoor shows in the Grand'Place.

September

Ongoing Festival of Wallonia (see June); Festival of Flanders (see June); Drive-in movies (see July)

Early Sept **Journées du Patrimoine**
Various venues, Brussels
www.monument.irisnet.be
A once-a-year chance to peek inside hundreds of historical buildings, usually closed to the general public.

Early-mid Sept **Brussels Gay Sports**
Various venues, Brussels
www.bgs.org
Started up in 1991, this gay sports day has become an institution, with hundreds of competitors. It's a social event too, with an after-party, a gay tour of the city and a closing Sunday brunch.

Late Sept **Jazz Brugge**
Various venues, Bruges
www.jazzbrugge.be

Zinneke p33

DON'T MISS

This biennial feast of jazz is a real must for fans of the genre, featuring performances, documentaries, workshops, vinyl exchange and exhibitions.

October

Ongoing Festival of Flanders
(see June)

Oct-Nov **Circuses**
Various locations, Brussels
Various circuses visit Brussels in late autumn, sometimes staying until Christmas and the New Year. Regulars include the Bouglione in place Flagey and the Florilegio at the Hippodrome de Boitsfort; look out for posters.

Oct-Dec **Skoda Jazz Festival**
Various venues across Belgium
www.skodajazz.be
An impressive array of jazz, blues, hip hop and avant-garde artists and bands perform in 16 Belgian cities, including Brussels, Antwerp and Ghent.

November

Ongoing Circuses (see Oct);
Skoda Jazz Festival (see Oct)

Early Nov **Independent Film Festival**
Centre Culturel Jacques Franck, St-Gilles, Brussels
www.centremultimedia.org
This indie festival began in 1974, when Super8 reigned supreme. It now incorporates a mix of media, but the philosophy remains the same: to give young directors a showcase for their work. Well worth checking out should your visit to Brussels coincide.

Late Nov-early Jan
Bruges Christmas Market
Markt Square, Bruges
www.brugesinfo.com
The Markt square is filled with seasonal revellers who come for a skate on the the ice rink. Surrounding it are stalls selling a range of Christmas specialities including *ghluwein* (mulled wine) and waffles.

December

Ongoing Skoda Jazz Festival (see Oct); Bruges Christmas Market (see Nov)

Dec **Christmas Market**
Groenplaats, Antwerp
Traditional yuletide food, drink, ice skating and a chance to try the juniper-flavoured local tipple, Jenever.
http://visit.antwerpen.be

Early Dec **December Dance**
Various venues, Bruges
www.decemberdance.be
A 12-day celebration of choreography and contemporary dance.

Dec-early Jan **Ice skating**
Place du Marché aux Poissons, Lower Town, Brussels
www.plaisirsdhiver.be
See box p38.

Dec-early Jan **Marché de Noël**
Grand'Place to place Ste-Catherine
www.plaisirsdhiver.be
See box p38.

6 Dec **St Nicholas**
Grand'Place & around, Brussels, see p52
Belgian children receive their main presents on 6 December, the feast of St Nicholas, rather than at Christmas. St Nicholas distributes gifts and *speculoos* (ginger biscuits), accompanied by Zwarte Piet – or Black Peter, the bogeyman. Political correctness aside, the parade takes place at 5pm.

31 Dec **New Year's Eve**
Grand'Place & around, Brussels see p52
High-spirited crowds pour into Grand'Place on 31 December; it's friendly, but not for the faint-hearted. The jollity extends to the streets around the square, where it's more relaxed. Later on, music is played over the speakers and folk start dancing – it all becomes magical from that moment on. There's also a fireworks display from the Parc de Bruxelles.

Itineraries

Le Jeune Albert p44

A Comic Turn

The comic strip or *bande dessinée* (BD) is a major part of Belgian culture – this is, after all, the homeland of blonde-quiffed boy hero Tintin. In 1993, Brussels had the bright idea of celebrating its rich comic heritage with a series of large-scale murals depicting popular characters. Over the years, more and more have been daubed on to the city walls, making for some deliciously surreal vistas and idiosyncratic photo opportunities. For a detailed outline of the six-kilometre route, download a map at www.brusselscomics.com, or pick one up at the Tourist Office on the Grand'Place (02 513 89 40, www.biponline.be).

This two to three-hour walk is designed to help you get your bearings around the muddle that is lower town Brussels – and get a cartoon fix at the same time. The starting point is **Le Cirio** (see p59), one of Brussels' finest cafés. After grabbing your coffee or beer, turn left out of the café and left again into rue de Tabora. Turn right into rue de l'Ecuyer and there you'll see the walk's first mural, Gaston Lagaffe leaning out of his window. This accident-prone office junior was created in 1957 by André Franquin for comic strip magazine *Spirou*. Turn left into rue Léopold and stroll to the front of **Théâtre de la Monnaie** (see p70), the Brussels opera house. It was here, in 1830, that the Belgian revolution started, triggered by the performance of a particularly rousing, patriotic aria.

Walk into the pedestrian rue Neuve, street of a thousand chain stores, and cut through the pretty little Passage du Nord on your left. As you emerge you'll see the **Métropole** (see p60) to your left. It's one of Brussels' grande dame hotels, with a café terrace that's perfect for people watching. This is place de Brouckère, once a smart square but now just madly busy.

Cross the place and turn right into Boulevard Jacqmain, where you'll see the glass edifice of the French-speaking **Théâtre National** (see p70). Stick your head into the foyer; it's a brilliant public space. Next, take a left into rue du Pont-Neuf and left again into rue de Laeken. You'll get a glimpse of the Flemish National Theatre to the right as you find yourself at the joyous mural of Bob et Bobette (Willy Vandersteen, 1945). They still appear in the *De Standaard* newspaper, where they are known as Suske en Wiske.

Cross the road and walk into rue du Grand Hospice, a lovely old part of town that was once home to the *béguines*, a religious community of widows and unmarried women. This ancient street brings you to the top part of the Ste-Catherine area; look up towards Ste-Catherine church and you'll see the remnants of the long-gone canal that once brought the fish to market. Keep going until the left turn into Rue d'Oppem. Here you'll find a relative youngster on the wall, Billy the Cat (Stéphane Colman and Stephen Desberg, 1979). The stories are darkly comic, as Billy has been reincarnated as a feline to pay for his misdeeds as a human.

A right turn into rue de Flandre brings you to a startling mural depicting Cubitus (Dupa, 1968) taking a pee in the manner of the Manneken Pis. Cubitus is a good-natured white dog, who made his first appearance in 1968 in the weekly *Tintin* comic.

Turn back on yourself and walk along rue de Flandre, with its odd shops, trendy delis and restaurants. It eventually brings you to place Ste-Catherine; turn right, past **De Markten** café (see p73) and you'll come to rue Antoine Dansaert.

You're now in the epicentre of designerville, sprinkled with boutiques from the Antwerp and Brussels fashion glitterati. At no.74 is **Stijl** (see p77), the shop that started it all. At no.16, the world's first Le Pain Quotidien is an ideal place to stop for lunch or afternoon tea. Next, turn the corner into rue des Chartreux, by design shop Kartell, and you'll find yourself in a different world of quirky second-hand and vintage shops.

Ahead of you, on a narrow strip of wall, is the enigmatic L'Ange de Sambre (Yslaire, 1986), with a jumble of graffiti at the bottom. Some is meant to be there, some

Tintin p44

isn't: your guess is as good as any. Sambre is based on the impossible love story of a rich aristocrat and poor farm girl in 19th-century revolutionary France. Walk the length of Charteux, past Zinneke the peeing dog and cross the little place du Jardin aux Fleurs into rue des Fabriques.

Here you'll find two murals: Cori le Moussaillon (Bob de Moor, 1951), who is an agent for Elizabeth I at the time of the Spanish Armada, and Les Rêves de Nic (Hermann, 1980), based on the dream adventures of its hero. Now turn down rue de la Senne and take the second left into rue T'Kint. On the next corner is one of the biggest murals, Lucky Luke (Morris, 1946), who can draw a gun faster than his own shadow. Luke is up there with Tintin and Asterix as one of Europe's bestsellers as he battles with the bumbling Dalton brothers.

Turning right into rue de la Buanderie brings you to a children's playground, where the plucky Asterix (René Goscinny and Albert Uderzo, 1959) has a colourful, action-packed wall of his own. Cross the main road into rue de la Verdure and gaze at the towering mural of Isabelle et Calendula (Will, 1970). Isabelle's adventures involve a wicked and a good witch (both called Calendula) and are full of fantasy and adventure. Walk to the busy boulevard Maurice Lemonnier and turn left towards place Fontainas, then right into rue des Bogards.

Above the army surplus shop is Monsieur Jean (Dupuy- Berberian, 1980), a Parisian bachelor forever looking for inspiration for his first novel. Continue a little way up the hill and to your right is the colourful Marolles resident Le Jeune Albert (Yves Chaland, 1985), lounging against a tram stop in a vibrant 1950s street scene.

Turn back down the hill then right into rue de l'Etuve, which brings you to the iconic Manneken Pis and his attendant tourist shops. Peer down rue du Chêne, though, and you'll see a fireworks shop. On the wall beside it is Olivier Rameau (Greg and Dany, 1968), a starburst of a mural showing Olivier and his future wife Colombe in the fantasy land of Rêverose, where boring people are banned.

Continue along rue de l'Etuve to see the granddaddy of them all, Tintin (Hergé, 1956), pictured with Snowy and Captain Haddock in a scene from *The Calculus Affair*. At the lights, turn left into rue du Lombard until you come to the café **Platesteen** (see p60). There's the young dreamer Broussaille (Frank Pé, 1978) walking arm-in-arm with his chum, an apt mural as you are now in the heart of Brussels' gay district. Across the road is Victor Sackville (François Rivière, 1985), a dapper World War I spy.

From here, cross rue du Midi and walk by the side of the police station to Grand' Place. Here you'll see the mysterious mural of Le Passage (François Schuiten, 1982), reflecting Schuitan's preoccupation with lost architectural treasures and urban fantasy.

Either stop on the square for a beer or, if you have the energy, walk alongside the Bourse and cross boulevard Anspach to place St-Géry. Nurse a cocktail at **Gecko Bar** (see p72) as you look at Nero (Marc Sleen, 1946), a heroic character who made his debut in 1946. Until his retirement in 2002, Sleen drew the comic strip every day – a feat that demonstrates just how deeply *bande dessinée* is engraved into the Belgian psyche. Sit back, relax and have another drink: not only have you seen some great art, but you've covered most of downtown Brussels. Santé!

Cathédral des Sts Michel et Gudule p47

Brussels Baroque

The Grand' Place in Brussels is arguably the world's greatest Baroque square, full of flounce and energy. Its ornate façades, statues and the pinnacles of the old guild houses set against the skyline are undeniably magnificent – but this itinerary takes you beyond the square to discover the city's other Baroque masterpieces, often overlooked by visitors. While they are listed here in a certain order – and we have included a map of the route – you can visit them in any combination you choose; each stands in a certain isolation, while at the same time being firmly embedded in its *quartier*.

A good place to start is at the **Eglise Notre-Dame du Finistère** (see p53), sitting all alone in the concrete blandness of rue Neuve, immediately opposite the modernist Inno department store. Its name is said to derive from the fact that the original chapel was built on the edge of the city limits (*finis terrae*); work on the current incarnation of the church began in 1617. It's a contemplative space, with the biggest, most overblown pulpit and cover you could ever hope to see and a fine collection of art, including the statues of Our Ladies of Finistère and Good Luck.

In spite of its surroundings, the church holds a special place in Brussels life. Shoppers drop in for a moment of peace and quiet reflection, especially in the Lady Chapel, while the free organ concerts that are sometimes held here on a Monday draw the crowds. The other free concert is the daily carillon, when the bells ring out across town.

A short walk across the boulevards Adolphe Max and Jacqmain brings you to the place du Béguinage in Ste-Catherine. Here, in the centre of a sundial of little streets is the **Eglise St Jean-Baptiste au Béguinage** (see p72) regarded as having the finest Italo-Flemish façade of any church in Belgium. It's a throwback to the time when the Lowlands were known as the Spanish Netherlands, and were under the control of Spain. This wasn't just a matter of political power: it was a statement of Catholic intention in this tricky, potentially Protestant part of Europe. The church is now all that remains of the Grand Béguinage, where lay sisters were offered homes in return for religious devotion.

In recent times, the church has achieved notoriety as a place of protest and a refuge for illegal immigrants. With the blessing of the church authorities, groups of *sans-papiers* have regularly set up home in the nave for a few nights to protest against government indifference to their situation; the role of the St Jean-Baptiste in offering shelter to those who need it continues across the centuries.

From here, walk along rue de Peuplier (make sure you look back, as the church's façade looks at its best from afar), cross the covered-over canal by the Métro station and head through the alleyway to rue de Flandre. At no.46 is the **Maison de Bellone** – unremarkable from the front, but with a splendid secret at the back.

Walk through to find a tiny Baroque façade, dating from 1697 and in the same imposing style as the Roi d'Espagne building on Grand' Place. With the wholesale destruction of swathes of the city in the 1960s and '70s, it's incredible that the building is still standing, never mind in such good repair. These days it's occupied by the administrative offices for various arts organisations, while concerts and special events are held in the courtyard, now protected by a soaring glass roof.

A good place to stop for lunch is the **Pré Salé** (see p75) – or, if you want something a little lighter or just a drink, **De Markten** (see p73). Across the square is the 19th-century **Ste-Catherine** church. To one side, standing alone, a 1629 Baroque tower is all that remains of an earlier church.

Turn your back on the church and walk across rue Antoine Dansaert and into rue du Vieux Marché aux Grains. This leads into rue St-Christophe, at the end of which you'll find **Notre-Dame aux Riches Claires** (see p70) to your left. This gem of a church is in classic Flemish Baroque style and once served two purposes: as a place of worship and as a convent for Riches Claires nuns. The original convent, attached to the church, now contains the church offices and some apartments.

Riches Claires is also known as the Spanish church; services are offered in Spanish and attract the area's sizeable Spanish community, along with Latin American locals. Notice the height of the church, and try to imagine it surrounded by much smaller houses huddled along the banks of the River Senne. In old Brussels, God and the Vatican were ever-present and ever-watchful.

Cross the boulevard Anspach (built over the river) and to your right you'll see the tower of **Notre-Dame du Bon Secours** (see p53), probably the most gracious of the city's Baroque churches. It's also the most untypical, in that it is hexagonal in shape and has a short nave. This little corner of Brussels is wonderfully atmospheric, with old houses clustering around the church and a stylish, vibrant bar scene. Inside the church, meanwhile, the magnificent altarpiece is a Baroque sunburst and all is cool and calm. This was one of the stops on the pilgrimage to Santiago de

Compostela; cast in bronze, the symbolic scallop shell of the pilgrimage appears on various city streets, marking the route that the pilgrims trod.

Next, walk back along Marché au Charbon to the Grand' Place, the greatest example of Flemish Baroque in Belgium. Before you settle down for a drink at **Le Roi d'Espagne** (see p63), which occupies the old bakers' guild headquarters, look up at the façade. There you'll see a bust of Charles II, the last Hapsburg King of Spain, from whom the bar takes its name.

Other touches of the flamboyant Baroque style are dotted all around Brussels, providing a striking contrast to its earlier Gothic symmetry and the rigid lines of traditional Dutch architecture. The famous statue of the **Manneken Pis** (see p52) stands beneath a Baroque seashell, while the **Cathédral des Sts Michel et Gudule** (see p82) has the Maes Chapel, with its 16th-century reredo of the Passion of Christ.

To round off your discovery of Baroque Brussels, you might like to visit the **Musées Royaux des Beaux-Arts** (see p83). Here you'll find a vast room devoted to Rubens' rich, sumptuous paintings, along with works by Anthony Van Dyck, Rembrandt, Jordaens and Jan Steen; a veritable visual feast.

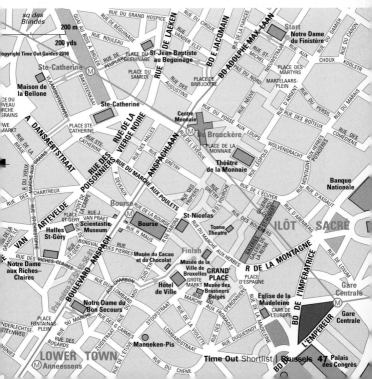

Beer, Glorious Beer

Belgium is justly lauded for its proud beer-brewing tradition, which is ingrained in the country's culture. The Brussels region has its own history when it comes to brewing, particularly the sour lambics (see box p94), although local production dwindled in the 19th century after the River Senne was covered over – and in more recent times, as multinationals took over some of the smaller producers.

This three-hour tour gives a glimpse into the history of beer, and takes you to the only working brewery in central Brussels. It's not a bar crawl, though: Belgian beer is generally much stronger than its European counterparts, and it's important to understand how the locals treat it. They tend to sip and appreciate rather than get ratted, and a good rule is to treat it more like wine than a pint of best. Keep an eye on the alcohol content, too; most menus in serious bars here show the percentage alongside the beer. As a benchmark, most standard lagers come in at around five per cent by volume.

As with so many things in Brussels, this walk starts on the Grand' Place. No.10, the **Maison des Brasseurs** is home to the Union of Belgian Brewers, with a museum devoted to the art of brewing down in its basement. The museum opens at 10am, so it's worth arriving bright and early to avoid the crowds – and to ensure that your walk ends at a good time for lunch and a glass.

While the museum gives a good historical overview of the brewing process, it's not stuck in the past. Instead, it uses new technology to reflect modern methodology, with touch screens and bright visuals in the old underground vaults. The museum visit ends with a beer tasting, so make sure you have a good breakfast in you.

Next, head to the **Cantillon Brewery** in Anderlecht. Leave

Moeder Lambic Fontainas

the Grand' Place via the narrow rue de la Tête d'Or and walk past the police headquarters. Cross rue du Midi and into rue du Marché au Charbon. If you fancy a coffee, try **Platesteen** (see p60). Nearby are a number of gay bars, renowned more for their atmosphere than their beer menus.

Marché au Charbon continues on the other side of rue du Lombard. In the evening, this is bar-crawl paradise, teeming with music bars, cocktail haunts and beery drinking dens – though you wouldn't know it by day, as you stroll by its quirky shops and enjoy the laid-back, local feel. Towards the end are **Au Soleil** (see p64) and **Fontainas** (see p60), both popular meeting places for locals and also good for a buzzy nightcap in the wee hours.

At the end of the street is place Fontainas. At no.8 here, **Moeder Lambic Fontainas** (see p58) is Brussels' latest beer temple, with 40 draught beers. Stop and sip if you wish, or mark it for a return visit later on. Its taps afford an insight into the future of Belgian brewing, with beers from younger brewers

such as Yvan de Baets and Bernard Leboucq of Brussels' artisan Brasserie de la Senne brewery.

At this juncture, you can walk one of two ways to get to the Grand Ecluse restaurant. The first entails heading left down boulevard Maurice Lemonnier; it's quicker but less attractive, with lots of traffic and noise.

The alternative route takes you through quieter backwaters: from Fontainas turn left into rue des Bogards, then right after the post office into rue du Midi. This takes you to place Rouppe, the site of the original Gare du Midi. Crossing the square you'll see Brussels' finest restaurant, **Comme Chez Soi** (see p59). Head straight across and into avenue de Stalingrad, a grand boulevard of massive townhouses built on the site of the old station platforms. At the end, cross the busy inner ring road and you'll see **La Grand Ecluse** (77 boulevard Poincaré, 02 522 30 25, www. grande-ecluse.be) to your right.

The restaurant is built around the old sluice gate of the River Senne, and parts of the operating machinery can still be seen inside. Breweries used to draw their water from the river, and the industrial Art Deco building opposite the restaurant was once the Caulier brewery. You can still see the tiled advertisement for one of its beers, Perle Caulier 28. By the mid 19th century, though, the river was choked with sewage and pollution, prone to flooding and a major source of cholera; in 1871, it was finally covered over with new public buildings and broad boulevards.

Walk past the restaurant to the square de l'Aviation, with its war memorial to fairground folk (each year, the Midi fair sets up along the middle of the boulevard du Midi; see p36). Across the square you'll see a grand old insurance building with bas reliefs and murals; walk to the right of this into rue Lambert Crickx, cross the square and turn right into rue Gheude. At no.56 is the Cantillon Brewery and the **Musée Bruxellois de la Gueuze** (see p135). Here, you can see the brewery in action, as it has been for over 100 years. The

Cantillon Brewery

original machinery is still in place, along with the cellars with their maturing vats and fermenting bottles, and the smell of bubbling lambic. A glass of beer is offered at the end of the tour; if this is your first taste of gueuze, be prepared for the sour kick.

It's now time for lunch, which means you need to get back to the centre. You can either reverse the walk (again, boulevard Lemonnier is the quickest route) or turn right into rue Brogniez, walk for a couple of minutes and pick up a 31 tram which will take you underground to Pré-Métro Bourse. Your destination is **A la Bécasse** (see p56) on rue de Tabora, at the back of the Bourse.

A tiny door and narrow passage lead to this authentic old hostelry, where you can order a wooden board of cheese, ham or steak tartare with hefty slabs of bread. Most important, though, is the punctuation mark that this place stamps on your beer tour. Here, staff serve draught Timmermans Gueuze, white lambic by the jug, or, if you prefer, a range of bottles including the sweeter fruit lambics.

Now may be a good time to take a rest and plan your onward beer discovery. In the evening, beer-drinkers favourites include **La Mort Subite** (see p60), **Delirium Café** (see p59), **Monk** (see p75) and **Chez Moeder Lambic Fontainas** (see p59). To buy some brews to take home, **Délices et Caprices** (see p67) is the best downtown place, while a Métro ride to Porte de Namur will take you to **Beer Mania** (see p117).

Finally, if your own intensive researches take you right through the night, soak it up with fried eggs at **A la Clef d'Or** (see p80), which opens at first light for the flea market crowd and club stragglers. There are times when a croissant simply doesn't cut the mustard.

By Area

Grand'Place

The Lower Town

Grand'Place & around

Described by Victor Hugo as
'the most beautiful square in the
world', the stately **Grand'Place** is
Brussels' ever-impressive set piece
– and a UNESCO World Heritage
Site. The tower of the **Hôtel de
Ville** is its distinctive landmark,
ringed by grand mercantile
guildhouses with glorious façades.

Just north of the Grand'Place,
around **petite rue des Bouchers**,
the Îlot Sacré (Holy Isle) is a
medieval maze of small streets,
packed with restaurants. Many
boast huge displays of fish on ice.

The south side of the Grand'
Place is quieter, characterised by an
urban tangle of touristy shops and
idiosyncratic boutiques. South of
the square, in rue de l'Etuve, is the
Manneken-Pis (see box p58) –
famous as a national symbol but
slightly disappointing as a tourist
spectacle, although it draws huge

crowds. A short walk west is gay-
friendly rue Marché au Charbon.
One of the loveliest of the Lower
Town's churches stands here:
Notre-Dame de Bon Secours.

Sights & Museums

Centre Belge de la
Bande Dessinée

*20 rue des Sables (02 219 19 80, www.
comicscenter.net). Métro/pré-métro De
Brouckère or Rogier.* **Open** 10am-6pm
Tue-Sun. **Admission** €7.50; €3-€6
reductions. No credit cards. **Map**
p55 E3 ❶
North of the Grand'Place, and set in a
beautiful Horta-designed department
store, the Comic Strip Museum greets
you with a statue of Tintin, Snowy and
the red and white rocket they took to
the moon. The Tintin collection is the
highlight of the museum, which covers
the history of comics and cartoons
from Gertie the Dinosaur (1914) to
modern-day heroes.

Hôtel de Ville

Grand'Place (02 279 43 65, tourist information 02 513 89 40). Pré-métro Bourse or métro Gare Centrale. **Open** *Guided tours* (in English) 3.15pm Tue, Wed. Apr-Sept also 10.45am & 12.15pm Sun. **Admission** €3. No credit cards. **Map** p55 D5 ❷

The left wing of this superb, sculpture-adorned edifice was built in 1406; for balance, a right wing was later added by an unknown architect. The old belfry was too small for the new structure, so Jan van Ruysbroeck added the octagonal tower; in 1455, a dramatic gilt statue of St Michael slaying the dragon was erected at its pinnacle. The tower seems to unbalance the rest of the building: legend has it that, in despair, the architect climbed to the top of his masterpiece and threw himself off. You can't climb the tower, but a series of elegant official rooms can be visited on the guided tour.

Musée des Brasseurs Belges

10 Grand'Place (02 511 49 87, www.beerparadise.be). Pré-métro Bourse or métro Gare Centrale. **Open** 10am-5pm daily. **Admission** €6. No credit cards. **Map** p55 D5 ❸

Run by the brewers' confederation, this permanent exhibition displays traditional techniques, and has a new high-tech brewing centre.

Musée du Cacao et du Chocolat

9-11 rue de la Tête d'Or (02 514 20 48, www.mucc.be). Pré-métro Bourse or métro Gare Centrale. **Open** 10am-4.30pm Tue-Sun. **Admission** €5.50; free under-12s. No credit cards. **Map** p54 C5 ❹

Founded by Jo Draps, a third generation Belgian chocolatier, the museum traces the history of chocolate, from its discovery by the Aztecs through its arrival in Europe, and on to the development of the praline and other Belgian specialities.

Musée de la Ville de Bruxelles

Grand'Place (02 279 43 50, www.brussels.be/artdet.cfm/4202). Pré-métro Bourse or métro Gare Centrale. **Open** 10am-5pm Tue-Sun. **Admission** €3. No credit cards. **Map** p55 D4 ❺

Constructed in the 13th century and thrice rebuilt, this place was owned by the bakers' guild, and is known in Dutch as the Broodhuis (bread house). Shored up after 1695, it was left to crumble until Mayor Jules Anspach rebuilt it in fashionable neo-Gothic style in 1860. It houses a slightly dowdy collection of photographs, models and documents chronicling the city's history, although paintings include Pieter Bruegel the Elder's *Wedding Procession*. Here, too, is the vast wardrobe of the Manneken-Pis (see box p58): of his 800 costumes, around 200 are on permanent display.

Notre-Dame de Bon Secours

Rue du Marché au Charbon (02 514 31 13). Pré-métro Anneessens. **Open** 9am-5.30pm daily. **Map** p54 C5 ❻

Built in the late 1600s, this Baroque masterpiece, designed as a collaboration between Jan Cortvrindt and Willem de Bruyn, remains a superb example of Flemish Renaissance style.

Notre-Dame du Finistère

Rue Neuve (02 217 52 52). Métro/pré-métro De Brouckère or Rogier. **Open** 8am-6pm Mon-Sat; 8am-noon, 3-6pm Sun. **Map** p55 D3 ❼

Largely built in the early 18th century on the site of a 15th-century chapel, the church's Baroque interior is most notable for its stupendously over-the-top pulpit.

St-Nicolas

1 rue au Beurre (02 267 51 64). Pré-métro Bourse. **Open** phone for details. **Map** p55 D4 ❽

Founded in the 11th century, this model of medieval sanctity survived

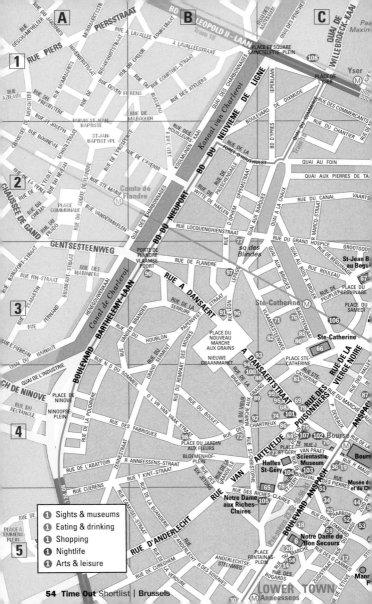

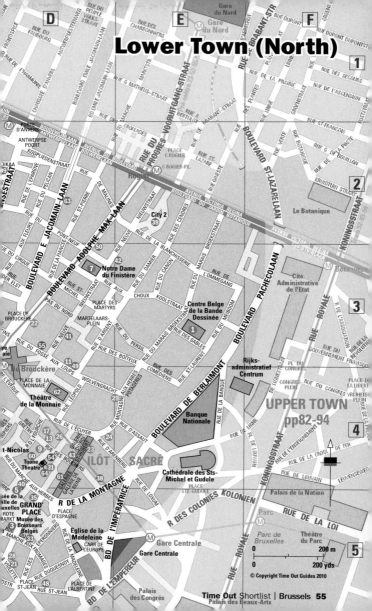

Lower Town (North)

D   **E**   **F**

Gare du Nord

1

RUE D'ANVERS
RUE DU FAUBOURG
CHAUSSÉE D'ANVERS
BOULEVARD EMILE JACQMAIN-LAAN
ANTWERPSESTEENWEG
RUE DU PEUPLE VOLKS STRAAT
RUE DES CHARBONNIERS
RUE DUPONT
RUE DUPONT DUPONT
GROEN
RUE DE BRABANT-STR
RUE DES SECOURS
RUE DE L'ASCENSION

PORTE D'ANVERS
ANTWERPSE POORT
KOOPLIEDENSTRAAT
BOEKDEWINELAAN
RUE DU PROGRÈS
VOORUITGANG-STRAAT
RUE G. MATHEUS-STRAAT
RUE MARTY-STR
RUE DES CROISADES
RUE DU MARCHÉ
RUE A. BERTOLF DE BRABANT-STRAAT
BOULEVARD ST-LAZARELAAN
RUE DE LA PRAIRIE
RUE ST-FRANÇOIS
RUE DES PLANTES
RUE VERTE
RUE DU NORD
RUE G. A POSTE
RUE DE BOTANIQUE
RUE DE BOUILLON

DIKAA
RUE DE L'ESPERANCE
RUE DU PELICAN
RUE ST-PIERRE
RUE DE MALINES
AVENUE DU BOULEVARD
PLACE C ROGIER
C ROGIER-PL
Rogier
AVENUE VICTORIA REGINA
BOULEVARD DU JARDIN BOTANIQUE
KONINGSSTRAAT

2

63
RUE DE LA FIANCÉE
PONT-NEUF
BOULEVARD E. JACQMAIN-LAAN
BOULEVARD ADOLPHE MAX-LAAN
NIEUWSTRAAT
NEUVE
RUE DE LA BLANCHISSERIE
RUE DES CENDRES
AVENUE VICTORIA REGINA
Le Botanique
KRUIDTUIN STRAAT

50
42
Notre Dame du Finistère
RUE DU DAMIER
RUE DU CANON
RUE DE L'OMMEGANG
City 2
39

RUE ST-MICHEL
NIEUWSTRAAT
RUE AUX
PLACE DES MARTYRS
MARTÉLAARS-PLEIN
CHOUX
KOOLSTRAAT
RUE DU MARAIS BROEKSTRAAT
Centre Belge de la Bande Dessinée
RUE DE L'OMMEGANG
BOULEVARD PACHECOLAAN
Cité Administrative de l'Etat
Botani

PLACE DE BROUCKÈRE
22
RUE NEUVE
41
RUE D'ARGENT
RUE DU PERSIL
RUE DU MARAIS
RUE DES SABLES
1
RUE ST-LAURENT
RUE DU MEIBOOM
RUE ROYALE
RUE DE L'ASSOCIATION

3

55
RUE DU FOSSÉ AUX LOUPS
49
RUE DES BOITEUX
RUE DES COMÉDIENS
RUE DU GOUVERNEMENT PROVINCIAL
PLACE DU CONGRÈS RUE DU CONGRÈS
PLEIN
PL DU CONGRÈS
PLACE DE LA LIBERT

e Brouckère
PLACE DE LA MONNAIE
62
Théâtre de la Monnaie
RUE LÉOPOLD
MONTAGNE AUX HERBES POTAGÈRES
WOLVENGRACHT
RUE D'ARGENT
Banque Nationale
RUE DE LIGNE
PLEIN
VRIJHEIDS PLEIN
RUE DE LA LI

RUE GRETRY
17
13
26
RUE DE L'ÉCUYER
RUE D'ARENBERG
24
BOULEVARD DE BERLAIMONT
RUE DE LA BANQUE
RUE DE L'ENSEIGNEMENT
DE FER

4
t-Nicolas
9
54
31
64
23
GALERIE DU ROI
GALERIE DE LA REINE
ILÔT SACRÉ
38
RUE DE LA MONTAGNE
Cathédrale des Sts-Michel et Gudule
PLACE STE-GUDULE
RUE DE LOXUM
RUE DES COLONIES KOLONIEN
Palais de la Nation
RUE DE LOUVAIN
RUE DE LA CROIX
LEIMENGEWER

ée de la ille de uxelles
MAISON DU ROI
BROODHUIS
GRAND PLACE GROTE MARKT
sée du Musée des Brasseurs Belges
RUE AU BEURRE
RUE DU MARCHÉ AUX HERBES
PLACE D'ESPAGNE
Eglise de la Madeleine
CARR DE L'EUROPE
UPPER TOWN
pp82-94
RUE DE LA LOI
Parc
Parc de Bruxelles
Théâtre du Parc

5
28
31
21
PLACE ST-JEAN
RUE ST-JEAN
48
PLACE DE L'ALBERTINE
RUE DU MARCHÉ AUX FROMAGES
RUE DUQUESNOY
BD DE L'IMPÉRATRICE
BD DE L'EMPEREUR
Gare Centrale
KONINGSSTRAAT
RUE ROYALE
200 m
200 yds
© Copyright Time Out Guides 2010
Palais des Congrès
Palais des Beaux-Arts

the 1695 bombardment. Its curved shape follows the old line of the River Senne and has tidy little houses (now shops) built into its walls. Over the centuries the church became gloomy and stained, but it has now been lovingly and painstakingly renovated, and sits again in warm, honeyed splendour.

Eating & drinking

The streets around the Grand'Place are alive with restaurants and bars. Their location in tourist central doesn't mean they're either of poor quality or overpriced; many have been here for decades, and used by generations of locals.

Aux Armes de Bruxelles

13 rue des Bouchers (02 511 50 50, www.armebrux.be). Métro Gare Centrale. **Open** noon-10.45pm Mon-Fri; noon-11.15pm Sat; noon-10.30pm Sun. **€€€**. **Belgian**. Map p55 D4 ❾
Sitting like a grounded galleon in a gaudy sea of fish restaurants, Aux Armes is a classically mullioned institution, beloved by business folk and middle-class Belgians since 1921. The art deco interior is as classy as the waiters, who glide around with the utmost professionalism, delivering creamy fish *waterzooi* and perfect moules-frites.

A la Bécasse

11 rue de Tabora (02 511 00 06, www.alabecasse.com). Pré-métro Bourse. **Open** 11am-midnight Mon-Thur, Sun; 11am-1am Fri, Sat. **Bar**. Map p55 D4 ❿
From the street, all that marks this bar's presence is a red neon light, hinting there's something tacky afoot. Not at all. Look down at your feet, where a stone and brass welcome mat is fixed to the pavement. Follow the alley through the houses and you'll see the Dickensian-style bottle windows. Behind is an ancient tavern, where customers sit at long tables and aproned waiters pour beer from jugs.

Belga Queen

32 rue du Fossé aux Loups (02 217 21 87, www.belgaqueen.be). Métro/pré-métro De Brouckère. **Open** noon-2pm, 7-10pm daily. **€€€**. **Belgian**. Map p55 D3 ⓫
Everything about this glitzy place is unashamedly Belgian; the design, the menu, the produce. It occupies a vast bank building with original pillars and a massive stained-glass skylight, giving it a lofty, spacious air. Heaving seafood platters are composed at the celebrated oyster bar, while other dishes are appealingly inventive.

Le Cercle des Voyageurs

18 rue des Grandes Carmes (02 514 39 49, www.lecercledesvoyageurs.com). Pré-métro Bourse. **Open** 11am-11pm Mon, Wed, Thur; 11am-midnight Fri; noon-midnight Sat; noon-10pm Sun. Closed Mon mid June-mid Aug. **Bar**. Map p54 C5 ⓬
As the name suggests, the Cercle is a place for travellers to meet. As well as drinking in a laid-back, colonial-inspired setting in a grand old house, there are events and talks about all aspects of travel. It's perfect for those on the road seeking inside information – speak to the regulars or consult the books and periodicals in the library.

Chez Léon

18 rue des Bouchers (02 511 14 15, www.chezleon.be). Métro Gare Centrale or pré-métro Bourse. **Open** 11.30am-11pm Mon-Thur, Sun; 11.30am-11.30pm Fri, Sat. **€€**. **Belgian**. Map p55 D4 ⓭
Chez Léon started as a tavern in 1893, then became a humble *frites* shop. Nowadays, it weaves through nine interconnecting houses and can seat 400 people. Its fast food feel keeps the nose-in-air locals away – or maybe it's the paper napkins and menu featuring photographed dishes. On the culinary front, this place is a temple to mussels and other Belgian classics such as rabbit in sour cherry beer.

Lower Town (South)

Dressed to impress

The Manneken as mannequin.

In fashion circles, Belgium is largely famed for Antwerp's crop of couture kings and queens (see box p143). But the capital has its own unlikely supermodel, whose outfits are gawped at and photographed by thousands, in the shape of the Manneken-Pis. The celebrated statue of a peeing boy has his attire changed on a regular basis: one day it might be a kilt, the next a diving suit.

What looks like the result of a drunken student night out is actually a tradition that started in the 1700s, when one of Louis XV's soldiers stole the statue and left him outside a brothel. Louis apologised by offering the boy his first outfit: a stylish gold brocade suit. From then on, Ketje (as he is fondly known in Bruxelloise) received sumptuous new outfits four times a year.

Today his wardrobe contains almost 800 costumes, the latest of which are displayed at the top of the grand staircase at the **Musée de la Ville de Bruxelles** (see p53). And much like his catwalk contemporaries, Ketje has a personal dresser, Jean-Marc Ahime, a security guard at the museum.

Ahime was trained by the previous *habilleur*, who held the post until retiring. The role requires an interest in costumes and in-depth knowledge of fabrics; many of the outfits (a Soviet cosmonaut's suit, say, or spangly Elvis jumpsuit) are fragile.

Anyone can offer to clothe the Manneken, who receives a new outfit about once a month; each proposal first goes before a committee for approval. If you're keen for Ketje to be seen in one of your creations, you need to think less loopy Lady Gaga get-up and more deserving achievements: a Nelson Mandela outfit and a Tour de France yellow jersey have both made the grade in the past.

If a bid is successful, Ahime dresses the statue at a formal ceremony, which famously involves turning Ketje's wee into wine or beer.

Chez Moeder Lambic Fontainas

NEW *8 place Fontainas (02 503 60 68, www.moederlambic.eu/sitebar/). Pré-métro Anneessens.* **Open** 11am-1am Mon-Thur, Sun; 11am-2am Fri, Sat. **Bar**. No credit cards. **Map** p54 C5 ⑭

The new and thoroughly modern daughter of St-Gilles Moeder Lambic (see p127) is a splendid addition to the city's bar scene. It sits in an old town-house on the unglamorous place Fontainas, at the end of the Marché au Charbon crawl, providing a punctuation mark to a long evening's drinking. Forty lesser-known draught Belgian beers make this a place of discovery.

Le Cirio

18-20 rue de la Bourse (02 512 13 95). Pré-métro Bourse. **Open** 10am-1am daily. €. No credit cards. **Café**. **Map** p54 C4 ⑮

Le Cirio is named after the Italian grocer, remembered on a million sauce cans, who shipped wagons of goodies over the Alps from Turin to his ornate delicatessen, set by the stock exchange. Both the Bourse and deli have since folded, but the decor remains – beautiful fittings, Vermouth promotions, cash registers and century-old gastronomy awards – along with the eternally popular *half-en-half* wine (half sparkling, half still, wholly Italian). Grandes dames and their lookalike poodles sip away the afternoon, the former from a stemmed glass, the latter from a bowl of tap water.

Comme chez Soi

23 place Rouppe (02 512 29 21, www.commechezsoi.be). Pré-métro Anneessens. **Open** noon-1.30pm, 7-10.30pm Tue, Thur-Sat; 7-10.30pm Wed. €€€€. **French**. **Map** p57 B1 ⑯

Begian super-chef Pierre Wynants has now passed the baton to his son-in-law, Lionel Rigolet, at this Michelin two-star establishment. Immaculate food is served in an art nouveau dining room: dishes might include sole fillets with a mousseline of riesling and shrimps, or lobster salad with black truffles. After a beautifully sculpted course arrives at your table, waiters return with an unassuming bowl of second helpings, proving that artistically small portions are never enough in Belgium.

Délirium Café

4A impasse de la Fidélité Carmes (02 514 44 34, www.deliriumcafe.be). Pré-métro Bourse. **Open** 10am-4am daily. **Pub**. **Map** p55 D4 ⑰

In a tiny alley off rue des Bouchers lies the big and brash Délirium, named after the powerful (8.5%) Belgian pale ale brew Délirium Tremens. The pink elephant tells you all you need to know. But don't think you're hallucinating when you see the menu of 2,000 beers and 500 genevers. The knowledgeable staff will help you around the menu, but keep an eye on the alcohol strengths unless you want to become a victim of the troublesome pachyderm.

Epicerie Fine de la Senne

NEW *4-6 rue de Bon Secours (02 502 2426, www.epiceriefinedelasenne.be). Pré-métro Bourse.* **Open** 9am-6pm Tue-Sat. €. No credit cards. **Café**. **Map** p54 C5 ⑱

Grab a Villo! urban bike, get yourself down to the Epicerie, grab some grub and head to the park for a picnic. The home-made quiches, panini or lasagne make a perfect lunch; alternatively, Valérie and Christian can assemble a hamper of goodies from their range of gourmet goods and wines. Food can be eaten in-house, too, from breakfast through to lunch and afternoon snacks. The odd art show adds a touch of culture to this homely but high-end deli.

Le Falstaff

19-25 rue Henri Maus (02 511 87 89, www.lefalstaff.be). Pré-métro Bourse. **Open** 10am-2am daily. €. **Café**. **Map** p54 C4 ⑲

This is probably the most famous café-restaurant in Brussels, and certainly the most evergreen. An awning on one side of the Bourse barely prepares the first-time visitor for the eye candy of the art nouveau interior, which has been attracting Bruxellois of every stripe for the better part of a century. Reasonably priced mains are but a side dish to the range of beers, while late opening hours are another major draw.

Fontainas

91 rue du Marché au Charbon (02 503 31 12). Pré-métro Anneessens or Bourse. **Open** 10.30am-1am Mon-Thur, Sun; 10.30am-2am Fri, Sat. No credit cards. **Bar**. **Map** p54 C5 ⑳

Possibly the best bar on Brussels' best stretch for bar crawling, the Fontainas is wonderfully understated. It's full of sweet retro touches – beaded curtains, Formica chairs – that would do justice to a 1950s milk bar. Yet this place is as determinedly 21st century as its gay/straight mixed clientele, with excellent sounds from resident DJs, strong cocktails and rare Orval and Maredsous brews. There are a few terrace tables for when the sun's out, too.

Goupil le Fol

22 rue de la Violette (02 511 13 96). Métro Gare Centrale. **Open** 7.30pm-5am daily. No credit cards. **Bar**. **Map** p55 D5 ㉑

Goupil can but cash in. He has his staff urge questionable house fruit wines upon many a tourist, while only providing standard Jupiler (at €2.50 a glass!) by means of any beer alternative. So, what is there to recommend? Well, Goupil is a kooky, labyrinthine junk-shop of a bar, where all trace of time can be lost thanks to a jukebox of 3,000 choice slices of vinyl. Eccentric and nostalgic, on the right night it is perfect – particularly à deux.

Métropole

31 place de Brouckère (02 217 23 00, www.metropolehotel.be). Métro/pré-métro De Brouckère. **Open** 9am-1am daily. **Bar**. **Map** p55 D3 ㉒

For a little fin-de-siècle finesse, pop into the café of the Hotel Métropole. It's of a different age: over-burdened chandeliers, mirrored walls, ornate ironwork and a hush that hasn't changed for a century. A pillar of guests' autographs features Vera Lynn; Sarah Bernhardt stayed here, too, and is reincarnated in the ladies with elaborate hairdos who sit on the terrace in sunglasses and fur coats year round. Aperitifs dominate the drinks menu, along with champagnes, delivered by bow-tied waiters.

Mokafé

9 galerie du Roi (02 511 78 70). Métro Gare Centrale. **Open** 7am-midnight Mon-Sat; 8am-midnight Sun. **€**. **Café**. **Map** p55 D4 ㉓

Located near the opera and opposite a superb classical music shop, Mokafé attracts a terrace full of arty types year round, protected by covered galleries. It's good for lunch, with reasonably priced café grub and pasta. On Sunday morning locals sit for hours with coffee and a paper, pretending to be in their own little world – but just watch eyes dart and ears prick when a newcomer takes a table.

A la Mort Subite

7 rue des Montagnes aux Herbes Potagères (02 513 13 18, www. alamortsubite.be). Métro Gare Centrale. **Open** 11am-12.30am Mon-Sat; 1pm-12.30am Sun. **Bar**. **Map** p55 D4 ㉔

Named after a card game and a variety of fruit beer whose hangovers easily assume the mantle of sudden death, the popularity of this dissolute café soon saw the name pass into legend. Earning such post-booze pain is a pleasure in this narrow haven of ensozzlement. It serves the local gueuze, which is to be handled with care.

Plattesteen

41 rue du Marché au Charbon (02 512 82 03). Pré-métro Anneessens. **Open** 11am-midnight daily. **€-€€**. **Café**. **Map** p54 C5 ㉕

Belga Queen p52

Hôtel de Ville p52

This multifunctional bar-café acts as both a neighbourhood bar and an inexpensive restaurant. It's something of a melting pot, joining shopping Brussels to gay Brussels and the rue du Marché au Charbon, so the clientele might include ladies with poodles, ladies with men and men with men.

Restaurant Vincent

8-10 rue des Dominicains (02 511 26 07, www.restaurantvincent.com). Métro/pré-métro De Brouckère. **Open** noon-2.45pm, 6.30-11.30pm Mon-Sat; noon-3pm, 6.30-10.30pm Sun. **€€€**. **Seafood**. Map p55 D4 ㉖

First-timers hesitate to enter Vincent, because there seems to be only a kitchen entrance. Correct. Be brave and walk past the steaming chefs, and the dry maître d' will meet you on the other side. When booking, ask to be seated in the tiled dining room (the fishing mural dates from 1905), or you could end up in the unexceptional space next door. Seafood and fish are cooked to perfection here, and it's one of those places where the final touches are rustled up at the table by epaulleted waiters, keen to show off their flambé skills.

Le Roi d'Espagne

1 Grand'Place (02 513 08 07, www.roidespagne.be). Pré-métro Bourse. **Open** 10am-1am daily. **Pub**. Map p55 D4 ㉗

The king of the guildhouses on the gilded square (it was the HQ of the bakers' guild), Le Roi is a classic spot, taking full advantage of the tourist trade by filling its warren of dark rooms and corners with dangling marionettes, old prints and pigs' bladders.

La Roue d'Or

26 rue des Chapeliers (02 514 25 54, www2.resto.be/rouedor). Pré-métro Bourse. **Open** noon-midnight daily. **€€-€€€**. **Belgian**. Map p55 D5 ㉘

The Golden Wheel takes its name from the gold motif at the heart of a stained-glass window above the open kitchen.

Life in the slow lane

Brussels puts the brakes on.

In September 2010, a shockwave coursed through the hearts of Belgian drivers as the unthinkable happened; central Brussels was imposed with a 30 kilometre per hour (20mph) speed limit.

The whole area within the Pentagon – the inner ring road – is now a go-slow zone, with exclusions for certain highways leading in and out of the city. The goal, says Christian Seux, Alderman for Town Planning and Mobility, is a 40 per cent reduction in pedestrian accidents, and a significant decrease in pollution and noise.

It's all part of a grand plan for a 20 per cent reduction in Belgium's road traffic by 2020. That's all well and good, but this is a country where driving is seen as an inalienable right, and drivers are wedded, if not welded, to their cars.

Alternatives to the car are being dangled like carrots, but it remains to be seen how much of a bite is taken. However, as in a number of other European cities with similar schemes, the response to a new urban cycling initiative (Villo!; see p185) has been encouraging.

By following the lead of other forward-thinking cities like Dublin and Lyon, Brussels could well be setting a Euro-trend. Now, much like smoking before it, the days of inner-city speeding look numbered.

Through the window you can watch the team of chefs toiling away at time-honoured Belgian classics such as mussels, oysters, lamb's tongue, pig's trotter and slabs of beef; vegetarians will feel rather left out. While the ingredients are no-nonsense, presentation and flavours are impeccable.

Sea Grill

Radisson SAS Royal, 47 rue du Fossé aux Loups (02 227 91 25, www.seagrill. be). Métro/pré-métro De Brouckère. **Open** noon-2pm, 7-10pm Mon-Fri. **€€€€**. **Seafood**. **Map** p55 E4 ㉙

This superb seafood restaurant is inside the five-star Radisson SAS Royal Hotel; while the entrance is rather corporate, the interior is seriously luxe. Chef Yves Mattagne seems to win every award going for his pairing of traditional French techniques with modern international touches.

Au Soleil

86 rue du Marché au Charbon (02 513 34 30). Pré-métro Anneessens or Bourse. **Open** 10am-1am Mon-Thur, Sun; 10am-2am Fri, Sat. No credit cards. **Bar**. **Map** p54 B5 ㉚

Set in an extravagant old tailor's premises, Au Soleil is filled with a constant buzz. Everyone seems to be talking on top of one another, when they're not looking impossibly interesting amid the fug of fumes. It's all a pose, of course, but it's quite fun.

Toone

21 petite rue des Bouchers (02 513 54 86, www.toone.be). Pré-métro Bourse. **Open** noon-midnight Tue-Sun. No credit cards. **Bar**. **Map** p55 D4 ㉛

This might be a well-known spot on the tourist trail, but to call it a trap would be doing the Toone family an injustice. This cosy, two-room dark-wood establishment is the old theatre bar. It's quirky enough (dangling marionettes and the like), quiet enough to enjoy in whispered intimacy, and not too quaint to put you off coming again.

Shopping

The lovely **Galeries St-Hubert** (see p23) consist of three glass-roofed arcades: Galerie du Roi, Galerie de la Reine and Galerie des Princes, each lined with shops.

Arlequin

7 rue du Chêne (02 514 54 28, www. arlequin.net). Pré-métro Anneessens or Métro Gare Centrale. **Open** 11am-7pm Mon-Sat; 2-7pm Sun. **Map** p57 C1 ㉜

Arlequin has all kinds of second-hand music, but focuses on rock, punk, import and jazz; its sister stores specialise in soul, funk, jazz, rap, reggae, classic and world music. Quality is high, and staff are friendly.

Balthazar

22 rue Marché aux Fromages (02 514 2396, www.balthazarstore.com). Pré-métro Bourse. **Open** 11am-6.30pm Mon-Sat. **Map** p55 D5 ㉝

A quietly refined, beautifully styled menswear emporium, Balthazar occupies three floors of an old gabled house, sitting discreetly among the garish kebab shops in what is known locally as the street of pittas. Under hefty wooden-beam ceilings are racks of Paul Smith, Comme des Garçons and John Smedley knitwear.

BCM

6 Plattesteen, Lower Town (02 502 09 72). Pré-métro Bourse. **Open** 11am-6.30pm Tue-Sat. No credit cards. **Map** p54 C5 ㉞

This is the best place in Brussels to find dance music on vinyl, running from techno, house and garage to drum 'n' bass. The staff are very helpful, and it's a good source of information for prospective clubbers.

La Boutique Tintin

13 rue de la Colline (02 514 51 52, www.tintin.com). Métro Gare Centrale. **Open** 10am-6pm Mon-Sat; 11am-5pm Sun. **Map** p55 D5 ㉟

Restaurant Vincent p63

Petite rue des Bouchers p52

The range includes clothes, stationery and soft toys, as well as the comic strip books themselves. Prices are high, but if you're a serious collector there are also some limited edition miniatures (and not-so-miniatures).

Brüsel

100 boulevard Anspach (02 511 08 09, www.brusel.com). Pré-métro Bourse. **Open** 10.30am-6.30pm Mon-Sat; noon-6.30pm Sun. **Map** p54 C4 ㉟

One of the finest comic shops in the city, with a huge choice of national favourites, as well as the most popular international strips in English, French and Dutch. The shop also stocks accompanying plastic and resin miniatures, posters and lithographs.

Dandoy

31 rue au Beurre (02 511 03 26, www.biscuiteriedandoy.be). Pré-métro Bourse. **Open** 8.30am-7pm Mon-Sat; 10.30am-6.30pm Sun. **Map** p55 D4 ㊲

The oldest cookie shop in town sells the best melt-in-your-mouth *speculoos* (traditional Belgian ginger biscuits), *pain d'amande* (wafer-thin biscuits), *pain d'épices* and *pain à la grecque*.

Délices et Caprices

68 rue des Bouchers (02 512 14 51). Pré-métro Bourse. **Open** noon-8pm Mon, Thur-Sun. **Map** p55 D4 ㊳

Délices et Caprices is run by Swiss Pierre Zuber, who's been in Belgium for 20 years and knows his beers. In addition to ale, beer glasses and other paraphernalia are sold, plus a few wines and genevers. Tastings are held on site.

Fnac

City 2, rue Neuve (02 275 11 11, www.fnac.be). Métro/pré-métro Rogier. **Open** 10am-7pm Mon-Thur, Sat; 10am-8pm Fri. **Map** p55 E2 ㊴

Head to the top of the City 2 shopping centre to find this mammoth store. The book stock is good in all disciplines and languages, and prices aren't bad. There are also CDs, DVDs, computer games

and audio-visual and computer equipment. By the door is a ticket office for concerts around town.

The Grasshopper

39 rue du Marché aux Herbes (02 511 96 22, www.thegrasshopper.be). Métro/pré-métro De Brouckère or métro Gare Centrale. **Open** 10am-7pm daily. **Map** p55 D4 ㊵

This fantastic toy store, with its eye-catching window displays, begins with a ground floor of trinkets and classics (yoyos, kaleidoscopes), novelty lamps and lots more. Upstairs are puzzles, educational and craft-based games, and larger items.

Hema

117 rue Neuve (02 227 52 109, www.hema.be). Métro/pré-métro De Brouckère. **Open** 9am-6.30pm Mon-Thur; 9am-7pm Fri, Sat. **Map** p55 D3 ㊶

Hema is like a Flemish Woolworths. Its two floors are filled with basics – candles, underwear, kitchenware and other random goods – of varying quality, but at ludicrously cheap prices.

Inno

111 rue Neuve (02 211 21 11, www.inno.be). Métro/pré-métro Rogier. **Open** 9.30am-7pm Mon-Thur, Sat; 9.30am-8pm Fri. **Map** p55 E3 ㊷

Inno is Brussels' main department store. Established in 1897, it has four shops in Brussels. This, the largest, has five floors with all the usual departments. The handbag, jewellery and lingerie departments are notably good.

Kaat Tilley

4 galerie du Roi (02 514 07 63, www.kaattilley.com). Métro Gare Centrale. **Open** 10am-6.30pm Mon-Sat. **Map** p55 D4 ㊸

Kaat Tilley's designs are ingeniously constructed out of delicate materials, sewn together in layers. The different lines include bridal and eveningwear, prêt-à-porter, knitwear, casualwear and womenswear.

Maison d'Art G Arekens

15 rue du Midi (02 511 48 08). Pré-métro Bourse. **Open** 10.30am-1pm, 2-6pm Mon-Sat. **Map** p54 C5 ㊹

You'll find a variety of religious icons such as crucifixes and triptychs. There are also small plaster-cast reproductions of non-religious statues, but the real highlights are the 55,000 postcards and reproduction etchings.

La Maison du Miel

121 rue du Midi (02 512 32 50, www.lamaisondumiel.be). Pré-métro Anneessens. **Open** 10.30am-6.30pm Mon-Fri, Sun; 10.30am-7pm Sat. **Map** p57 B1 ㊺

Make a beeline for this shop, which was founded in 1887 and sells all things honey-themed, scented and flavoured, from edibles to toiletries.

Pêle-Mêle

55 boulevard Maurice Lemonnier (02 548 78 00, www.pele-mele.be). Pré-métro Anneessens. **Open** 10am-6.30pm Mon-Sat. No credit cards. **Map** p57 B1 ㊻

Pêle-Mêle is stuffed with books, comics, magazines, CDs, records, videos, DVDs and computer games, to buy and sell. There's a decent English section and patient delving usually proves rewarding. Prices are good.

Planète Chocolat

24 rue du Lombard (02 511 07 55, www.planetechocolat.be). Pré-métro Bourse or Anneessens. **Open** 11am-6.30pm Tue-Sun. **Map** p54 C5 ㊼

As well as being a chocolate shop and tea house, Planète Chocolat offers (bookable) group demonstrations of chocolate-making. The chocolate itself is among the funkiest in town: chocolate lips and bouquets of chocolate 'flowers' are specialities.

Ride All Day

39 rue St-Jean, Lower Town (02 512 89 22, www.rideallday.be). Métro Gare Centrale. **Open** noon-6.30pm Tue-Sat. No credit cards. **Map** p55 D5 ㊽

Ride All Day kits out the local Mont des Arts skaters with boards, shoes and clothing. The staff are happy to advise about hardware.

Sterling

38 rue du Fossé aux Loups (02 223 62 23, www.sterlingbooks.be). Métro/pré-métro De Brouckère. **Open** 10am-7pm Mon-Sat; noon-6.30pm Sun. **Map** p55 D3/4 ㊾

The ground floor of this bookshop has an excellent range of contemporary fiction, children's books, magazines and newspapers in English; the first floor stocks classic fiction and non-fiction (such as computer and travel books).

Waterstone's

71-75 boulevard Adolphe Max (02 219 27 08). Métro/pré-métro Rogier. **Open** 9am-7pm Mon-Sat; 10.30am-6pm Sun. **Map** p55 D3 ㊿

The local Waterstone's has a good collection of English-language reading material (books, magazines and newspapers) on its two floors. The prices are on the steep side, though.

Nightlife

Ancienne Belgique

110 boulevard Anspach (02 548 24 24, www.abconcerts.be). Pré-métro Bourse. **Map** p54 C4/5 (51)

Once down-at-heel, but now shiny and new, l'Ancienne is a rare example of a renovation that transforms a venue without losing any of its spirit. Its main hall can hold 2,000, mostly standing, with an adjacent side bar poignantly decked out in posters for shows by performers no longer with us, including Joe Strummer and Johnny Thunders.

Le Belgica

32 rue du Marché au Charbon (no phone, www.lebelgica.be). Pré-métro Bourse. **Open** 10pm-3am Thur-Sat; 8pm-3am Sun. No credit cards. **Map** p54 C5 (52)

A must-visit bar, La Belgica is packed to the rafters with gay men and their friends of both sexes. It doesn't get buzzing until 11pm, but then it buzzes some. Looking over it all is a bust of Léopold II, who is clearly not amused.

Boy's Boudoir

25 rue du Marché au Charbon (02 614 58 38, www.leboysboudoir.be). Pré-métro Bourse. **Open** 6pm-5am daily. **Map** p54 C5 ❸

This stalwart of the busy Charbon gay scene is an all-in-one, made-to-measure delight. The main bar becomes a wild dance fest as DJs take over after midnight. Upstairs is a more genteel restaurant, serving food until the wee hours.

Dali's Bar

35 petite rue des Bouchers (no phone, www.myspace.com/dalisbar). Métro/pré-métro De Brouckère or métro Gare Centrale. **Open** 10pm-5am Thur-Sat. No credit cards. **Map** p55 C4 ❹

This compact club has become a byword for partying on a smaller scale. Trip hop, jazz, house and even didgeridoo competitions give proceedings a pleasingly varied flavour.

Factory

12 rue Fossé aux Loups (no phone). Métro/pré-métro De Brouckère. **Open** 10pm-6am Sat. No credit cards. **Map** p55 D3 ❺

It may only hold around 400 people, but Factory rocks on Saturday nights, pumped up to the nines by progressive house tunes and heavy one-off parties. Keep an eye on www.noctis.com for details of forthcoming events.

L'Homo Erectus

57 rue des Pierres, Lower Town (02 514 74 93, www.lhomoerectus.com). Pré-métro Bourse. **Open** 3pm-3am daily. No credit cards. **Map** p54 C5 ❻

You can't miss this tiny gay bar, with its Darwin-like window of apes slowly evolving into macho man. It's a victim of its own success – you need to evolve

into a snake to be able to squeeze to the bar at peak times. But L'Homo is fun, especially when the chaps start jumping on the bar for a song.

Music Village

50 rue des Pierres (02 513 13 45, www.themusicvillage.com). Pré-métro Bourse. **Open** 7pm-late Wed-Sat. *Concerts* 8.30pm Wed, Thur; 9pm Fri, Sat. **Map** p54 C5 ❼

The club provides a home for more traditional jazz styles, as well as the occasional avant-garde act. Weekdays attract a lot of business visitors, but on Fridays and Saturdays well known performers mean it fills up with jazz aficionados. Dinner is optional.

Smouss Café

NEW *112 rue du Marché au Charbon (0476 28 85 40, www.smousscafe.be). Pré-metro Anneessens.* **Open** 4.30pm-5am Thur, Fri; 6pm-5am Sat; 4-10pm Sun. No credit cards. **Map** p54 C5 ❽

This gay bar-café is one of the newest places to open on the street of dreams. It's a stylish place, with industrial design, stripped-back brickwork and a smart, clubby and cocktaily crowd. Sunday's tea dance is a massive hit.

Le Soixante

60 rue du Marché au Charbon (mobile 0477 70 41 56, www.myspace.com/barsoixante). Pré-métro Bourse. **Open** 9pm-late Fri, Sat, 1st Sun of mth. No credit cards. **Map** p54 C5 ❾

Inside the Soixante, twenty- and thirtysomethings knock back cocktails and flirt to retro house and electronica. It's an unpredictable place – sometimes safe and sound, sometimes frenetic.

Arts & Leisure

Actors Studio

16 petite rue des Bouchers (02 512 16 96, information 0900 27 854, http://actorsstudio.cinenews.be). Métro/pré-métro De Brouckère. No credit cards. **Map** p55 D4 ❿

Tucked into a hotel basement among the restaurants near the Grand'Place, this two-screen studio is one of Brussels' little gems. If your taste leans towards foreign cinema rather than Hollywood hits, the Actors is for you.

Arenberg Galeries

26 galerie de la Reine (02 512 80 63, www.arenberg.be). Métro Gare Centrale. No credit cards. **Map** p55 D4 ⑥①
These two 1895 arthouse screens still constitute Brussels' poshest cinematic address. Eclectic programming mixes good-looking world cinema with the French avant-garde, and there's an annual summer film bash, Ecran Total.

Théâtre de la Monnaie

Place de la Monnaie, 4 rue Léopold, Lower Town (070 23 39 39, www. lamonnaie.be). Métro/pré-métro De Brouckère. **Map** p55 D4 ⑥②
The national opera house is the jewel in Brussels' cultural crown, balancing contemporary work and classics with on-the-up performers and accessible prices.

Théâtre National

111-115 boulevard Emile Jacqmain (02 203 53 03, www.theatrenational.be). Métro/pré-métro De Brouckère. **Map** p55 D2 ⑥③
Though only serving the French-speaking community, this is one of Belgium's most important producing houses, with a mix of classical, modern, satirical and youth theatre in a beautiful performance space.

Théâtre du Toone

21 petite rue des Bouchers (02 511 71 37, www.toone.be). Métro/pré-métro De Brouckère. No credit cards. **Map** p55 D4 ⑥④
This is a world-famous, world-class marionette theatre with productions in Bruxellois dialect. The atmosphere balances out incomprehension, though you may be lucky enough to catch *Hamlet* in Brussels English.

St-Géry & Ste-Catherine

Restaurants, bars and churches are the key features of sassy St-Géry and former quayside Ste-Catherine, two small, self-contained quarters across boulevard Anspach from the Bourse. Both neighbourhoods have undergone major renovations, turning once-shabby districts into likeable but somewhat sterile and sanitised versions of their former selves. The area has also become the city's fashion centre, with a throng of choice boutiques on chic rue Antoine Dansaert and along rue des Chartreux.

St-Géry centres on the square of the same name, composed mostly of a great number of swanky designer bars, whose busy terraces create a Mediterranean atmosphere on summer nights.

By contrast, set around the quays of the old harbour, Ste-Catherine still feels like a port. The knock-on effect of St-Géry has crossed over, though, and now everyday Belgian bars, cafés and shops are becoming interspersed with nods to minimalist chic.

Sights & museums

Notre-Dame aux Riches Claires

23 rue des Riches Claires (02 511 09 37). Pré-métro Bourse. **Open** 4-6pm Sat; 9.30am-2pm Sun. **Map** p54 C4 ⑥⑤
This charming asymmetrical structure, built in 1665, is probably the work of Luc Fayd'herbe, a pupil of Rubens.

Ste-Catherine

Place Ste-Catherine (02 513 34 81). Métro Ste-Catherine. **Open** 8.30am-5pm (summer until 6pm) Mon-Sat; 9am-noon Sun. **Map** p54 C3 ⑥⑥
Almost as unkempt as its surroundings (and with an ancient pissoir built

Galeries St Hubert p64

between the buttresses), Ste-Catherine was designed in 1854 in neo-Gothic style by Joseph Poelaert, and almost became the stock exchange before becoming a church in 1867. One treasure is a 15th-century statue of a Black Madonna, supposedly rescued from the river Senne after being thrown in by angry Protestants.

St-Jean-Baptiste au Béguinage

Place du Béguinage (02 217 87 42). Métro Ste-Catherine. **Open** 10am-5pm Tue-Sun. **Map** p54 C3 ⑰

One of the best examples of Flemish Baroque architecture in the city, this large church, attributed to Luc Fayd'herbe, has a fluid, honey-coloured façade. Its light-filled interior houses a beautiful pulpit and 17th-century paintings by Theodoor van Loon.

Eating & drinking

Bonsoir Clara

22-26 rue Antoine Dansaert (02 502 09 90, www.bonsoirclara.be). Pré-métro Bourse. **Open** noon-2.30pm, 7-11.30pm Mon-Thur; noon-2.30pm, 7pm-midnight Fri; 7pm-midnight Sat; 7-11.30pm Sun. €€€. **Modern European**. **Map** p54 C4 ⑱

Bonsoir Clara is the restaurant that started it all off for Antoine Dansaert, a beacon of streamlined cool in an area that was just waiting to happen. It still pulls in the crowds with its understated sophistication and an eclectic menu that borrows from around the world with Asian spices, Italian delicacies and Californian reductions.

Comocomo

19 rue Antoine Dansaert (02 503 03 30, www.comocomo.com). Pré-métro Bourse. **Open** noon-2.30pm, 7pm-late daily. €. **Tapas**. **Map** p54 C4 ⑲

Comocomo owes its popularity to both the food and its concept: it's a Basque *pintxo* (tapas) bar with a sushi-style conveyor belt. The restaurant feels

inviting and up-to-the-minute (there's Wi-Fi, too). *Pintxos* wind their way around the snaking belt in colour codes: purple for pork, blue for fish, green for veggie and so on.

Le Coq

14 rue Auguste Orts (02 514 24 14). Pré-métro Bourse. **Open** 10am-late daily. No credit cards. **Bar**. **Map** p54 C4 ⑳

Le Coq's wood panelled walls and flat lighting resemble any bar in any town. But there's magic inside, from the professionalism of the older staff to the eclectic mix of daytime boozers and night owls, all there for an drink and deep philosophical banter.

Au Daringman

37 rue de Flandre (02 512 43 23). Métro Ste-Catherine. **Open** noon-1am Tue-Thur; noon-2am Fri; 4pm-2am Sat. No credit cards. **Bar**. **Map** p54 C3 ㉑

Also known as Chez Haesendonck or Chez Martine, this retro brown bar is hidden between the fashion quarter and the canal. It attracts an enjoyably varied clientele, with theatregoing older couples sharing tobacco smoke and squeezed-in tables with folk of a younger, more boho bent.

Divino

56 rue des Chartreux (02 503 39 09, www.restodivino.be). Pré-métro Bourse. **Open** noon-2.30pm, 6.30-11.30pm Mon-Fri; 6.30-11.30pm Sat. €. **Italian**. **Map** p54 B4 ㉒

Owner Moses Guez has created a retro-minimalist dining space where eager diners attack gigantic pizzas topped with goats' cheese and parma ham or carpaccio of beef. The pasta dishes are brilliantly subtle and make liberal use of seafood and fresh vegetables, and there's a lovely, brick-walled terrace.

Gecko

16 place St-Géry (02 502 29 99, www.geckococktailbar.be). Pré-métro Bourse. **Open** 9am-2am Mon-Thur;

10am-3am Fri; 10am-3am Sat, Sun.
No credit cards. **Bar**. Map p54 C4 **73**
This once in-the-know splinter of St-Géry, narrow of interior and thin in customers, is now a full-blown bar attracting an across-the-board clientele with cut-price lunches, zingy cocktails and – after a welcome expansion – cosy alcoves and casual furnishings.

Le Greenwich
7 rue des Chartreux (02 511 41 67).
Pré-métro Bourse. **Open** 10.30am-1am Mon-Thur; 10.30am-2am Fri, Sat.
No credit cards. **Bar**. Map p54 C4 **74**
The Greenwich is one of Brussels' institutions: a brown bar whose raison d'être is the studied patience of chess. Grab a chair, a beer, a board and a Tupperware box of chess pieces and become part of the furniture. Or order up a drink, open up a book and observe the regulars at play.

Hotel Orts Café
38-40 rue Auguste Orts (02 517 07 00, www.hotelorts.com). Pré-métro Bourse.
Open 9am-2am daily. **€**. **Café**.
Map p54 C4 **75**
Tourists and locals use the belle époque, ever-packed Orts for different purposes throughout the day – breakfast, lunch, evening drinks or for a good late-night booze-up on Guinness or the excellent collection of Belgian brews. The terrace is open year-round, despite the traffic.

Jacques
44 quai aux Briques (02 513 27 62, www.restaurantjacques.be). Métro Ste-Catherine. **Open** noon-2pm, 6.30-10pm Mon-Sat. **€€€**. **Seafood**.
Map p54 C3 **76**
A favourite with locals, Jacques oozes traditional, old-fashioned, Belgian charm, especially in summer when the huge windows are open. Jacques is famous for its sublimely light and buttery turbot with sauce mousseline, but the moules-frites make an excellent alternative. Booking is essential.

Jaloa
NEW *4 quai aux Barques (02 513 19 92, www.jaloa.com).* Métro Ste-Catherine.
Open noon-2.30pm, 7-10.30pm Tue-Fri; 7-10.30pm Mon, Sat. **€€€-€€€€**.
French. Map p54 B2/3 **77**
French-born chef Gaëtan Colin opened Jaloa in a classy 17th-century townhouse. Small and cosy, with a covered terrace, it exudes understated style. Set menus come in four-, six- or nine-course versions. Prices are lower at lunchtime, and at its offshoot on place Ste-Catherine, Jaloa Brasserie (nos.5-7, 02 512 18 31, www.brasseriejaloa.com).

Le Java
22 rue de la Grand Ile (02 512 37 16).
Pré-métro Bourse. **Open** 5.30pm-4am Mon-Thur, Sun; 5.30pm-5am Fri, Sat.
No credit cards. **Bar**. Map p54 C4 **78**
An imposingly cool bar composing the bow of St-Géry as it meets rue de la Grande Ile, Le Java makes the best of its corner plot. The interior is dominated by a round bar counter, footrailed by Gaudi-esque metalwork and offset by half a tree and half a globe.

Kafka
21 rue des Poissonniers (02 513 54 89). Pré-métro Bourse. **Open** 4pm-2am daily. **Bar**. Map p54 C4 **79**
If it's late and you're lashing back the vodkas, chances are you're in the Kafka. Not that you'll remember the next day, but this place boasts a heady array of vodkas, genevers and other assorted white spirits, plus all the usual beers to chase the chasers down with.

De Markten
5 rue Vieux Marché aux Grains (02 512 91 85, www.demarkten.be). Métro Ste-Catherine. **Open** 8.30am-midnight Mon-Sat; 10am-6pm Sun. **€**. No credit cards. **Café**. Map p54 C3 **80**
Before you enter this ground-floor café, take a step back and admire the magnificent building. The café is part of a cultural centre, and as such attracts young arty types from the Flemish

Le Greenwich p73

school of thought. Inside, the style is postmodernist industrial chic (it looks like a school canteen). In summer, a terrace looks over the square.

Monk

42 rue Ste-Catherine (02 503 08 80).
Métro Ste-Catherine. **Open** 11am-2am
Mon-Thur; 11am-4am Fri, Sat; 4pm-2am Sun. No credit cards. **Bar**.
Map p54 C4 ③
Monk occupies a 17th-century gabled house close to the main square. Inside, there's a long, dark-wood bar, softly lit by railway carriage wall lights above a row of mirrored panels. Jazz sounds go with the territory – hence the name.

Le Pré Salé

20 rue de Flandre (02 513 65 45).
Métro Ste-Catherine. **Open** noon-2.30pm, 6.30-10.30pm Wed-Sun.
€€€. **Belgian**. Map p54 C3 ②
There's no subtlety at the Pré Salé – it's all bright lights, big noise and vast plates of meat and fish, which is why we love it. A white tiled dining room leads through to the open kitchen, where madame chef cooks everything to order. Friday night is cabaret night, a decades-old tradition with Bruxellois jokes, bawdy humour and a bit of a knees-up (book way ahead).

La Tentation

28 rue de Laeken (02 223 22 75,
www.latentation.org). Métro/pré-métro
De Brouckère. **Open** 9am-4am Mon-Fri;
5pm-4am Sat, Sun. **Bar**. Map p54 C3 ③
Oozing chic, this converted drapery warehouse has huge windows, brick walls and low lighting. Staff are relaxed and friendly, and there's a stylish and civilised vibe. It's run by Brussels' Galician community, hence the menu (Spanish liqueurs, various tapas, cheese and cold meats) and the odd flamenco night.

Thiên-Long

12 rue van Artevelde (02 511 34 80).
Pré-metro Bourse. **Open** noon-3pm,
6-11pm Mon, Tue, Thur-Sun. **€**.
No credit cards. **Vietnamese**.
Map p54 C4 ③
First impressions of this Vietnamese restaurant are of a wooden-tabled caff incongruously set in a jungle of kitsch artefacts from the Far East. Steaming bowls of hot chilli soup, beef with bamboo and crunchy stir-fried vegetables sum up a long menu. The food is sublime and the portions huge.

Le Vistro

16 quai aux Briques (02 512 41 81).
Métro Ste-Catherine. **Open** noon-2.30pm, 7pm-midnight Mon-Fri;
6.30pm-midnight Sat. **€€-€€€**.
Seafood. Map p54 C3 ③
Occupying the narrowest house of a terrace of fish restaurants, this is a compact and welcoming bistro. The fish is on the traditional French side – think buttery sauces – but what makes Vistro special is its mighty platters of fresh seafood, groaning with oysters, mussels, clams, winkles and whelks, crowned with crab or lobster.

Shopping

AM Sweet

4 rue des Chartreux (02 513 51 31).
Pré-métro Bourse. **Open** 9am-6.30pm
Tue-Sat. No credit cards. **Map** p54 C4 ③
This lovely old-fashioned tea house and sweet shop sells biscuits, chocolate, cakes, sweets, teas and coffees, some of which are made in-house. Foodstuffs range from traditional *pain d'épices* to innovative concoctions such as French crystallised flowers, made from real rose, lavender and violet.

L'Ame des Rues – Librairie de Cinéma

49 boulevard Anspach (02 217 59 47).
Métro/pré-métro De Brouckère. **Open**
noon-6pm Mon-Sat. **Map** p54 C4 ③
A real mecca for film buffs, packed as it is with film stills, posters and postcards, plus television- and film-related books and memorabilia.

Annemie Verbeke

64 rue Antoine Dansaert (02 511 21 71, www.annemieverbeke.be). Pré-métro Bourse. **Open** 11am-6pm Mon, Wed-Sat. **Map** p54 C4 **⑱**

Fashionistas flock to Annemie Verbeke's shop, in a beautiful old building, for her classic clothes and exquisite knitwear.

Annick Tapernoux

28 rue du Vieux Marché aux Grains (02 512 43 79). Pré-métro Bourse. **Open** 1-6pm Fri; 11am-6pm Sat. **Map** p54 B4 **⑲**

Annick Tapernoux studied in Antwerp and at London's RCA prior to setting up her shop, which displays her silver jewellery (inspired by the elegance of the 1920s and '30s) and homeware, such as bowls and vases.

Christa Reniers

196 rue Antoine Dansaert (02 510 06 60, www.christareniers.com). Pré-métro Bourse. **Open** 11am-1pm, 2-6.30pm Mon-Sat. **Map** p54 B3 **⑳**

Since she sold her first piece of jewellery in the early 1990s, Christa Reniers has become Belgium's most famous jewellery designer. Self-taught, she creates several new designs each season; each piece is hand-cast and finished in the workshop above the store.

Christophe Coppens

2 rue Léon Lepage (02 512 77 97). Métro Ste-Catherine. **Open** 11am-6pm Tue-Sat. **Map** p54 B3 **㉛**

Flemish Christophe Coppens' hats are mainly for women, using all kinds of materials and ranging in price from around €150 to seriously pricey. His A-list fans include the likes of Rihanna and Beth Ditto.

Gabriele Vintage

27 rue des Chartreux (02 512 67 43). Pré-métro Bourse. **Open** noon-6pm Tue-Fri; 1-7pm Sat. **Map** p54 B4 **㉜**

This vintage clothing boutique sells hats, elegant evening dresses, coats and shoes, all dating from the 1920s onwards. Look out for the lopsided dummy standing on the street.

Hatshoe

89 rue Antoine Dansaert (02 512 41 52). Pré-métro Bourse. **Open** 12.30-6.30pm Mon; 10.30am-6.30pm Tue-Sat. **Map** p54 B3 **㉝**

Covetable designer footwear for both sexes by Patrick Cox, Costume National, Dries van Noten and Veronique Braquinho. The hats and scarves are by Cécile Bertrand.

Idiz Bogam

76 rue Antoine Dansaert (02 512 10 32, www.myspace.com/idizbogam). Pré-métro Bourse. **Open** 11am-7pm Mon-Sat. **Map** p54 B3/4 **㉞**

A quirky second-hand and vintage boutique for both men and women. Stock comes from London, New York and Paris, much of it customised with sequins, ruffs and so on. There are also some wacky wedding dresses, as well as shoes, hats and retro furniture.

Kat en Muis

33 rue Antoine Dansaert (02 514 32 34). Pré-métro Bourse. **Open** 10.30am-6.30pm Mon-Sat. **Map** p54 C4 **㉟**

This is the children's version of cutting-edge fashion store Stijl, which you'll find further along the street – so expect designer clothes at high prices. It's ideal for muddy weather, as the wellies and hats are rather fetching.

Mapp

5 rue Léon Lepage (02 551 1767, www.thisismapp.com). Métro Ste-Catherine. **Open** 11am-7pm Mon-Sat. **Map** p54 B3 **㊱**

This calm, white space on a little side street off the main fashion drag is good for art, CDs and vinyl, exhibitions and parties. Here, fashion is part of the bigger design picture. A mini blog on the website gives you news updates on the latest products and events. It's all very cool, but still accessible.

Martin Margiela

114 rue de Flandre (02 223 75 20, www.martinmargiela.com). Métro Ste-Catherine. **Open** 11am-7pm Mon-Sat. **Map** p54 B3 ⑤⑦

Keep an eye on the street numbers: Martin Margiela's store, like his clothes, is unlabelled. This first store of the Paris-based Flemish designer is an all-white space housing understated attire for men and women.

Own Shop

5 place du Jardin aux Fleurs (02 217 9571, www.own.be). Pré-métro Bourse. **Open** 11am-6.30pm Mon-Sat. **Map** p54 B4 ⑥⑧

Own Shop stocks high-end mens- and womenswear from the likes of Belgian demi-god Raf Simons (who also has a new line for Fred Perry), APC and Swedish trendsters Whyred. To top it all off, there's stunning silver jewellery from Belgian designer Atelier 11.

Rue Blanche

39-41 rue Antoine Dansaert (02 512 03 14, www.rueblanche.com). Pré-métro Bourse. **Open** 11am-6.30pm Mon-Sat. **Map** p54 C4 ⑨⑨

Belgian designers Marie Chantal Regout and Patrick van Heurck, launched Rue Blanche in 1987, with seven different styles of cotton jersey. Their business has expanded to include more than 100 items in gorgeous fabrics, as well as evening bags, scarves and shoes.

Stijl

74 rue Antoine Dansaert (02 512 03 13). Pré-métro Bourse. **Open** 10.30am-6.30pm Mon-Sat. **Map** p54 B4 ⑩⓪

The stark interior of Stijl contains some of the most cutting-edge design that Belgium has to offer – at a price. Owner Sonia Noël has a knack for spotting home-grown talent, having signed up first-time collections from Ann Demeulemeester, Dries van Noten and Martin Margiela, as well as Olivier Theyskens and Xavier Delcour.

Nightlife

L'Archiduc

6 rue Antoine Dansaert (02 512 06 52, www.archiduc.be). Pré-métro Bourse. **Open** 4pm-5am daily. **Map** p54 C4 ⑩①

This little art deco jewel on Antoine Dansaert was built in the 1930s, and Nat King Cole used to drop by for an après-gig drink and a tinkle on the ivories. It was resurrected in 1985; nowadays, doorbell entry, pre-dawn drinking and demi-monde regulars add to the allure.

Beursschouwburg

20-28 rue Auguste Orts (02 550 03 50, www.beursschouwburg.be). Pré-métro Bourse. **Open** Bar 7.30pm-late Thur-Sat. No credit cards. **Map** p54 C4 ⑩②

The Beurs is a centre of excellence for modern cross-form art, hosting a colourful range of events (concerts, club nights and so on) with an often eccentric vibe. The bar – more like a club, truth be told – opens at weekends and is pulsing until late. The roof terrace is packed in summer.

Box

7 rue des Riches Claires (no phone, www.boxclub.be). Pré-métro Bourse. **Open** 10pm-dawn daily. **Admission** free. No credit cards. **Map** p54 C4 ⑩③

The Box has become a stalwart of the Brussels gay scene. At the weekend, all three floors open up and resident DJs Dre and Andre1 play a mix of electro pop, techno and deep house. Special party nights add a sense of occasion – see the website for details.

Café Central

14 rue de Borgval (no phone, www.lecafecentral.com). Pré-métro Bourse. **Map** p54 C4 ⑩④

Café Central has become one of the capital's most fashionable venues, and an epicentre of cool. There are around three concerts here each month, along with DJ nights and cult film screenings. The Central is also a participating venue in various music festivals, including the legendary Jazz Marathon.

Le Coaster

28 rue des Riches Claires (02 512 08 47). Pré-métro Bourse. **Open** 8pm-5am Mon-Thur; 8pm-7am Fri, Sat. No credit cards. **Map** p54 C5 **105**

Not a club per se, the Coaster is a wild blip in the regularised St-Géry bar scene. Two rooms crammed into a 17th-century house fill up with young guys and gals out for a night of danceable music without the rigmarole of a nightclub. There's even table football. Reasonable drinks prices, an easygoing crowd and dancing on the tables when there's no more space make Le Coaster soar like a rocket.

Madame Moustache et son Freakshow

NEW *5-7 Quai au Bois à Brûler (02 485 534 494, www.madamemoustache.be). Métro Ste-Catherine.* **Map** p54 C3 **106**

This newcomer to the city's drinking scene is about as far removed from those tired clichés of boring Brussels as a bar can get. It's part circus, part Mexican cantina, a little bit burlesque and a lot trendy; unsurprisingly, it has proved a big hit with the party crowd. Expect bands, DJs, quirky cabaret and minor mayhem.

MP3 Disco Bar

17-19 rue du Pont de la Carpe (no phone, www.mp3bar.be). Pré-métro Bourse. **Open** 6pm-late Mon-Sat. No credit cards. **Map** p54 C4 **107**

MP3 is a busy late-night DJ bar in the heart of St-Géry, with a stylish interior featuring a curving bar, a row of brown stools and a bar-length mirror. Facing this is a stretch of banquettes leading to a more raised dancefloor, two semicircles of seats and a disco ball. All of this is mere decoration – a hindrance, even – to the buzz of activity by the decks at the far end of the bar counter, and the confined but enthusiastic dancing post-midnight.

Arts & Leisure

Kaaitheater

20 square Sainctelette (02 201 59 59, www.kaaitheater.be). Métro Yser. **Map** p54 C1 **108**

The art deco Kaai is one of Brussels' most invigorating performance spaces, at the forefront of the avant-garde. Along with Flemish-speaking theatre productions, it has a solid stable of visiting theatre and dance companies from around the globe, including Forced Entertainment and the Wooster Group. The medium-sized hall also hosts opera and concerts; Ictus is the resident ensemble. Smaller theatre productions and dance performances are also staged at its more intimate studio complex, Kaaitheaterstudio's (81 rue Notre-Dame du Sommeil, 02 201 59 59)

Koninklijke Vlaamse Schouwburg

146 rue de Laeken, Lower Town (02 210 11 12, www.kvs.be). Métro Yser. **Map** p55 D2 **109**

Known as the KVS, the Royal Flemish Theatre is one of the big subsidised houses providing serious theatre in Dutch. Productions here range from weirdly modern to firmly classical, with a sprinkling of guest productions from Belgium and Europe. There's a more experimental black box studio next door, the KVS Box.

The Marolles

The Marolles area is Brussels' traditional working-class district – albeit one that is being rapidly gentrified. It is a mix of shabby shops, restored antique boutiques and interior design palaces, with a largely immigrant population now peppered with nouveau-riche interlopers and even a few deep-rooted locals who still speak odd words of Marollien, a fantastically rude dialect that is a mélange of world languages.

Rue des Chartreux

At night, trendy drinkers gather in the adjoining Sablon district before making their way down the hill to eat, drink and party. As they tip out at daybreak, and the market sets up, so the cyclical life of the Marolles starts all over again.

At the north end of the district is place de la Chapelle, where **Notre-Dame de la Chapelle** stands. The Marolles' epicentre, though, is **place du Jeu de Balle**, whose daily flea market is surrounded by earthy bars and cafés.

Sights & Museums

Notre-Dame de la Chapelle

Place de la Chapelle (02 512 07 37). Prémétro Anneessens or bus 20, 48. **Open** 9.30am-4.30pm Mon-Fri; 12.30-5pm Sat; 8am-7pm Sun. **Map** p57 C2 ⑩
Parts of Notre-Dame de la Chapelle date from the 12th century, while the transepts are Romanesque and the nave 15th-century Gothic. Most of the paintings are 19th-century works.

Eating & drinking

Chez Marcel

20 place du Jeu de Balle (02 511 13 75). Métro/pré-métro Porte de Hal or bus 27, 48. **Open** 6am-midnight daily. No credit cards. **Bar. Map** p57 B3 ⑪
Of all the venues on the downbeat flea market square, this one is the most true to local life. As tatty as the traders it serves, Marcel's offers Cantillon Gueuze, a rarity from the Anderlecht brewery of the same name, along with cheaper, more standard beers, toasted sarnies and heavy lunches. Order a beer and enjoy the banter.

A la Clef d'Or

1 place du Jeu de Balle (02 511 97 62). Métro/pré-métro Porte de Hal or bus 27, 48. No credit cards. **Café. Map** p57 B3 ⑫
This loud caff is a favourite with locals. Sunday morning is best and busiest,

thanks to the accordionist and party atmosphere. The interior sports vinyl chairs and pink neon advertising signs; food is of the croque monsieur ilk.

La Grande Porte

9 rue Notre-Seigneur (02 512 89 98). Bus 27, 48, 95, 96. **Open** noon-3pm, 6pm-2am Mon-Fri; 6pm-2am Sat. **€€. Belgian. Map** p57 B2 ⑬
This cosy room, with a bar running along one wall (avoid the soulless backroom) is great for late-night Belgian classics: mussels, steaks and *waterzooi*, served with deep bowls of frites.

L'Idiot du Village

19 rue Notre-Seigneur (02 502 55 82). Bus 27, 48, 95, 96. **Open** noon-2pm, 7.15-11pm Mon-Fri. **€€-€€€. Modern European. Map** p57 C2 ⑭
Book ahead at this small bistro, in a side street off rue Blaes. The chairs and tables are of the type you'd hope to find in the nearby flea market, the flowers dried, the chandeliers camp. It sounds clichéd but works perfectly, as does chef Alain Gascoin's down to earth but well executed food; try the succulent rabbit and leek stew.

Au Stekerlapatte

4 rue des Prêtres (02 512 86 81, www.stekerlapatte.be). Métro Hôtel des Monnaies. **Open** noon-2.30pm, 7-11pm Tue, Wed; noon-2.30pm, 7pm-midnight Thur-Sat. **€€. Belgian. Map** p57 B4 ⑮
A late-night restaurant, serving traditional food at no-nonsense prices and occupying a warren of rooms and corridors. Steaks and sauces with great fat fries, grilled pig's trotter, spare ribs and black pudding are prepared in the time-honoured way (vegetarians beware).

Shopping

If you're looking for home furnishings, the best places for a browse are the two main streets of rues Blaes and Haute, leading to the well-attended daily flea market on place du Jeu de Balle.

Bernard Gavilan

146 rue Blaes (02 502 01 28, www. bernardgavilan.com). Métro Porte de Hal. **Open** 2-7pm Mon; noon-7pm Tue-Sat. No credit cards. **Map** p57 B3 ⑯
Local gay celeb Bernard reopened his stylish shop in 2010, selling classy designer second-hand and customised vintage clothes, including trainers, sports bags and accessories.

Les Memoires de Jacqmotte

92-96 rue Blaes (02 502 50 83, www. lesmemoiresdejacqmotte.com). Métro/ pré-métro Porte de Hal or bus 27, 48. **Open** 10am-6pm Mon, Tue, Thur-Sat; 10am-4pm Sun. **Map** p57 B3 ⑰
About ten years ago the warehouse of the Jacqmotte coffee emporium was converted into this space, where dealers can rent a pitch and display their goods. Expect to find art deco antiques, including furniture, porcelain and jewellery, plus earlier pieces.

Modes

164 rue Blaes (02 512 49 07). Métro/ pré-métro Porte de Hal or bus 27, 48. **Open** 10am-2.30pm Tue-Fri; 10am-3.30pm Sat, Sun. **Map** p57 B3 ⑱
Modes specialises in vintage clothing made prior to 1950. Most pieces are for women, but there's a small children's section and a room at the back for men. The amazing collection includes furs, coats, dresses, shirts, skirts and hats, plus glasses, gloves, hat pins, purses and boas. There's also a limited range of linens, laces, ribbon and fabric.

Nightlife

Bazaar

63 rue des Capucins (02 511 26 00, www.bazaarresto.be). Bus 27. **Open** *Restaurant* 7.30pm-midnight Tue-Thur. *Club* 7.30pm-4am Fri, Sat. **Map** p57 B3 ⑲

At Bazaar, a clubby, ethnic-inspired bar and restaurant is set above a small but regularly heaving party space, which occupies the cellar of the old Capucin monastery. Packed with beautiful people, it boasts some great one-off clubbing specials such as Catclub.

Fuse

208 rue Blaes, Lower Town (02 511 97 89, www.fuse.be). Métro/pré-métro Porte de Hal or bus 27, 48. **Open** 10pm-5am Thur; 11pm-7am Fri, Sat. **Map** p57 A4 ⑳
Fuse is the only club in Brussels with a truly international reputation, and the current residents draw crowds from all over. It attracts international stars, with the likes of Sven Väth making regular guest appearances. Fuse also hosts La Démence, Brussels' biggest and best-known gay night.

Havana

4 rue de l'Epée, Lower Town (02 502 12 24, www.havana-brussels.com). Tram 92, 94. **Open** 7pm-2am Thur; 7pm-5am Fri; 7pm-7am Sat. **Map** p57 C3 ㉑
In the shadow of the Palais de Justice, Havana is a classy joint carved out of an old Marollien house, attracting an international, professional crowd. You can eat, drink (three bars) or dance to Latin-based live acts, degenerating into a popular free-for-all later.

Recyclart

Gare de Bruxelles-Chapelle, 25 rue des Ursulines (02 502 57 34, www. recyclart.be). Métro Gare Centrale or bus 95. No credit cards. **Map** p57 B2 ㉒
Part of an urban regeneration project under the old Chapelle railway station, Recyclart is a hotbed of discovery. Often varied and inventive, this place is always throbbing; the DJ line-ups lean towards electro sounds and attract a young crowd. Occasional exhibitions, children's puppet shows and philosophical debates are also held here.

Place du Petit Sablon

The Upper Town

It's quite a climb from the Lower Town to the Upper Town – home of the seats of royalty and government, along with grand squares and imposing public spaces. Here, too, is the Gothic **Cathédrale des Sts Michel et Gudule**, which would have dominated the medieval city skyline – and acted as a constant reminder to the lower orders of the power of the Church.

A clutch of illustrious museums and galleries completes the picture, from the new **Musée Magritte** to the city's splendid pair of fine art galleries, the **Musées Royaux des Beaux-Arts**. The **Palais des Beaux-Arts**, better known as Bozar, is another cultural big-hitter; just across rue Royale, the Upper Town's dignified main artery, the 18th-century **Parc de Bruxelles** is an elegant spot for a stroll.

Meander south past the Musées Royaux des Beaux-Arts to reach the sophisticated enclave of Sablon.

Its landmark is the lovely **Notre-Dame au Sablon**, just across the road from the place du Petit Sablon; at the square's centre is a small but pretty park with railings by art nouveau architect Paul Hankar and a series of statuettes representing Brussels' ancient guilds. Behind Notre-Dame is the larger **place du Grand Sablon**, lined with upmarket restaurants, antique and chocolate shops and galleries.

Sights & museums

Cathédrale des Sts Michel et Gudule

Place Ste-Gudule (02 217 83 45, www.cathedralestmichel.be). Métro Gare Centrale or Parc or tram 92, 93, 94. **Open** 7am-6pm Mon-Fri; 8.30am-3.30pm Sat; 2-6pm Sun. **Admission** free. **Map** p84 C2 **①**
Work on this Gothic cathedral began in 1226, and was completed in 1499 – though chapels were added in the 16th

and 17th centuries. It is dedicated to the city's patron saints; St Michel is the better known, but Ste Gudule is far more popular in local lore. Her symbol is a lamp, blown out by the devil but miraculously relit as she prayed. The Cathédrale's darkest moments came with the mass defacement in 1579, perpetrated by Protestant iconoclasts, and in the late 18th century, when French revolutionary armies largely destroyed the interior along with priceless works of art. Still, the splendidly proportioned interior retains a host of treasures – not least the 13th-century choir and some stunning 16th-century stained glass.

Musée BELvue

7 place des Palais (070 22 04 92, www.musbellevue.be). Métro Trône or tram 92, 94. **Open** 10am-5pm Tue-Fri; 10am-6pm Sat, Sun. **Admission** €5; €3 reductions. Combined ticket with Palais Coudenberg €8; free-€5 reductions. No credit cards. **Map** p85 C4 ❷

The museum has become of wider interest since the Fondation Baudouin added an exhibition on the life of the last king, including his office and relics of his childhood. It's all rather voyeuristic, which makes it bizarrely irresistible.

Musée du Cinéma

Palais des Beaux-Arts, 9 rue Baron Horta (02 511 19 19, www.cinematheque.be). Métro Gare Centrale or Parc or tram 92, 94. **Open** from 4.30pm Mon, Tue, Fri; 2.30pm Wed, Sat, Sun; 12.30pm Thur. **Admission** €3. No credit cards. **Map** p84 C3 ❸

This modest but fascinating museum traces the early days of cinema, and the inventions that led to the development of cinematography by the Lumière brothers. It's also still used as a marvellous working cinema (see p92).

Musée des Instruments de Musique

2 rue Montagne de la Cour (02 545 01 30, www.mim.be). Métro Gare Centrale or tram 92, 94. **Open** 9.30am-4.45pm Tue-Fri; 10am-4.45pm Sat, Sun. *Restaurant* until 11pm Thur-Sat. **Admission** €5; free-€4 reductions. **Map** p85 C4 ❹

Designed by Paul Saintenoy in 1899, with curving wrought ironwork framing the windows, the Old England department store emerged a century later – and after a decade of restoration – as a museum housing a 6,000-strong collection of instruments, of which 1,500 are on display at any one time. Look out for the bizarre saxophone types dreamed up by the instrument's inventor, Adolphe Sax. The top floor restaurant offers panoramic city views.

Musée Magritte

NEW *1 place Royale (02 508 32 11, www.musee-magritte-museum.be). Métro Gare Centrale or tram 92, 94.* **Open** 10am-5pm Tue, Thur-Sun; 10am-8pm Wed. **Admission** €8; free-€5 reductions. Combined ticket with Musées Royaux des Beaux-Arts €13; €9 reductions. No credit cards. **Map** p85 C4 ❺

Until June 2009, the only place of homage to René Magritte was the museum in his little house in Anderlecht (see p136). That all changed with the opening of this new museum, in a stunning building on place Royale. On entering you are elevated up to the third floor, then work your way back down, with each floor representing a period in the artist's life. It's all very theatrical, and you get to see some of Magritte's most famous works. The museum has been wildly successful; book online to avoid the inevitable queues. See box p86.

Musées Royaux des Beaux-Arts

3 rue de la Régence (02 508 32 11, www.fine-arts-museum.be). Métro Gare Centrale or tram 92, 94. **Open** 10am-5pm Tue-Sun. **Admission** €8; free-€5 reductions. Combined ticket with Musée Magritte €13; €9 reductions. **Map** p85 C4 ❻

BRUSSELS BY AREA

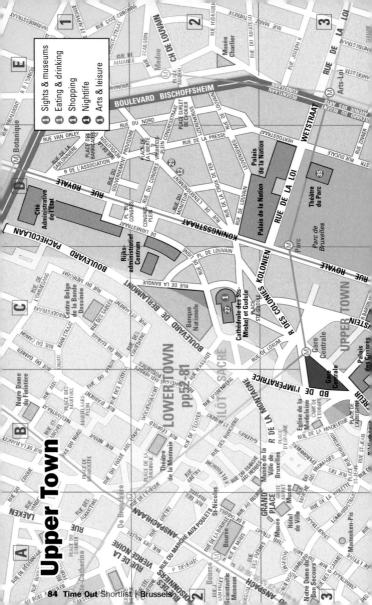

Upper Town

LAEKEN

Legend
- 1 Sights & museums
- 1 Eating & drinking
- 1 Shopping
- 1 Nightlife
- 1 Arts & leisure

LOWER TOWN pp52-81

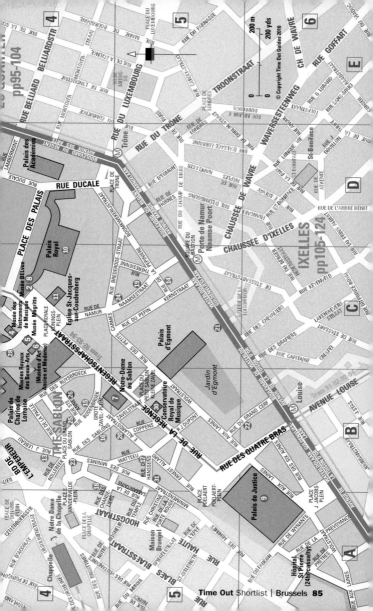

The great Magritte

Brussels' big new art museum lives up to the hype.

Musée Magritte

Anticipation was high in the run up to the opening of the new Musée Magritte (see p83) – a long-awaited, high-profile addition to the clutch of prestigious museums around place Royale.

As works on its chosen site, the grandly neo-classical Hôtel Altenloh, were taking place, the entire building was shrouded in a giant canvas. Its tantalising trompe l'oeil design showed the walls of the hôtel being drawn back like curtains, to reveal one of Magritte's magnificent paintings.

When, at last, the museum opened its doors in summer 2009, it met with a glowing reception. Visitors descended in droves – some 300,000 in the first six months alone – and the city fathers heaved a huge sigh of relief. In some ways, its success comes as no surprise; Magritte is, after all, one of the best-known artists in the world. Nonetheless, the bowler-hatted surrealist can't take all the credit: from the start, this has been a slickly planned and carefully realised project.

Occupying over 26,000 square feet and set over five spacious levels, the museum houses the largest collection of Magritte's work in the world, from drawings and paintings to photographs, sculptures and even amateur films shot by the artist.

But beyond its collections, this is a shining example of a modern, single-subject museum, ranking alongside Amsterdam's Van Gogh Museum and Berne's Zentrum Paul Klee. Culture chiefs around the world are also looking closely at the museum's innovative model of public-private partnership.

Energy company GDF Suez acted as 'founding sponsor', providing over six million euros' worth of expertise in the museum's construction – described by the director of the Fine Arts Museum as a 'decisive and inestimable element' in the project's realisation. And the end result? A combination of crowd-pleasing culture and low-energy, eco-friendly credentials that has given a hefty boost to Brussels' profile.

The Fine Arts Museum showcases the art of the Low Countries over the past six centuries, from masterworks by Rogier van der Weyden, Pieter Bruegel the Elder and Hans Memling to the work of the surrealists. A new wing carved out of two landmark buildings (one art nouveau, the other neo-classical) houses a bookstore, restaurant and café; the expansion made more room for the museum's superb collection of 17th- and 18th-century Flemish paintings, while the Patio gallery displays a rare series of Renaissance tapestries.

Notre-Dame au Sablon

38 rue de la Régence (02 511 57 41). Métro Porte de Namur or tram 92, 94. **Open** 9am-7pm Mon-Sat. **Admission** free. **Map** p85 B5 **7**

Built in the 15th and 16th centuries, Notre-Dame au Sablon was once home to a statue of Mary shipped in from Antwerp on account of its reputed healing powers. A carving of the boat can be seen in the nave, but the statue was destroyed by Protestants during the Iconoclastic Riots. The church itself boasts some stunning 14m (46ft) high stained-glass windows.

Palais Coudenberg

Entrance through Musée BELvue, place des Palais (070 22 04 92, www. coudenberg.com). Métro Trône or tram 92, 94. **Open** 10am-5pm Tue-Fri; 10am-6pm Sat, Sun. **Admission** €5; €3 reductions. Combined ticket with Musée BELvue €8; free-€5 reductions. No credit cards. **Map** p85 C4 **8**

Begun in the 11th century and enlarged by Philip the Good in the 15th century to become one of Europe's finest palaces, the Coudenberg was razed by fire in 1731. It was built over to create place Royale, but excavated in recent times to allow visitors a glimpse of its past glory. The cellars of the Aula Magna, a vast reception chamber with a capacity of 1,400 where Charles V gave his farewell address in 1555, are among the relics.

Palais de Justice

Place Poelaert (02 508 64 10). Métro Louise or tram 92, 94, 97 or bus 20, 48. **Open** 8am-5pm Mon-Fri. **Admission** free. **Map** p85 A6 **9**

The largest of Léopold II's grandiose projects, this intimidating colossus caused the demolition of 3,000 houses and the demise of its architect Poelaert, driven mad by his need for symmetry. Few critics agree on its style, even today: the 'Assyro-Babylonian' exterior is really a mish-mash of styles that has suffered some ridicule over the centuries. The interior is imposing – and flawlessly symmetrical – with grand magisterial statues of Demosthenes and Cicero, and an echoing waiting room, the Salle des Pas Perdus (Hall of Lost Steps). Kafka would have loved it.

Palais Royal

Place des Palais (02 551 20 20, www.monarchie.be). Métro Trône or tram 92, 94. **Open** *Late July-early Sept* 10.30am-5.30pm Tue-Sun. **Admission** free. No credit cards. **Map** p85 C4 **10**

The current, charmless building is an amalgam of styles created originally by Dutch king William I, remodelled in 1825 and again in 1904. As this is a residential palace, there's nothing much of historic interest here, so don't expect to see a fur wrap thrown casually over a Louis XV chair.

Eglise St-Jacques-sur-Coudenberg

1 impasse Borgendael, place Royale (02 511 78 36). Métro Trône or tram 92, 93, 94. **Open** 1-6pm Tue-Sat; 8.45am-5pm Sun. *Services* 5.15pm Tue-Thur; 9am, 9.45am (English), 11am Sun. **Admission** free. **Map** p85 C4 **11**

This late 18th-century church was built to resemble a Roman temple, although an incongruous belltower was later tacked on, giving it a strange Pilgrim Fathers-New England air. The interior is as peculiarly imposing as the exterior, and you can imagine that it served perfectly as a temple of reason and then as a temple of law when Brussels was under the sway of revolutionary France, before being returned to Catholicism in 1802.

Eating & drinking

Le Bier Circus
89 rue de l'Enseignement (02 218 00 34, www.bier-circus.be). Tram 92, 94. **Open** noon-2.30pm, 6-11pm Tue-Fri; 6-11pm Sat. **Bar. Map** p84 D2 ⑫
This somewhat bland brick bar would not merit mention, save for its astonishing range of beers. There are around 200 to pick from, filling 17 pages of the impressively lengthy menu. Vintage beers – gueuze aged in Cognac barrels, say, at €20 – warrant four pages, and there's a blackboard of seasonal beers. Delve a little deeper and you'll find an intimate side room, and a back room decorated with cartoon characters.

Le Cap Sablon
75 rue Lebeau (02 512 01 70, http://sites.resto.com/capsablon). Métro Gare Centrale or bus 95. **Open** noon-midnight daily. **€-€€. Modern European. Map** p85 B4 ⑬
Amid the glitz of the Sablon, this understated little brasserie continues to shine – and to resist any pressure to trendify. Its simple art deco interior gives it a homely feel, reflected in the menu. Succulent roasts and grills, fish livened up by oriental spices and wicked desserts all make for a satisfying meal. If you'd like to dine on the small terrace, specify when booking.

The Flat
NEW *12 rue de la Pépinière (02 502 74 34, www.theflat.be). Métro Porte de Namur.* **Open** 6pm-2am Wed-Sat. **Bar. Map** p85 C5 ⑭
This quirky bar may seem a bit theme park-ish at first, but works well as a sophisticated drinking den. Rooms are laid out as if they are part of someone's home, so you can quaff a beer in the lounge, the candlelit bedroom or even

the bathroom. Meanwhile, TV screens flash a stock market-type pricing index for drinks, which change according to how they're selling; get stuck into the margaritas and the price comes down.

Le Grain de Sable
15-16 place du Grand Sablon (02 513 18 44, www.legraindesable.be). Bus 95 or tram 92, 94. **Open** 8.30am-2.30am daily. **Bar. Map** p85 B4 ⑮
Outside Le Grain, the pavement terrace snakes its way around a corner, and in warm weather becomes a right-angle of convivial chatter. Inside, funky Latin jazz plays in the tiny bar, while the flickering candles seem to find their own bossa rhythm. The customers tend towards the vodka-Schweppes rather than the beer bottle, while the staff are friendly and easy on the eye.

Lola
33 place du Grand Sablon (02 514 24 60, www.restolola.be). Bus 95. **Open** noon-3pm, 6.30-11.30pm Mon-Fri; noon-11.30pm Sat, Sun. **€€€. Modern European. Map** p85 B4 ⑯
Lola is one of those institutions loved by urban professionals. It has the name, it has the location, it has the right clientele. The food is absolutely fine, in a modern brasserie way: rabbit with almonds and orange blossom or, for vegetarians, risotto and parmesan chips. It's a loud, gregarious place – so not a spot to whisper sweet nothings.

Le Perroquet
31 rue Watteeu (02 512 99 22, http://newsites.resto.com/leperroquet). Bus 95. **Open** 10am-1am daily. **€. Café. Map** p85 B5 ⑰
This art nouveau café features mirrors aplenty, plus a striking black and white tiled floor and a summer terrace. It's a stylish complement to the bland terrace bars of place du Grand Sablon, but quite dinky inside; expect a scramble for tables after office hours on Friday. Plentiful salads and stuffed pittas form the core of the menu.

Le Perroquet

Pierre Marcolini

Soul

NEW *20 rue de la Samaritaine (02 513 52 13, www.soulresto.com). Bus 48, 95.* **Open** noon-2.30pm, 7-10pm Wed-Fri; 7-10pm Sat, Sun. **€€. Organic. Map** p85 B4 🔞

The dining room at Soul is small but cosy, while the menu is all about nutritious, often organic ingredients. Typical mains might run from the wholesome likes of carrot and nut falafel with spiced lentils and raita to salmon fillet and quinoa risotto with green beans, seeds, feta and dill.

Shopping

Autour du Monde (Bensimon Collection)

70 rue de Namur (02 503 55 92, www.bensimon.com). Métro Porte de Namur. **Open** 10am-6.30pm Mon-Sat. **Map** p85 C5 🔞

The Brussels branch of a perennially popular Parisian lifestyle boutique sells a nicely co-ordinated mix of clothes, bags, toiletries, home furnishings, stationery and accessories.

Claire Fontaine

3 rue Ernest Allard (02 512 24 10). Tram 92, 93, 94. **Open** 10am-6.30pm Tue-Sat. No credit cards. **Map** p85 B5 🔞

It's near impossible to walk past Claire Fontaine without popping in to sample some delight. As well as sandwiches, soups, quiches and pastries to take away, there's a host of international delicacies such as olives, tisanes, absinthe and Belgian fruit wines.

Delvaux

27 boulevard de Waterloo (02 513 05 02, www.delvaux.com). Métro Louise or Porte de Namur. **Open** 10am-6.30pm Mon-Sat. **Map** p85 C5 🔞

Delvaux is an institution in Belgium, creating fine leather goods since 1829. The range includes covetable handbags, wallets, belts, a small range of hand luggage, silk scarves and ties.

Greta Marta

11 rue du Grand Cerf (02 648 62 24, www.gretamarta.be). Métro Louise. **Open** noon-6.30pm Mon; 10am-6.30pm Tue-Sat. **Map** p85 B6 🔞

The shop may bear the owner's name, but 80% of the stock carries the label of Belgian-born designer Diane von Furstenberg, famed for her classic wrap dress. The boutique aims to sell unique pieces within Belgium, stocking just one size of each design.

Pierre Marcolini

1 rue des Minimes (02 514 12 06, www.marcolini.be). Bus 95, 96. **Open** 10am-7pm Mon-Thur; 10am-8pm Fri; 9am-8pm Sat; 9am-7pm Sun. **Map** p85 B4 🔞

Pierre Marcolini is Brussels' biggest and brightest international name in chocolate, with branches dotted across the city. Mini macarons in every hue, tonka bean truffles and chocolates infused with orange blossom are among the temptations.

Toni & Guy

28 rue de Namur (02 213 70 90, www.toniandguy.be). Tram 92, 94 or bus 95. **Open** 10am-7pm Mon-Wed; 10am-8pm Thur, Fri; 9am-7pm Sat. **Map** p85 C5 🔞

Prices at Toni & Guy depend on who cuts your hair, ranging from a lowly stylist to the dizzy heights of the creative director. This Brussels outpost comes with multilingual staff, with English, French, Dutch, Spanish and Italian all spoken.

Wittamer

12 place du Grand Sablon (02 512 37 42, www.wittamer.com). Tram 92, 94 or bus 95. **Open** 9am-6pm Mon; 7am-7pm Tue-Sat; 7am-6.30pm Sun. **Map** p85 B4 🔞

Wittamer is a renowned chocolate dynasty on the Sablon, with a café along the street at no.6. In the shop, stock up on heart-shaped pralines, champagne truffles and other treats.

BRUSSELS BY AREA

Nightlife

Marquee

*20-22 rue Ste-Anne (no phone,
www.themarquee.be). Bus 95.* **Open**
10pm-late Thur; 11pm-late Fri, Sat;
9pm-late Sun. No credit cards. **Map**
p85 B4 ㉖

This stylish club, just off the posh
Grand Sablon, attracts a fashionable
crowd. Regular club nights Ottati's on
Thursdays and Borderline Corp on
Sundays give way to one-off specials
on Friday and Saturday nights. If you
want to hang with the beautiful people,
this is the place to be.

Arts & leisure

Cathédrale des Sts Michel et Gudule

*Place Ste-Gudule (02 217 83 45,
www.cathedralestmichel.be). Métro
Gare Centrale or Parc. No credit
cards.* **Map** p84 C2 ㉗

Brussels' most grandiose church is too
large for music more complicated than
Gregorian chant. Nevertheless, it's the
venue for a number of major events,
especially organ concerts. Audiences of
a thousand or so help absorb some of
the ten-second echo. Sunday 12.30pm
mass (10am in summer) often features
concerts; evening concerts are rarer.

Chapelle Royale

*Eglise Protestante, 2 rue du Musée
(02 213 49 40, www.eglisedumusee.be).
Métro Gare Centrale. No credit cards.*
Map p85 C4 ㉘

A pleasure, both acoustically and
architecturally. Too small for anything
larger than a baroque chamber orchestra, the venue is ideal for recitals featuring period instruments. As the
maximum audience size is 150, early
booking is highly advisable.

Cirque Royale

*81 rue de l'Enseignement, Upper Town
(02 218 20 15, www.cirque-royal.org).
Métro Madou.* **Map** p84 D2 ㉙

This is the nearest thing Brussels has
to the Royal Albert Hall: plush and
spherical, with great acoustics.
Classical concerts are held here, but
rock bands also take to the stage.
There's no dancing though – you're
expected to sit down and look enrap-
tured. Even talking to your neighbour
can draw disapproving looks.

Conservatoire Royal de Bruxelles

*30 rue de la Régence (02 511 04 27,
www.conservatoire.be). Tram 92, 94.*
No credit cards. **Map** p85 B5 ㉚

The Conservatory's fine hall is a little
too narrow for full-size symphonic
orchestras, but perfect for chamber for-
mations and solo recitals. Ignore the
peeling paint; the acoustics are excellent, in a hall partially designed by
French organ-builder Cavaillé-Coll.

Eglise des Sts Jean et Etienne aux Minimes

*62 rue des Minimes (02 511 93 84).
Bus 27, 48. No credit cards.* **Map** p85
B5 ㉛

This high-Baroque church has rather
average acoustics but hosts a wealth of
concerts. The Philharmonic Society
performs early music recitals here,
while the summer Midis-Minimes festival (www.midis-minimes.be) draws
locals and tourists alike. One Sunday
morning a month, the Chapelle des
Minimes ensemble presents fine performances of Bach cantatas, as it has done
for the last 20 years.

Musée du Cinema

*Palais des Beaux-Arts, 9 rue Baron
Horta (02 507 83 70, www.cinema
theque.be). Métro Gare Centrale or
Parc, tram 92, 93, 94 or bus 38, 60,
71. No credit cards.* **Map** p84 C3 ㉜

With programming that draws on the
50,000 reels sitting in its vaults, and
live piano accompaniment to silent
films, the Film Museum is the closest
you'll get to cinema heaven. Each
month, three or four movie cycles focus

Palais des Beaux-Arts (Bozar)

The beer necessities

Know your gueuze from your lambic.

The choice of beers in Brussels' myriad bars can be deeply confusing – not least if you're not sure what lambic beer is. Here's a quick beginners' guide to get you started.

Specific to the Brussels region, lambic was the staple beer of the Belgians in the early 19th century. In its original form, it is a cloudy, viciously tart draught brew – rarely seen nowadays, though you can find it at A la Bécasse (see p56).

Instead, Brussels' bars serve new-style lambics, mostly in the guise of gueuze or kriek; knowing the difference between them can put you on nodding terms with the locals. Gueuze is a careful blend of young and old lambics, matured in oak barrels for one and three years respectively. Gueuze needs at least a year to mature, but can last for up to twenty years; this is reflected in prices at bars like Delirium Café (see p59).

Add cherries to the mix and you get kriek. Like gueuze, it continues to ferment in the bottle and maintains a subtle, sour taste. Variants include raspberry or peach, but beware of imposters: some breweries simply add fruit syrups to the beer, and some are not really lambics at all. Lindemans, Cantillon or Timmermans will always give you the authentic experience, while Belle-Vue is a sweeter option.

on a director or a theme – anything from ethnographic shorts from the silent period to *Dirty Harry*-era Clint Eastwood. Book ahead.

Palais des Beaux-Arts (Bozar)

23 rue Ravenstein (02 507 84 44/ 02 507 82 00, www.bozar.be). Métro Gare Centrale or Parc or tram 92, 94. **Open** 10am-6pm Tue, Wed, Fri-Sun; 10am-9pm Thur. **Map** p84 C3 ❸❸
The once moribund Palais des Beaux-Arts has been transformed by director Paul Dujardin into the Bozar, a modern, multi-purpose cultural institute not unlike the Barbican in London. Designed by Victor Horta in 1928, the art deco building has also been restored. Home of the National Orchestra and seat of the renowned Philharmonic Society, Bozar is Brussels' most prestigious venue.

Théâtre du Rideau de Bruxelles

Palais des Beaux-Arts, 23 rue Ravenstein (02 507 83 61, www. rideaudebruxelles.be). Métro Gare Centrale or Parc. **Map** p85 C4 ❸❹
Resident at the Palais since 1943, the Rideau is an integral part of the French-language theatre scene. It appeals to the middle-class, middle-brow set, with modern classics and safe costume dramas, but stages an eyebrow-lifting modern piece every now and then.

Théâtre Royal du Parc

3 rue de la Loi (02 505 30 30, www. theatreduparc.be). Métro Arts-Loi or Parc. **Map** p84 D3 ❸❺
This stunner was built as a playhouse for the rich in 1782, and has managed to hang on to its genteel audience ever since. Most of what is staged here is described as comédie, but this doesn't mean funny; even Eugene O'Neill's darkly compelling *Long Day's Journey Into Night* is described as a 'comédie dramatique'. Expect a healthy mix of classic and contemporary plays.

Berlaymont

EU Quarter

In the 1960s, an attractive 19th-century quarter around the Schuman roundabout was torn down to allow the construction of office buildings for the burgeoning European institutions. Then, in the 1980s, the once-lively Quartier Léopold suffered a similar fate when the European Parliament complex was built. Most Bruxellois were appalled at the damage done to the fragile fabric of their city, with soaring office blocks nudging out lovely townhouses, and local communities gone forever.

Still, change is afoot, with some ambitious plans for improvement on the cards (see p101). Recent times have also seen a more decisive architectural style, with heavy grey office blocks being replaced by more daring buildings. One such structure is the (in)famous Berlaymont, by Schuman métro station. It is a high-tech, star-shaped symbol not just of the EU,

but of the bureaucratic nightmares associated with it – it now houses the whole Commission and 3,000 officials. Opposite is the Justus Lipsius building, where the world's media gather on high days. Away to the south, shining like a crystal palace in the distance, is the European Parliament, known locally as the *Caprice des Dieux* (Folly of the gods).

For the best views of this impressive set of buildings head to parc Léopold, home to the **Institut Royal des Sciences Naturelles** and the weird but wonderful **Musée Wiertz**. Turn right out of the park and you'll come to place Jourdain, lined with bars and restaurants in the old style; here, too, is Maison Antoine, the most famous *friterie* in town.

The area's loveliest green space is parc du Cinquantenaire. The vast Arc de Triomphe stands at its centre, flanked by museums

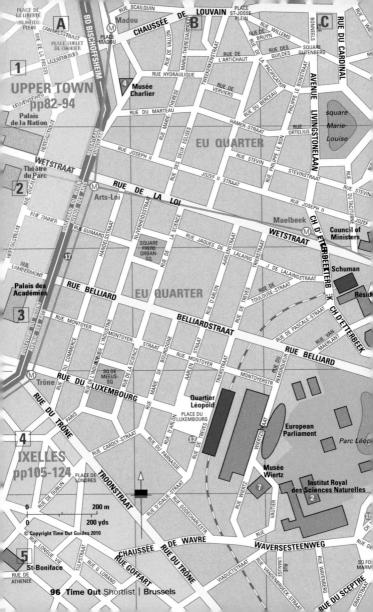

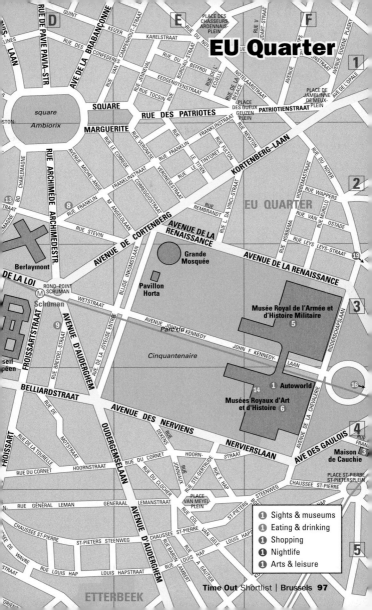

EU Quarter

Sights & museums

Eating & drinking

Shopping

Nightlife

Arts & leisure

DIT MONUMENT IS IN 1905
OPGERICHT TER VERHEERLIJKING
VAN BELGIE'S ONAFHANKELIJKHEID

EU Quarter

– including the **Musées Royaux d'Art et d'Histoire**. A short stroll away is the beautiful, art nouveau **Maison de Cauchie**.

Sights & museums

Autoworld

11 parc du Cinquantenaire (02 736 41 65, www.autoworld.be). Métro Mérode. **Open** Apr-Sept 10am-6pm daily. Oct-Mar 10am-5pm daily. **Admission** €6; €3-€4.70 reductions. No credit cards. **Map** p97 F4 ❶

The venue for Belgium's motor show since 1902, this is one of the biggest automobile museums in Europe. Enthusiasts will be thrilled by its collection, which runs from horse drawn carriages to natty little '50s sports cars and gleaming, look-at-me limousines.

Institut Royal des Sciences Naturelles

29 rue Vautier (02 627 42 38, www.naturalsciences.be). Métro Trône or bus 34, 80. **Open** 9.30am-5pm Tue-Fri; 10am-6pm Sat, Sun & school hols. **Admission** €7; free-€6 reductions. **Map** p96 C5 ❷

The child-friendly Royal Natural History Museum contains one of the world's finest collections of iguanodons, as well as a deep-sea diving vessel that plunges down to see a scrap between a sperm whale and a giant squid. These now vie for visitors' attentions with the sumptuous Arctic and Antarctica Room.

Maison de Cauchie

5 rue des Francs (02 733 86 84, www. cauchie.be). Métro Mérode. **Open** 10am-1pm, 2-5.30pm 1st weekend of mth & by appt. **Admission** €5; free under-12s. No credit cards. **Map** p97 F4 ❸

The former home of renowned painter and architect Paul Cauchie was built in 1905, in the twilight of Brussels' art nouveau period. Its geometric shapes show the influence of the Vienna Secession; the richly gilded exterior

mural of maidens in long, flowing gowns is reminiscent of Gustav Klimt, and designed to act as an advertisement for Cauchie's art. Following a 15-year restoration project the house is in fine fettle, inside and out; in the cellar and studio, a gallery space exhibits Paul and Lina Cauchie's paintings.

Musée Charlier

16 avenue des Arts (02 220 26 91, www.charliermuseum.be). Métro Arts-Loi or Madou or bus 29, 63, 65, 66. **Open** noon-5pm Mon-Thur; 10am-1pm Fri. **Admission** €5. No credit cards. **Map** p96 A1 ❹

Sculptor Guillaume Charlier was an active figure in Brussels in the early 1900s, when he was taken under the wing of Henri van Cutsem, a patron of the arts. Charlier moved into van Cutsem's house, the site of the museum, where he hosted concerts and salon discussions. The house, whose interior was redesigned by Horta, is filled with rich tapestries, gilded mirrors, antiques and works by Ensor, Meunier and Charlier himself.

Musée Royal de l'Armée et d'Histoire Militaire

3 parc du Cinquantenaire (02 737 78 11, www.klm-mra.be). Métro Mérode. **Open** 9am-noon, 1-4.45pm Tue-Sun. **Admission** free. No credit cards. **Map** p97 F3 ❺

A few years ago, a revamp added a new section covering international conflict from 1918 to the present day – the European Forum on Contemporary Conflicts. The display dealing with the 1830 Belgian uprising and the hangar filled with aircraft from the two world wars are also particularly striking.

Musées Royaux d'Art et d'Histoire

10 parc du Cinquantenaire (02 741 72 11, www.kmkg-mrah.be). Métro Mérode. **Open** 9.30am-5pm Tue-Fri; 10am-5pm Sat, Sun. **Admission** €5; free-€4 reductions. **Map** p97 F4 ❻

The museum's antiquity department has a huge array of artefacts from the ancient worlds of Egypt, Greece, the Near and Far East, and pre-Columbian America. Other collections include European art from the Middle Ages, art deco glass and metalwork, lace and 18th-century carriages.

Musée Wiertz

62 rue Vautier (02 648 17 18, www.fine-arts-museum.be). Métro Trône or bus 34, 38, 54, 59, 80, 95. **Open** 10am-noon, 1-5pm Tue-Fri. **Admission** free. No credit cards. **Map** p96 B4 **7**

A somewhat controversial figure, Antoine Wiertz (1806-65) painted vast canvases of deeply gruesome subjects: often biblical and mythical scenes, with plenty of gratuitous violence and shock value. Well regarded in his time (not least by himself – he put his own work on a par with that of Michelangelo and Rubens), Wiertz persuaded the state to buy him this house and studio in return for his artworks when he died. The museum contains 160 pieces and makes for an unusual, if bizarre, diversion.

Eating & drinking

L'Atelier Européen

28 rue Franklin (02 734 91 40, www.atelier-euro.be). Métro Schuman. **Open** noon-2.30pm, 7-10pm Mon-Fri. **€€.** **Modern European**. **Map** p97 D2 **8**

This former wine warehouse, with a leafy courtyard out front, was first converted into a studio, then a restaurant. The studio feel remains – it's light and airy, with a beamed roof and white-washed brick walls. The food is a mix of Belgian and French, with a focus on seafood (own-made grey shrimp croquettes, say, or roasted sea bass). Prices are reasonable for the area, which makes the place lively.

Au Bain Marie

46 rue Breydel (02 280 48 88). Métro Schuman. **Open** noon-2pm Mon-Fri. **€.** **Italian**. **Map** p97 D3 **9**

The little, weekday lunch-only Au Bain Marie prides itself on its meatless, frite-less menu. Instead, it serves up great wedges of freshly made quiches, home-made pastas and verdant salads. Such is its popularity, it's near-impossible to get in without a reservation.

Chez Bernard

47 place Jourdan (02 230 22 38). Métro Schuman. **Open** 7am-2am daily. No credit cards. **Bar**. **Map** p96 C5 **10**

Sitting unfazed amid all the mock-nouveau wine bars and brasseries on this busiest of squares, Bernard's remains rock-solid traditional. A long mirrored room leads to an unlikely glass conservatory, giving the impression that a tearoom has been stuck on the back of a beer hall. The crowd includes Eurocrats feeling good about mixing with locals, locals feeling indifferent about mixing with Eurocrats and Sunday morning shoppers. You can buy chips from Maison Antoine, the famous *frites* stall opposite, and eat them here; staff will offer you a napkin and a beer list.

L'Esprit de Sel Brasserie

52-54 place Jourdan (02 230 60 40, www.espritdesel.be). Métro Schuman. **Open** noon-2.30pm, 7-10pm midnight daily. **€€.** **Brasserie**. **Map** p96 C4 **11**

What used to be two restaurants have now become one. The menu is the same, but the looks are different: one section is slightly more trad, with an amazing Murano glass chandelier, while the other is all wood, marble and copper. But it matters not a jot when you get round to tucking into the best of Belgian, from simple roast chicken and chips to rabbit in sour beer or beef tournedos with port. Popular with artistes, free thinkers and the odd celeb.

Fat Boy's

5 place du Luxembourg (02 511 32 66, www.fatboys-be.com). Métro Trône. **Open** 11am-late daily. **Bar**. **Map** p96 B4 **12**

European Parliament p95

Fat Boy's is Brussels' main expat sports bar, conveniently set in the considerable shadow of the European Parliament. Although it is categorically American in style, Brits flock here in droves to spend beery Sunday afternoons gawping at any of nine screens showing Premiership action and scoffing their way through the meaty menu of ribs and burgers. Fat Boy's improves when the post-work crowd descends to fill its long interior, spilling on to the terrace on summer evenings.

Kafenio

134 rue Stevin (02 231 55 55, www.kafenio.be). Métro Schuman. **Open** noon-3pm, 6-11pm daily. **€.** **Greek. Map** p97 D2 ⑬

It's at lunchtimes that this Greek-inspired restaurant and bar really swings into action, with every table taken and a queue forming at the door. The reason is the buffet meze bar, where – accompanied by a waiter – you can make your selection from 50 hot and cold dishes, sit down with a drink and await delivery.

Le Midi Cinquante

Musées Royaux d'Art et d'Histoire, 10 Parc du Cinquantenaire (02 735 87 54). Métro Mérode. **Open** 10.30am-4.30pm Tue-Sun. **€.** **Modern European. Map** p97 E4 ⑭

This inviting establishment attracts not just visitors to the museum, but the movers and shakers of the EU Quarter. Renowned for its pasta dishes, Le Midi is all about generous portions, perfectly prepared and cleanly presented. Also on offer are flavoursome soups. Moroccan tagine and oriental-inspired salads. As befits so grand a building, the dining room is delightfully elegant; the lovely terrace overlooking the park is packed in summer.

Schievelavabo

344 Chaussée de Wavre, place Jourdan (02 280 00 83, www.leschievelavabo.be). Métro Schuman. **Open** 11am-2.30pm,

7pm-midnight Mon-Fri; 7pm-midnight Sat, Sun. **Bar. Map** p96 C5 ⑮

The Schievelavabo (literally translating as 'Wonky Washbasin', or – if you prefer – 'Skewiff Sink') now has several outposts across the city. This one is fairly typical, with its solid wooden furniture, enticing variety of well-sourced local beers and amiable staff. There's food to soak up the brews, too: think giant burgers and chips, substantial salads and pasta.

La Terrasse

1 avenue des Celtes (02 732 28 51, www.brasserielaterrasse.be). Métro Mérode. **Open** 8am-midnight Mon-Wed; 8am-1am Thur-Sat; 10am-midnight Sun. **€.** **Belgian. Map** p97 F4 ⑯

Thanks to its proximity to Mérode métro and its sun-dappled terrace, this place makes an ideal meeting spot. On the other side of the Parc de Cinquantenaire from the EU institutions, it's set far enough back from the traffic of avenue de Tervueren to give the illusion of rustic supping. It's more than just a summer retreat, though; in autumn, when the kitchen cooks up mussels in eight varieties, the clientele moves inside to a chatty, old-style brasserie of wooden furnishings beneath globe light fittings.

Shopping

Filigranes

39-40 avenue des Arts (02 511 90 15, www.filigranes.be). Métro Arts-Loi. **Open** 8am-8pm Mon-Fri; 10am-7.30pm Sat; 10am-7pm Sun. **Map** p96 A3 ⑰

This labyrinthine bookstore has a decent English books section, as well as assorted international magazines and newspapers. The art department is outstanding, and the kids will love the children's area. You can also stop for a drink in the central café, surrounded by books and browsers. Filigranes is totally un-Belgian in that it's open 365 days a year.

The sky's the limit

High-rise plans to reinvent the EU.

Rue de la Loi

The creation of the EU Quarter was a frankly traumatic affair, as the close-knit community and classic townhouses of the old quartier Léopold vanished in a flurry of Compulsory Purchase Orders, demolitions, digging up and relocations, leaving locals understandably resentful.

In the quartier's place came the EU institutions. They arrived bit by bit – as did the buildings, resulting in a mish-mash of styles. Rather souless by day, the quarter can be eerily empty by night, with little to endear it to locals' hearts.

The ongoing PR problem of how to marry the demands of the EU and the investment it brings with the needs of the city and its people has taxed planners and politicians for decades, with numerous schemes coming to nothing over the years.

Then, in 2008, an architectural competition was launched, calling for a radical redevelopment of the area around the unlovely, traffic-packed rue de la Loi. Not only would it expand the EU

administrative centre, but it would also bring new housing and leisure facilities, open to everyone.

So far, so good – until the announcement of the winning design, from a consortium led by French architect Christian de Portzamparc, in early 2009. Its high-rise nature has led to words like brutal, ugly and inhuman being bandied on blogs, and concerns are also being raised about the project's timescale and cost. With estimates that the work could take up to 15 years to complete, its opponents fear a vast construction site in the heart of the city.

On the other hand, it could be just what Brussels needs. It's hard to love rue de la Loi as it is now, and it's hard to imagine anyone mourning its passing. The four lanes of traffic will be cut to two, with a central tram line, and the plan includes plenty of green space as well as new housing (though doubters fear high-cost flats for the EU elite). As ever, the balance remains delicate – but change is most definitely afoot.

Soaring ambitions

The ruler of Belgium from 1865 until 1909, Léopold II left Brussels with a dizzying legacy of overblown buildings and monuments.

There's certainly no missing the huge **Arc de Triomphe**, at the centre of the EU Quarter's **parc du Cinquantenaire**. Some 300 labourers toiled day and night to finish it in time for Belgium's 50th anniversary celebrations in 1880; alas, it was too much of a stretch, and a wooden stand-in had to be deployed. The whole thing was only completed in 1910 – a year after the king's death.

Among the oddest of his whims were the Japanese Tower and Chinese Pavilion (see p130), two extravagant follies. He was also behind Tervuren's Musée du Congo – which brings us to the question of how the king's grand schemes were funded.

Léopold extracted a fortune from ivory and rubber in the Congo, under the guise of philanthropy. In fact the regime ran on fear, with whippings and brutal mutilations to keep workers in line; when the truth emerged, it unleashed an international scandal. The king's Congo museum, now renamed the Musée Museum Royal de l'Afrique Centrale (13 chaussée de Louvain, 02 769 52 11, www.africamuseum.be) was long a celebration of imperial arrogance. It's now being given a much-needed overhaul – so it'll be interesting to see what it has to say about its founder.

Gallaecia

6 rue Charles Martel (02 230 33 56). Métro Maelbeek. **Open** 11am-7pm Mon-Fri; 11am-3.30pm Sat. No credit cards. **Map** p96 C2 ⑱
If you're looking for superior Spanish produce, then this is the place to come. It sells tasty empañadas, as well as olive oils, hunks of manchego cheese, salty serrano ham, tinned fish and various jars of preserves. Sweet treats such as *turrones* and *polvorones* (crumbly shortbreads) are popular, as are the wines and cava.

Anthony-And

165 rue de Linthout (02 736 45 35, www.anthony-and.com). Métro Mérode. **Open** 9am-7pm Mon-Sat. No credit cards. **Map** p97 F3 ⑲
Just to the south of parc du Cinquantenaire, this fashionable but unpretentious salon has some talented hairdressers, and very reasonable prices. Book on a Saturday and there's a musical accompaniment to the sound of snipping scissors, as a resident DJ spins the vinyl.

Nightlife

Espace Senghor

366 chaussée de Wavre (02 230 31 40, www.senghor.be). Métro Maelbeek or Schuman. **Open** varies; call for details. Tickets €8-€12. No credit cards. **Map** p96 C5 ⑳
The French-speaking community restored this old cinema (formerly the Rixy) and re-opened it as a cultural centre, the Espace Senghor, in 1988. Set on a pedestrianised street just off busy place Jourdain, it runs an imaginative and popular programme of jazz and world music concerts, usually three or four times a month. The programme also takes in contemporary dance performances, film screenings, theatre (including children's shows) and debates. It's not the place for a riotous night out, but there are generally some gems on the line-up.

Matongé

Ixelles

Covering a swathe of southern Brussels before it becomes forest, the commune of Ixelles represents what living in this city is all about. Here, simply turning a corner can take you from one world to another: from fine belle époque and art nouveau townhouses to the vibrancy and bustle of the African quarter of the **Matongé**, which takes its name from an area of Kinshasa in the Congo, and the stylish bars of the Châtelain, Ixelles is Brussels at its most diverse.

The quarter grew up around the imposing, broad **avenue Louise**, built in the mid 19th century and named for Léopold II's daughter. The first stretch, flanked with smart shops and galleries, makes for enjoyable browsing; after place Stéphanie, traffic dominates and it's better to take a tram. Many run all the way to the avenue's end and the **Bois de la Cambre** – Brussels' answer to Central Park.

A vast wooded parkland on the edge of the city centre, it was once part of the vast Forêt de Soignes.

Hop off the tram halfway down the avenue to visit the **Fondation pour l'Architecture**, tucked down a sidestreet. On the other side of the avenue, to the west, rue du Châtelain leads to **place du Châtelain**, with its chic eateries and buzzy nightlife. The square also hosts a brilliant food market on Wednesday afternoon from 2pm.

For a grittier take on Ixelles, head east from avenue Louise to Porte de Namur, where the twin chaussées of Wavre and Ixelles fan out. Between the two spread the colourful shops and cafés of the Matongé. Chaussée d'Ixelles ends at the **Etangs d'Ixelles**, or Ixelles Ponds, which are filled with ducks and fishermen, and lovely in spring and summer. Here, too, is the multi-purpose arts venue **Flagey**, set in splendid 1930s premises.

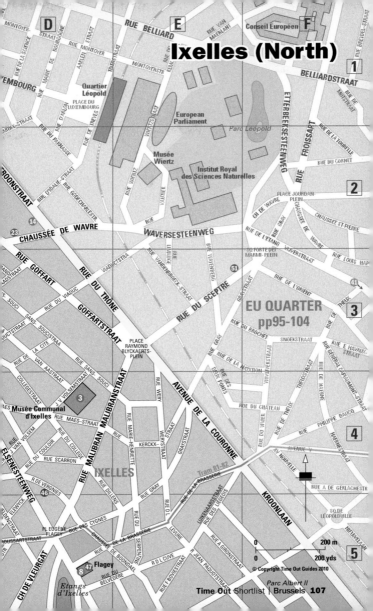

Ixelles (North)

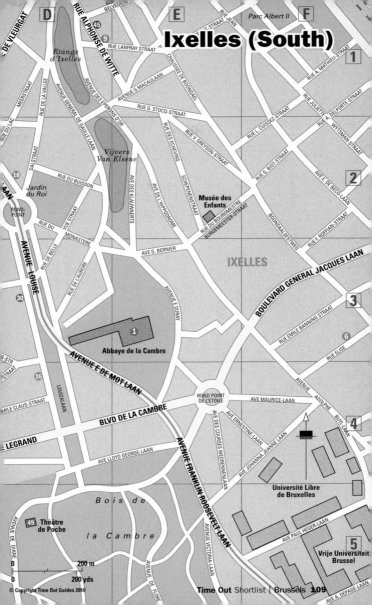

Ixelles (South)

D E F

1

2

3

4

5

Parc Albert II

Etangs d'Ixelles

RUE ALPHONSE DE WITTE

RUE LANFRAY STRAAT

CHAUSSÉE DE BOONDAEL

AVENUE G. MACAULAAN

RUE G. STOCQ-STRAAT

RUE V. GREYSON-STRAAT

RUE L. CUISSEZ-STRAAT

RUE A. MATHIEU-STRAAT

RUE A. DE PORTE-STRAAT

RUE JULIETTE-STRAAT

RUE A. WYTSMAN-STRAAT

AVENUE DES ÉPERONS D'OR

RUE DES ÉCHEVINS

RUE DE LA VALLÉE

MEERSTRAAT

RUE DU LAC

DALSTRAAT

Vijvers Van Elsene

RUE DU BUISSON

AVE DES KLAUWAERTS

SCHEPENSTRAAT

AVE DE L'HIPPODROME

RUE DU BOURGMESTRE
BURGEMEESTER-STRAAT

Musée des Enfants

RUE G. BIOT-STRAAT

AVE E. DE BECO-LAAN

Jardin du Roi

ROND-POINT

18

VILE STRAAT

RUE DU MONASTÈRE

AVE G. Bernier

BOONDAALSESTWEG

RUE F. ROFFIAN-STRAAT

IXELLES

RUE DE BELLE

RUE DE L'AURORE

AVENUE E. DURAY

AVENUE LOUISE

BOULEVARD GENERAL JACQUES LAAN

30

RUE EMILE BANNING STRAAT

6

RUE ELISE

Abbaye de la Cambre

1

AVENUE E DE MOT LAAN

16

ROND POINT DE L'ÉTOILE

AVE MAURICE-LAAN

AVENUE ADOLPHE BUYL-LAAN

EMILE CLAUS-STRAAT

LOUIZALAAN

BLVD DE LA CAMBRE

AVE DES COURSES WEDRENNENLAAN

AVE ERNESTINE-LAAN

LEGRAND

AVENUE FRANKLIN ROOSEVELT-LAAN

AVE LLOYD GEORGE-LAAN

AVE JOHANNA JEANNE-LAAN

Université Libre de Bruxelles

Bois de la Cambre

49 **Théâtre de Poche**

200 m

200 yds

AVENUE DE DIANE

AVENUE DE FLORE

AVENUE VICTORIA-LAAN

AVE PAUL HEGER-LAAN

Vrije Universiteit Brussel

AVE A. DEPAGE-LAAN

© Copyright Time Out Guides 2010

Sights & museums

Abbaye de la Cambre

11 avenue Emile Duray (02 648 11 21). Tram 23, 94 or bus 71. **Open** 9am-noon, 3-6pm Mon-Fri, Sun; 3-6pm Sat. **Admission** free. No credit cards. **Map** p109 E3 **❶**

Founded in the 12th century by the noble Gisèle for the Cîteaux Order, the Abbaye de la Cambre was badly damaged during the Wars of Religion and rebuilt in both the 16th and 18th centuries, although the 14th-century church attached to the abbey survives. It's all set in elegant French gardens, alongside the National Geographical Institute and an exhibition centre.

Fondation pour l'Architecture

55 rue de l'Ermitage (02 642 24 80, www.fondationpourlarchitecture.be). Tram 81, 82, 94 or bus 38, 54, 60. **Open** noon-6pm Tue-Fri; 10.30am-6pm Sat, Sun. **Admission** €6; €5 reductions. No credit cards. **Map** p106 C4/5 **❷**

This converted pumping house should be the first port of call for anyone interested in Brussels' architectural heritage. Exhibitions are varied and well put together, with models, photos, videos and furniture, and there is a first-class bookshop.

Musée Communal d'Ixelles

71 rue Van Volsem (02 515 64 21, www.musee-ixelles.be). Bus 38, 54, 60, 71, 95. **Open** 11.30am-5pm Tue-Sun. **Admission** €7; €5 reductions. **Map** p107 D4 **❸**

This excellent little museum, founded in 1892 and set in a former abattoir, is renowned for its exhibitions of mainly modern art. Its permanent collection is impressive, too, with works by local greats such as Magritte, Delvaux, Spilliaert and Van Rysselberghe, along with original posters by Toulouse-Lautrec. Two wings blend perfectly for a well-lit and interesting space.

Musée Meunier

59 rue de l'Abbaye (02 648 44 49, www.fine-arts-museum.be). Tram 94 or bus 38. **Open** 10am-noon, 1-5pm Tue-Fri. **Admission** free. No credit cards. **Map** p108 C3 **❹**

The house and studio of the renowned 19th-century Belgian sculptor and painter is home to over 170 of his sculptures and 120 of his paintings (from an output of 800), the best known being his bronze figures of workers. Meunier began painting religious scenes, but turned to sculpture inspired by social realism: farmers, miners and workers labour heroically in grim surrounds.

Eating & drinking

L'Ancienne Poissonnerie

65 rue du Trône (02 502 75 05, www.anciennepoissonnerie.be). Métro Trône. **Open** noon-3pm, 7-11pm Mon-Fri; 7-11pm Sat. **€€**. **Italian**. **Map** p106 C2 **❺**

Now a listed monument, the art nouveau Poissonnerie began life as a baker's, then became a seafood emporium. In its third reincarnation, owner Nicola Piscopo has created a beautiful Italian restaurant, whose elegant interior is a harmonious blend of old and new. Classic meat, fish and own-made pasta dishes are served from an open kitchen; the food is Italian, but with a nod to French and world influences. It attracts suits at lunchtime and the well-heeled in the evening, but the AP remains a bastion of democratic eating.

L'Atelier

77 rue Elise (02 649 19 53). Tram 94 or bus 71. **Open** 4pm-3am Mon-Thur, Sun; 4pm-4am Fri; 4pm-5am Sat. No credit cards. **Bar**. **Map** p109 F3 **❻**

Tucked away amid drab streets 'twixt Ixelles lakes and cemetery, L'Atelier is a gem: a cosy, candlelit wood and brick scout hut of a bar, with a broad counter separating a conspiratorial back room from the front of house. Behind the dividing line is a vast fridge

African beat

Welcome to the Matongé.

Hidden in suburban Ixelles, beyond the bland glitz of avenue Louise, Brussels is home to a small corner of Africa. Taking its name from an area of Kinshasa in the Congo, the Matongé is located between chaussée d'Ixelles and rue de Trône, bringing a welcome infusion of music and vitality to what is otherwise still a gently decaying district.

A wave of students came to Brussels in the early 1960s, after independence was declared in the former Belgian colony of Congo. Congolese intellectuals gathered in clubs such as Les Anges Noirs and bars around Porte de Namur métro, and this became the main jumping off point for the Matongé.

At the area's heart is Galerie d'Ixelles, which links chaussées de Wavre and d'Ixelles. The arcade's two sides take their names from Kinshasa's main streets, Inzia and Kanda-Kanda. Inzia is filled with snack bars,

while Kanda-Kanda's myriad hairdressers double up as packed social centres, where customers debate local goings-on as well as the latest hair extensions. Also here is Musicanova (no.24), a superb African music shop.

Chaussée de Wavre is lined with grocer's shopfronts, piled high with plantains, manioc leaves, yams and guava; inside, the shelves are stacked with sacks of rice, drums of palm oil and heaps of dried fish. Traders thrust forward cheap shoes 'direct from Abidjan', cotton *kangas* (shawls) and colourful *bazin* (wraps).

At night, the upbeat bars and restaurants on rue Longue Vie, between chaussée de Wavre and rue de la Paix, blaze forth the sounds of African artists. Head here for a change from *moules-frites*: spicy stews, fiery chicken piri-piri, *foufou* and *chikwangue*, a starchy cassava root mash, washed down with Congolese Tembo beer or palm wine.

Ixelles Ponds p105

of bottled beers. Draught options – Kriek, Barbar and Chouffe among them – are chalked up, as are local genevers and wines. It's popular with beer buffs, who mingle with intellectual types from the nearby university.

Banco!

79 rue du Bailli (02 537 52 65, www. bancobar.be). Tram 92, 94. **Open** 9am-2am daily. **Bar.** **Map** p108 B1 ❼
This old bank building used to house an Irish pub; sporting a new look to better fit this happening street and a vaguely international name, it has now been reborn as Banco! The young Châtelain crowd loves this place for its informal drinking and big sports screen; cocktails are the early-evening preference, but there's no getting away from the past – Guinness, Kilkenny and Celtic Irish Cider remain at the core of the beer menu.

Café Belga

18 place Flagey (02 640 35 08, www. cafebelga.be). Bus 71. **Open** 9.30am-2am Mon-Thur, Sun; 9.30am-3am Fri, Sat. **€.** No credit cards. **Café.** **Map** p107 D5 ❽
Café Belga is spread over the ground floor of the prestigious Flagey arts complex, its zinc and chrome 1950s look another attractive design by leisure guru Fred Nicolay. It's sleek and spacious, certainly, but not without charm, and always busy. Unless you're eating – options include soups, salads and sandwiches – it's counter service only, and not cheap, but that doesn't stop the flow of young arty sorts through its rather grandiose doors.

Chez Marie

40 rue Alphonse de Witte (02 644 30 31). Tram 81, 82 or bus 71. **Open** noon-2.15pm, 7.30-10.30pm Tue-Fri; 7.30-10.30pm Sat. **€€-€€€.** **French.** **Map** p109 D1 ❾
Marie's has become a shining star in the restaurant scene, especially since chef Lilian Devaux won herself a

Michelin sparkler. Sitting by the ponds, the diminutive restaurant smacks of country living, with wood panels, an old bar and homely curtains. The contrast comes in the modern take on French cooking, which eschews heavy, cream-laden sauces in favour of fresh reductions and bold flavours. Book ahead.

Cose Cosi

16 chaussée de Wavre (02 512 11 71, www2.resto.be/cosecosi). Métro Porte de Namur. **Open** noon-3pm, 6-11.30pm daily. **€€.** **Italian.** **Map** p106 B2 ❿
There are surprises in store behind Cose Cosi's unremarkable exterior. The first is the size of the place, and how many diners it manages to pack in. Then you notice the antelope heads, Zulu spears, faux shuttered windows and tropical plants; you could be in a safari lodge, except there's a baby grand piano where staff step up for a quick song. Somehow, it works: the wine flows, the chatter is loud, and on-the-ball staff deliver generous plates of Italian staples, grilled meats and fish.

Le Deuxième Element

7 rue St-Boniface (02 502 00 28, www.2emeelement.be). Métro Porte de Namur. **Open** noon-2.30pm, 7-11.30pm Mon-Fri; 7-11.30pm Sat, Sun. **€.** **Thai.** **Map** p106 C2 ⓫
Instead of bamboo and Buddhas, this place favours chic minimalism, with wooden café tables and stylish modern art. The food is authentic Thai, though, with no meddling with time-honoured flavours; plenty of ginger, lemongrass and fresh basil ensure a perfect red curry. Le Deuxième gets mobbed every mealtime, so it's always best to book.

L'Elément Terre

465 chaussée de Waterloo (02 649 37 27, www.resto.com/lelementterre). Tram 92. **Open** noon-2.30pm, 7-10.30pm Tue-Fri; 7-10.30pm Sat. **€€.** **Vegetarian.** **Map** p108 A2 ⓬
The 'Elementary' is a small vegetarian eaterie that also serves fish dishes.

BRUSSELS BY AREA

Confused? This is Brussels. The food is both excellent and eclectic, running from babaganoush with sesame pitta to vegetable tagine with falafel or cheese-topped enchiladas. The 'discovery plate' is a good way into the menu, offering a taste of this and that.

Le Fils de Jules

35 rue du Page (02 534 00 57, www.filsdejules.be). Tram 81, 92, 97. **Open** noon-2.30pm, 7-11pm Tue-Thur; noon-2.30pm, 7pm-midnight Fri; 7pm-midnight Sat, Sun. **€€**. **French**. **Map** p108 B2 ⑬

Jules is an integral part of the Châtelain scene, pulling in classy urbanites hungry for its authentic French foodie experience; set Sunday menus invariably ensure a full house. The menu is firmly based in the Landais and Basque region, with lots of duck products, chunks of fish, thick lentils and Salardais potatoes drenched in garlic. The wine list is a discovery, too, with its illegible local-language labels.

L'Horloge du Sud

141 rue du Trône (02 512 18 64, www.horlogedusud.be). Métro Trône or bus 95, 96. **Open** 11am-3pm, 6pm-midnight Mon-Fri; 6pm-midnight Sat. **€**. **Bar-Restaurant**. **Map** p107 D2 ⑭

Near the vibrant heart of the Matongé, L'Horloge is a far cry from the tacky, perpetually crowded bars of nearby rue de Longue Vie. Spacious and comfortable, the bar comprises a loose collection of old tables and chairs, plants, warrior statues, musical instruments and a massive mirror, all of which merge woozily as the drum rhythms and plentiful selection of Caribbean rums and cocktails kick in. There's African and Belgian cuisine, the odd gig and regular DJ sets at weekends.

Ma Cabane Bambou

11 rue du Prince Royal (02 512 26 86, www.macabanebambou.be). Tram 92, 94. **Open** 7pm-late Tue-Sat. No credit cards. **Bar**. **Map** p106 B2/3 ⑮

For 20 years this was Le Requin Chagrin, where Marlène Dépêche offered the exotic cuisine of Réunion, running a little rum as a side attraction. Marlène then transformed the Despondent Shark into a merry rum bar of broader provenance, with cane spirits from Réunion and other former French territories, including those in the Caribbean. They are put to excellent use in a vibrant cocktail selection, and a variation of a strong Antillean punch known as 'Le P'tit Pépé Loulou'.

La Porte des Indes

455 avenue Louise (02 647 86 51, www.laportedesindes.com). Tram 97. **Open** noon-2.30pm, 7-10.30pm Mon-Thur; noon-2.30pm, 7-11pm Fri, Sat; 7-10.30pm Sun. **€€**. **Indian**. **Map** p109 D4 ⑯

Decorated in Maharaja baroque fashion with vast palms and over-the-top lighting and artefacts, La Porte has a refined, hushed air. The opulent decor is the perfect backdrop for top-notch southern Indian food (with nods to the north). A dish from the royal court of Hyderabad – lamb cutlets soaked in garam masala, ginger and lemon – is an example of the finesse and careful balance achieved in the kitchen.

La Quincaillerie

45 rue du Page (02 533 98 33, www. quincaillerie.be). Tram 81, 92, 97. **Open** noon-2.30pm, 7pm-midnight Mon-Sat; 7pm-midnight Sun. **€€-€€€**. **Brasserie**. **Map** p108 A2 ⑰

The name means ironmonger – and sure enough, the fine interior is largely untouched, its tables set with the original wooden drawers for holding nails, screws and widgets. A cast-iron gallery circles the ensemble, overlooked by a giant clock. The seafood bar, piled with crustaceans, is considered one of the best in the city, and the restaurant attracts a wealthy set. Service is often abrupt, even rude, but that doesn't seem to deter anyone – it's best to book on any night of the week.

Place du Châtelain market p105

La Quincaillerie p114

Rick's Bar

344 avenue Louise (02 647 75 30).
Métro Louise then tram 97. **Open**
11am-midnight Mon-Sat; 10am-4pm
Sun. **€. American. Map** p109 D2 ⑱
The swish, chic Rick's is by far the
best-known American bar in Brussels
– almost as well known in these parts
as the *Casablanca* bar that spawned its
concept. Housed in a magnificent three-
storey townhouse on avenue Louise, it
serves what is arguably the best bar
brunch in town. There are full meals,
too – T-bone steaks, ribs and the like –
but it's mainly used as a networking
bar and after-office haunt. The rear terrace is glorious in summer.

Roxi

82 rue du Bailli (02 646 17 92,
www.roxi.be). Métro Louise then tram
93, 94. **Open** 8am-1am Mon-Wed, Sun;
8am-2am Thur-Sat. **Bar. Map** p108
B1 ⑲
This trendy bar and gathering place
attracts the chic urbanites of the
Châtelain quarter with three floors of
stark decor, all-day cuisine and
unfussy background sounds. Metal
staircases link the floors, from the
ground-floor bar with its wide windows to the dinky red stools of the tearoom, and on up to the modest balcony.

Saint Boniface

9 rue St-Boniface (02 511 53 66).
Métro Porte de Namur or bus 71.
Open noon-2.30pm, 7-10pm Mon-Fri.
€€. French. Map p106 C2 ⑳
The Boniface looks as if it has stood on
its little plot forever, beamed up from
a distant Dordogne village, and cares
not a jot for its trendier neighbours.
Old posters and oil lamps stand guard over
a menu of hearty Périgordine classics:
duck, puy lentils, foie gras, lamb stud-
ded with garlic and sliced potatoes
soaked in goose fat. Notices pinned to
the wall warn that mobile phones are
not welcome. All well and good: you
won't want to be distracted from the
authentic food in this timewarp joint.

De la Vigne à l'Assiette

51 rue de la Longue Haie (02 647 68
03, http://sites.resto.com/delavignea
lassiette). Métro Louise. **Open** noon-
2pm, 7-10pm Tue-Fri; 7-10pm Sat. **€€.**
Modern European. Map p106 B4 ㉑
Eddy Dandimont, joint owner of this
tiny brasserie, is an award-winning
sommelier. His splendid, reasonably
priced wine list complements the menu
perfectly; dishes are French based but
make quirky use of spices and herbs.
The dining room is pleasingly rustic,
with globe lamps and scrubbed walls,
while the youngish Ixelles clientele
adds to the atmosphere.

Winery

18 place Brugmann (02 345 47 17,
www.winery online.be). Tram 92.
Open 11am-8pm Mon-Sat. **Bar.**
Map p108 A2 ㉒
This clever little venture is attached to
a wine shop in the shadows of the old
church on the square. Wine bars are
not that big in Brussels, but this place
manages to attract a goodly local
crowd, who appreciate its unpretentious decor (a black and white tiled
floor and tall, bleached wood stalls)
and down to earth prices.

Shopping

Beer Mania

174-178 chaussée de Wavre (02 512
17 88, www.beermania.be). Métro Porte
de Namur. **Open** *Jan-Nov* 11am-9pm
Mon-Sat. *Dec* 11am-9pm daily. **Map**
p107 D2 ㉓
Beer Mania has been open for over 20
years and boasts a range of over 400
beers, along with matching glasses,
gift packages, accessories and books.
There's a bar, too, so you can sit down
and sample the brews in comfort.

Chine Collection

82-84 avenue Louise (02 512 45 52,
www.chinecollection.com). Métro Louise
then tram 94. **Open** 10am-6.30pm
Mon-Sat. **Map** p106 B3 ㉔

Designer Guillaume Thys launched this upmarket Belgian chain in 1991, with a feminine but functional prêt-à-porter womenswear range. Printed and plain silks sourced from the Far East are a mainstay, although fur, leather, denim, wool and cashmere also feature.

Les Enfants d'Edouard

175-177 avenue Louise (02 640 42 45, www.lesenfantsdedouard.net). Métro Louise then tram 94. **Open** 10am-6.30pm Mon-Sat. **Map** p106 B5 ㉕
This two-floor avenue Louise boutique sells second-hand designer labels and end-of-line stock from the likes of Paul & Joe, Hussein Chalayen, Marni and Lanvin. All of it is in excellent condition, and as a result prices can lean towards the expensive – though there are some choice pieces to be had.

Eva Luna

41 rue du Bailli (02 647 46 45, www.evaluna.be). Tram 92, 94. **Open** 1-6.30pm Mon; 11am-6.30pm Tue-Sat. **Map** p106 B5 ㉖
Eva Luna describes itself as a 'love shop' rather than a lingerie retailer. As such, it sells fragrant massage oils and cheeky sex toys as well as romantic, sexy and sassy underwear.

Francis Ferent

60 avenue Louise (02 545 78 30, www.ferent.be). Métro Louise. **Open** 10am-6.30pm Mon-Sat. **Map** p106 B3 ㉗
This is the flagship store of a small empire of boutiques stocking high-end labels for men, women and children. Brands include Dolce & Gabbana, DKNY, Sonia Rykiel, Miu Miu, Marc Jacobs, Helmut Lang and Prada. You might get an icy reception, though – the assistants seem to think that they own the place.

Isabelle Baines

4 rue de la Longue Haie (02 502 13 73, www.isabellebaines.com). Métro Louise. **Open** 2-6.30pm Mon; 10.30am-6.30pm Tue-Sat. **Map** p106 B4 ㉘

Local designer Baines opened her first boutique in Brussels in 1986, selling machine-knitted but hand-finished jumpers, cardigans and gilets. The winter collection is made from wool and cashmere, and the summer clothes cotton. Expect top-quality, classic pieces with a modern twist.

Look 50

10 rue de la Paix (02 512 24 18). Métro Porte de Namur or bus 71. **Open** 10.30am-6.30pm Mon-Sat. No credit cards. **Map** p106 C2 ㉙
Look 50 is vintage at its rawest, with no horrifying price tags attached. Here, customers dig through the tightly packed mess of clothes in search of sartorial gems. The dominating era is the 1970s, with leather jackets, polyester dresses and fun hats.

Maison Degand

415 avenue Louise (02 649 00 73, www.degand.be). Métro Louise. **Open** 10am-7pm Mon-Sat. **Map** p109 D3 ㉚
Maison Degand, housed in a grand fin-de-siècle mansion, sells luxury clothes and accessories, including made-to-measure suits and soft cashmere sweaters in myriad hues. It also stocks accessories such as cufflinks, cravats and hip flasks.

Massimo Dutti

47 avenue de la Toison d'Or (02 502 23 91, www.massimodutti.com). Métro Porte de Namur or Louise. **Open** 10am-6.30pm Mon-Sat. **Map** p106 A2 ㉛
Another successful Spanish clothing export, Massimo Dutti serves up elegant, classically styled attire for men, women and children.

Nicole Jocelyn

37 chaussée de Wavre (02 511 28 74). Métro Porte de Namur. **Open** 9.30am-7pm Mon-Sat. No credit cards. **Map** p106 C2 ㉜
Nicole's is one of the largest and most popular hairdressers in the area, specialising in Afro hair.

Abbaye de la Cambre p110

Flagey p124

Nijinski

15-17 rue du Page (02 539 20 28).
Tram 81, 82 or bus 54. **Open** 11am-
7pm Mon-Sat. No credit cards.
Map p108 B1 ③③
Staff are relaxed and friendly and
prices reasonable in this generously-
proportioned second-hand bookstore.
Stock includes English language
books, and there's a play area to keep
small fry entertained.

Nina Meert

1 rue St-Boniface (02 514 22 63).
Métro Porte de Namur. **Open** 2.30-
6.30pm Mon; 10.30am-6.30pm Tue-Sat.
Map p106 C2 ③④
Born into a family of painters, Nina
Meert worked for Pucci in Florence and
Cacharel in Paris before opening her
own shop in Brussels in 1979. Among
the admirers of her artfully simple
designs, made from natural fibres such
as wool and silk, is Isabelle Adjani.

Rose

56-58 rue de l'Aqueduc (02 534 9808).
Tram 91, 92. **Open** 10.30am-6.20pm
Tue-Sat. **Map** p108 A1 ③⑤
Run by Elodie Gleis, this sweet bou-
tique sells a mix of decorative objects,
fashion accessories and small gifts.
Designers include Cath Kidston and
Atelier LZC, famed for their delicate
floral motifs, printed on to mirrors.

Serneels

69 avenue Louise (02 538 30 66,
www.serneels.be). Métro Louise.
Open 9.30am-6.30pm Mon-Sat.
Map p106 A3 ③⑥
Just about every toy a little heart could
desire is stocked at this deluxe store,
from tutus, teddies and tea sets to pup-
pets, board games, gaily-painted train
sets and traditional toy soldiers.

Tarlatane

22 rue Ernest Solvay (02 502 79 29).
Métro Porte de Namur or bus 54, 71.
Open 11am-6.30pm Tue-Sat.
Map p106 C2 ③⑦

Valérie Janssens' range of accessories
has an appealingly feminine feel.
Goodies include cloche hats and berets,
scarves, recycled wool day bags and
jewellery made from sparkly cut glass
stones and buttons.

Le Tartisan

27 rue de la Paix (02 503 36 00, www.
tartisan.be). Métro Porte de Namur or
bus 54, 71. **Open** 10am-7pm Mon, Tue;
10am-10pm Wed-Sat. **Map** p106 C2 ③⑧
The speciality of the house is, suffice
to say, tarts. Made on site according to
traditional recipes, they are astonishingly light. There are vegetarian and
meat options, plus lemon, walnut and
chocolate or frangipane for sweet-
toothed customers.

Z'art

223 chaussée d'Ixelles (02 649 06
53, www.zart-shop.com). Bus 54, 71.
Open 10.30am-6.30pm Tue-Sat.
Map p106 C4 ③⑨
Z'Art specialises in novelty items with
a function, some more useful than others – think octopus salt shakers, snail-
shaped Sellotape dispensers, flower
printed bike bells and the like.

Nightlife

Grain d'Orge

142 chaussée de Wavre (02 511 26 47).
Métro Porte de Namur. **Open** 11am-
3am Fri. *Concerts* 9pm. **Map** p107 D2 ④⓪
If you sport a flared denim suit with
beer towels sewn in, you'll love this
ultimate spit-and-sawdust bar. The
Grain d'Orge hosts gigs every Friday
night, with most of the acts tending
towards American-style rock, blues or
country sounds. Everyone has a good
time and – this being Belgium – a certain knowing sense of irony is all part
of the fun.

Kultuurkaffee

Vrije Universiteit Brussel (Flemish
University), boulevard de la Plaine 2
(02 629 23 25, www.vub.ac.be/cultuur).

Tram 23, 90. **Open** *Concerts* 8pm or 8.30pm Thur. No credit cards. **Map** p107 F3 ⓷

Although it's slightly off the beaten track, on the university campus, this is a good place to sample the rather hidden but often quite adventurous culture of Brussels' minority Flemish student community, akin to their British counterparts when it comes to liking late nights and a good drink. The Kultuurkaffee, with support from radio station Studio Brussel, puts on rock acts (including semi-well-known groups such as Traktor), jam sessions, world music and the occasional Flemish oddity.

Louise Gallery

Level 1, Galerie Louise, avenue Louise, (mobile 0478 79 79 79, www.louise gallery.com). Métro Louise. **Open** 11pm-7am Fri-Sun. No credit cards. **Map** p106 A2/3 ⓸

This glamorous nightspot is like an underground Greek temple, decked out with columns and mirrors, while its website features snaps of Blu Cantrell, Eric Cantona and David Copperfield (which says a lot about the vibe inside). A powerful lighting set and thumping sound system give it a hefty but highly enjoyable edge. Phone to book a table if you'd like to reserve a refuge. On Sunday, the predominantly gay Strong Cabaret takes over.

New York Café & Jazz Club

5 chaussée de Charleroi (02 534 85 09). Métro Louise. **Open** 10pm-1.30am Fri, Sat. **Map** p106 A3 ⓹

Table service pushes the drinks prices up in this smart little establishment, which also serves bistro-style food; still, it's balanced out by the fact that there's no entry fee. The programme tends towards smooth, dinner-style jazz – not to everyone's taste, perhaps, but popular with a well-dressed crowd, keen to warm up for a late night elsewhere in the capital.

Sounds Jazz Club

28 rue de la Tulipe (02 512 92 50, www.soundsjazzclub.be). Métro Porte de Namur or bus 54, 71. **Open** 8pm-4am Mon-Sat. *Concerts* 10pm. No credit cards. **Map** p106 C3 ⓺

Sounds continues to be a compulsory port of call for local jazz fans. Far enough from the centre of town to discourage tourists (though only 15 minutes by bus), it attracts expats and eurocrats who like to swap their dull grey suits for glad rags. It favours modern-ish jazz, but there's also the odd big band night; Wednesdays usually bring Latino concerts. It stays open very late, too.

La Soupape

26 rue Alphonse de Witte (02 649 58 88, www.lasoupape.be). Tram 81, 82 or bus 38, 60, 71. **Open** 8.30pm-midnight concert days only. No credit cards. **Map** p109 D1 ⓻

Set in a side street in the ever more lively area near place Flagey and the Ixelles ponds, this intimate, idiosyncratic venue specialises in *chanson française*, and holds heats for a national competition. La Soupape is a great place for discovering new talent, with many acts destined to be seen later by far more than the 50 people squeezed around its rickety tables.

Théâtre Marni

23-25 rue de Vergnies (02 639 09 80, www.theatremarni.com). Tram 81, 82 or bus 71. **Open** 8pm-2am Tue-Sat. *Concerts* 8.30pm. No credit cards. **Map** p107 D4 ⓼

This renovated theatre, a former bowling alley near place Flagey, has a wonderfully varied programme of quality jazz and world music from Belgium and beyond. Gigs take place in the large and comfortable main theatre or in the entrance hall. The organisers of the late and much-lamented Travers jazz club continue to host innovative new performers here, mainly during two seasons in May and September.

Rebel with a cause

The man who took on the Gestapo.

The innocuous-looking apartment building at 453 avenue Louise has a dark past. It was here that the occupying Nazi forces of World War II installed the dreaded Gestapo, converting the building into a base for surveillance and a detention centre. Locals knew what it was and what went on in there, but there was little they could do in the face of brutal security. But one heroic Belgian changed all that, and brought some much-needed cheer to the dark days of war.

Baron Jean-Michel de Selys Longchamp fled Belgium after German troops arrived in May 1940. He made it safely to England, where he joined a Belgian air force squadron attached to the RAF. In January 1943, he took off with another pilot from Manston airfield in Kent, on a mission to strafe German railway movements in north Belgium. Their mission safely accomplished, the planes returned to England – but not

Selys Longchamp, who turned and headed for Brussels. He had already approached RAF bosses about an idea he had to destroy the Gestapo HQ, but had been given no answer. This, he decided, was his big chance.

Flying in low, he sped towards the building in his Typhoon and set off his guns, destroying great lumps of the façade in a cloud of concrete and glass. As he soared away, he let the flags of Belgium and Britain fall on to the wreckage before flying back to Manston. His audacious attack killed a top Gestapo officer and, perhaps more importantly, massively boosted morale within the Resistance. Selys Longchamp was both demoted and awarded the Distinguished Flying Cross, in recognition of his insubordination and his bravery. Seven months later he was killed in a mission over Ostend, but the baron had already entered Brussels lore as the man who took on the Gestapo and won.

Like many venues, the Marni also has a splendid bar attached, so there's no need to rush off home once the gig has come to an end.

Arts & leisure

Flagey

Place Ste-Croix, next to place Flagey (02 641 10 20, www.flagey.be). Tram 81, 82 or bus 38, 60, 71. Map p107 D5 **47**
Flagey, the former home of the National Radio Orchestra, folded during the 1990s, then reopened after a great deal of lengthy and very expensive renovation work. In its heyday, the main studio was acoustically one of Europe's finest, and hosted some truly memorable world premières. Now it hosts a range of contemporary and classical concerts. The building itself is a magnificent 1930s construction, with the sleek curves of an ocean liner.

Styx

72 rue de l'Arbre Bénit (02 512 21 02, http://cinema-styx.wikeo.be). Métro Porte de Namur or bus 54, 71. No credit cards. Map p106 C3 **48**
Now over 40 years old, the Styx is Brussels' most adorable fleapit. The sound quality may be less than perfect, but the programming is truly irresistible – from Truffaut retrospectives and *Amores Perros* to modern Belgian classics in the making.

Théâtre de Poche

1A chemin de Gymnase (02 649 17 27, www.poche.be). Tram 23, 90, 93, 94. No credit cards. Map p109 D5 **49**
The little Pocket Theatre was founded by Roger Domani in 1951, and first opened its doors on the chaussée d'Ixelles, until being demolished to make way for a shopping gallery. Since then it has sat in a small building in the Bois de la Cambre, which has been the making of it. The work staged here is demanding and hard-hitting and always pushes limits, taking world politics as its starting point.

Théâtre de la Toison d'Or

396 galeries de la Toison d'Or (02 510 05 10, www.theatredelatoisondor.be). Métro Porte de Namur. Map p106 B2 **50**
This place is a magnet for camp, madcap comedy and revue, with offbeat takes on Eurovision, piss-takes of the sci-fi genre, irreverent stand-up comedians and café-theatre.

Théâtre Varia

78 rue du Sceptre (02 640 82 58, www.varia.be). Bus 38, 60, 95, 96. Map p107 E3 **51**
Firmly French in nature, the Varia mixes up a programme of new writing (Belgian and Moroccan) with modern takes on Shakespeare in translation as well as a varied dance programme. It's a space that makes a concerted effort to welcome everyone, and even has a babysitting service.

UGC Toison d'Or

8 avenue de la Toison d'Or (0900 10 440, www.ugc.be). Métro Porte de Namur. Map p106 B2 **52**
With 15 screens (rather confusingly, at two not-quite-adjacent locations), the UGC Toison d'Or is the only serious competition to Kinepolis (see p130) – and its more adventurous programming often carries the day. First-class sound and fabulous picture quality make this the best address to randomly turn up at without knowing what you want to see. On the whole, tickets aren't cheap, except for the lunchtime shows.

Vendôme

18 chaussée de Wavre (02 502 37 00, www.cinema-vendome.be). Métro Porte de Namur. No credit cards. Map p106 B2 **53**
Round the corner from the Toison d'Or, this five-screen independent is a treasure, and has smartened itself up after a considerable government grant. The films are mainly European and US indie releases, but the cinema is also a regular on the local festival circuit, and home to a well-loved short film festival.

Espace Photographique Contretype

St-Gilles

St-Gilles is easily one of Brussels' most beautiful residential areas. It is built on a hill that climbs roughly north to south, and as the altitude increases, so the area changes. Rooming houses and tacky shops give way to row upon row of well-groomed, middle-class townhouses, culminating in the magnificent mansions around avenue Brugmann.

Like the wider neighbourhood, the main square, the **parvis de St-Gilles**, has a quiet, contemplative air – except for the bustling market on Sunday mornings. This is very much a residential part of town: if you move away from the main thoroughfares, you'll find yourself in small, quiet streets, most with their own bars and local shops.

St-Gilles' golden age came at the end of the 19th century, when wealthy residents commissioned fabulous art nouveau residences. Most are closed to the public, but

one striking exception is architect Victor Horta's home, now the **Musée Horta**. It's set in the heart of the art nouveau area in rue Américaine, heading into Ixelles.

Sights & museums

Espace Photographique Contretype

1 avenue de la Jonction (02 538 42 20, www.contretype.org). Tram 81, 91, 92, 97 or bus 54. **Open** *11am-6pm Wed-Fri; 1-6pm Sat, Sun.* **Admission** €2.50. No credit cards. **Map** p127 D5 ❶
Jules Brunfaut built this art nouveau house for industrialist Edouard Hannon, who was also a keen amateur photographer. His photographs are on display, along with works by various photographers in residence. The interior features lofty salons and a staircase with a vast fresco. Stripped of its original furniture, the house has the echoing impersonality of a grand showpiece studio.

BRUSSELS BY AREA

Musée Horta

*25 rue Américaine (02 543 04 90,
www.hortamuseum.be). Tram 81, 91,
92, 97 or bus 54.* **Open** 2-5.30pm daily.
Admission €7; €4 reductions. No
credit cards. **Map** p127 D5 ❷

Horta built his home and studio in
1899-1901. Although the exterior is
nothing compared to the Hankar-
designed house in nearby rue Defacqz,
the interior is astonishingly light and
harmonious. Every element, down to
the door handles, is designed in his
fluid, sensuous style. The staircase and
stairwell are breathtaking: an extravaganza of iron and mirrors, topped by
a stained-glass canopy. The museum
is often crowded, though – come early.

Eating & drinking

Bosquet 58

*58 rue Bosquet (02 544 13 15). Métro
Hôtel des Monnaies.* **Open** noon-3pm,
6-10pm Mon-Fri; 6-10pm Sat, Sun. **€**.
French. **Map** p127 D3 ❸

Hidden away in a quiet residential
street, Bosquet has a reputation based
on word of mouth alone. French chef
Marc Louradour serves two- or three-

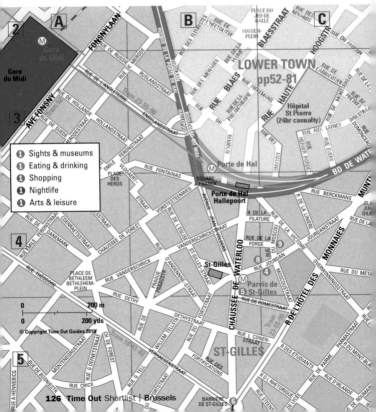

course *menu restos*, and what menus they are: duck breasts, leg of lamb and sole, all served with masses of veggies. It's only him cooking and his wife serving out front, so it can be a bit slow at weekends when it's busier.

Brasserie de l'Union

55 parvis de St-Gilles (02 538 15 79). Pré-métro Parvis de St-Gilles. **Open** 7.30am-1am daily. No credit cards. **Bar**. **Map** p126 C4 **④**

A tatty-round-the-edges bohemian bar, happy to serve the local community at large – some befriended solely by

spaniels, and deep in one-way conversations – the Union comprises one large, busy room propping up a corner of the focal parvis de St-Gilles. Sunday morning market browsing is accompanied by an accordionist squeezing out tunes – though nothing can drown out the din of children running amok. After they depart, along with the spaniels, the squeezeboxer and the eccentrics, the night is claimed by characters from the covers of pulp fiction novels.

Brasserie Verschueren

11-13 parvis de St-Gilles (02 539 40 68). Pré-métro Parvis de St-Gilles. **Open** 8am-2am daily. No credit cards. **Bar**. **Map** p126 B4 **⑤**

The classier of the corner bars serving the parvis, the Verschueren twinkles with art deco touches. Three rows of tables and banquettes are waited on by rather erratic staff, safe in the knowledge that few of the boho-intellectual regulars are paying much attention; the Verschueren is simply their natural habitat. If they cared to look up, they'd find a more than adequate selection of beers – including bottled rarities such as Pecheresse.

Chez Moeder Lambic

68 rue de Savoie (02 539 14 19, www.moederlambic.eu). Pré-métro Horta or Albert. **Open** 4pm-3am daily. No credit cards. **Bar**. **Map** p126 B5 **⑥**

Happy to collect dust in its own little corner, the collectors' cavern of Chez Moeder Lambic hides from the soaring St-Gilles town hall behind beer-labelled windows. Inside it's a dark hive, with three long shelves of obscure bottles framing the bar counter and wooden tables. It would take a lifetime to sample every cobwebbed variety here, but to pass the time, racks of comic books line one wall.

Ma Folle de Soeur

53 chaussée de Charleroi (02 538 22 39, www.mafolledesoeur.be). Métro Louise or tram 92. **Open** noon-2.30pm,

6-10.30pm Mon-Sat. €-€€. **Modern European**. Map p127 E4 **7**
Run by two sisters, this small restaurant has a mellow dining room, its wooden bar and tables softened by yellow walls and candlelight in the evening. The menu has flair – it's Belgian in nature, with French bistro influences. Meat (duck, steak and even horse) is to the fore, and dressed with imaginative sauces. Suits give way to young lovers and groups of friends in the evening, and there's a back garden.

Maison du Peuple
39 parvis de St-Gilles (02 850 09 08, www.maison-du-peuple.be). Pré-métro Parvis de St-Gilles. **Open** 8.30am-1am daily. **€. Café. Map** p126 B4 **8**
Situated on the ground floor of a wonderful turn of the century building, MdP is a vibrant blend of café culture, music and art. Exhibitions and parties are attended by a cool but friendly crowd, and there's an early-evening happy hour. Breakfast is available first thing, then the kitchen turns its attention to well-made antipasti, croque monsieurs, quiches and panini.

Aux Mille et Une Nuits
7 rue de Moscou (02 537 41 27, www.milleetunenuits.be). Pré-métro Parvis de St-Gilles. **Open** noon-3pm, 6-11.30pm Mon-Sat. **€€. Tunisian.** Map p126 C4 **9**
Kitsch decor gives this Tunisian restaurant an edge in an area packed with North African eateries. Oriental rugs adorn the walls, and thousands of tiny lights sparkle like stars. Service is impeccable, and the food is out of this world; start with *harira* chickpea soup or honey-soaked chicken in crisp pastry. For mains, you can't go far wrong with caramelised lamb couscous or chicken tagine with grapes and honey.

Salons de l'Atalaïde
89 chaussée de Charleroi (02 538 29 29, http://lessalons.be). Tram 92. **Open** 11.30am-11.30pm Mon-Fri; 7pm-

midnight Sat. **€€. Modern European**. Map p127 D4 **10**
This former auction house is now an off-the-wall, over-the-top restaurant. Baroque mirrors, ornate chandeliers, oversized paintings, Gothic candles and ostentatious palms combine to give it a slightly unreal edge. The menu reflects a fresh take on Franco-Belgian cooking, so seasonal ingredients replace the old year-round staples.

Shopping

There is a lively food market at parvis de St-Gilles on Sundays.

Dille & Kamille
16 rue Jean Stas (02 538 81 25, www.dille-kamille.be). Métro Louise or tram 91, 92, 94. **Open** 9.30am-6.30pm Mon-Sat. **Map** p127 D3 **11**
This chi-chi garden and home store is great for browsing. Plants and baskets are at the front, while foodstuffs (olive oils, mustards, herbs, teas) are at the back. There are also household basics, kitchen gadgets, cookbooks and traditional wooden toys.

Mig's World Wines
43 chaussée de Charleroi (02 534 77 03, www.migsworldwines.com). Métro Louise then tram 92. **Open** 11am-7pm Mon-Sat. **Map** p127 D3 **12**
Best known for its Australian wines (owner Miguel Saelens stocks around 100), this store also sells wines from 30 other regions and countries, including Belgium and Eastern Europe, plus fruit wines, grappa and whisky. Go on a Saturday for a spot of wine tasting.

Schleiper
149 chaussée de Charleroi (02 541 05 41, www.schleiper.com). Tram 92. **Open** 9.30am-6.30pm Mon-Sat. **Map** p127 E4 **13**
An excellent choice of all types of art supplies, as well as an efficient framing service, framed art for sale and some office supplies.

Atomium

Beyond the centre

Laeken

Laeken stretches over a huge green area some distance north of the centre, divided into a royal estate (the **Château Royal** itself, home to the Belgian royal family, is very much closed to the public, although you can wander the glorious **Parc du Laeken**) and the public leisure complex of Heysel.

It seems an unreal, artificial city, hovering outside Brussels proper, and while each of its main sights are in themselves worthy of a visit, they make unlikely neighbours. Among them are the national stadium, the **Kinepolis** multiplex, the offbeat **Bruparck** theme park and two Léopoldine follies, the **Tour Japonais** and the **Pavillon Chinois**. Perhaps most surreal of all is the iconic **Atomium** – a giant, 1950s replica molecule.

To get there, take the metro to Heysel or the 18, 23 or 81 tram.

Sights & museums

Atomium

Boulevard du Centenaire (02 475 47 75, www.atomium.be). Métro Heysel or tram 23, 81. **Open** 10am-6pm daily. **Admission** €11; €4-€8 reductions. **Map** p131 B2.

Designed for the 1958 World Fair, this iconic structure has a deliciously retro appeal. After years of neglect, dynamic curator Diane Hennebert negotiated a €24 million renovation, and the molecule reopened in 2005 with a new visitors' centre and a restaurant at the top.

Notre-Dame de Laeken

Parvis Notre-Dame (02 479 23 62, www.ndlaeken-olvlaken.be). Métro Bockstael or tram 81, 94 or bus 53. **Open** 2-5pm Tue-Sun. **Admission** free. **Map** p131 E3.

Although opening times are restricted, the church's huge, neo-Gothic exterior, designed by Joseph Poelaert in 1851, is worth seeing. In the cemetery are the tombs of important Belgians – Poelaert among them. Inside, look out for the 13th-century Madonna on the altar.

Pavillon Chinois

44 avenue Jules van Praet (02 268 16 08, www.kmkg-mrah.be). Tram 23, 52. **Open** 9.30am-5pm Tue-Fri; 10am-5pm Sat, Sun. **Admission** €4 combined tour with Tour Japonaise. No credit cards. **Map** p131 D1.

Built as a restaurant for Léopold II (see box p104), then left to its own devices for years, the pavilion is now home to a collection of fine Chinese porcelain.

Serres Royales

61 avenue du Parc Royal (02 513 89 40). Métro Heysel. **Open** May; call for details. **Admission** €2; free under-18s. No credit cards. **Map** p131 D1.

These magnificent greenhouses were built by Balat and the young Victor Horta in the 1870s, and are a soaring iron and glass cathedral to botany. Léopold II moved into one on his deathbed, and other royals have in the past set up writing desks and seating areas in others. They are open in May each year; ask at the tourist information office for details.

Tour Japonaise

44 avenue Jules van Praet (02 268 16 08, www.kmkg-mrah.be). Tram 23, 52. **Open** 9.30am-5pm Tue-Fri; 10am-5pm Sat, Sun. **Admission** €4 combined tour with Pavillon Chinois. No credit cards. **Map** p131 D1.

This mock pagoda, set around Japanese gardens, was built on the orders of Léopold II (see box p104). These days, it houses Japanese-themed art exhibitions.

Arts & leisure

Bruparck

1 avenue du Football (02 474 83 83, www.bruparck.com). Métro Heysel. **Open** hours vary; check online for details. **Map** p131 A/B2.

The main draw at this attraction park at the foot of the Atomium is Mini-Europe, with its small-scale replicas of European landmarks such as the Eiffel Tower and Big Ben (listen out for its sonorous chimes). Bruparck also takes in the Océade water park, with its child-friendly slides and chutes.

Kinepolis

Bruparck, avenue du Centenaire, (bookings 02 474 26 00, information 0900 00 555, www.kinepolis.com). Métro Heysel. No credit cards. **Map** p131 A2.

Don't be fooled by its run-down look: Kinepolis is state of the art. With its 24 giant screens and futuristic sound systems, this is total cinema, Flemish-style. Cutting-edge technology also includes one of the few servers powerful enough to download entire movies by satellite for the big screen.

Stade Roi Baudouin

Avenue du Marathon, Laeken (02 474 39 40). Métro Heysel or Roi Baudouin. **Map** p131 A2.

Formerly the Heysel, Belgium's national stadium was a crumbling ruin when it closed after the tragedy of 1985, when 39 fans died at a European Cup Final. Ten years later it reopened as the Roi Baudouin, a 50,000-capacity all-seater with its own métro stop. It hosts athletics events, cycling races, football matches and rugby games.

Schaerbeek & St-Josse

Once a wooded hunting ground, and later famed for its cherry orchards, Schaerbeek covers a vast swathe of northern Brussels. Before the Gare du Nord was built in 1841, it was a mellow backwater of bakeries and breweries. These days, it's a rather gloomy mix of industry and grand avenues, and home to significant immigrant

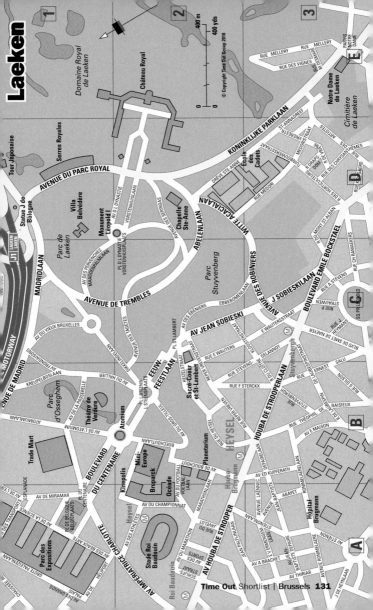

Laeken

Time Out Shortlist | Brussels **131**

populations; along its spine, Chaussée de Haecht, you'll find Turkish bakeries, Muslim butchers and cafés filled with Turkish football flags. At no.266, Maison Autrique (www.autrique.be) was art nouveau architect Victor Horta's first design commission. It is now half-museum, half-theatrical mise-en-scène; you walk through the rooms, from the laundry to the attic, experiencing local life the way it was lived a century ago. The area's other attractions include the **Halles de Schaerbeek** and the thriving **Théâtre 140**.

Schaerbeek touches on the smaller, poorer commune of St-Josse, which hugs the north-east portion of the Petit Ring and is almost completely North African and Turkish in character. Full of bustling fruit shops and intimate little ethnic eateries, its standout venue is **Le Botanique**, another vibrant arts complex.

Eating & drinking

Senza Nome

22 rue Royale Ste-Marie, Schaerbeek (02 223 16 17, www.senzanome.be). Tram 92, 93, 94. **Open** noon-2pm, 7-9.30pm Mon-Fri; 7-9.30pm Sat. **€€-€€€. Italian**
Senza Nome steers clear of predictable Italian fare with a short, seasonal menu, offering the likes of squid-inked pastas or sea bass, bursting with citrus flavours. Book ahead: it's popular with audiences at the Halles de Schaerbeek.

Nightlife

Le Botanique

236 rue Royale, St-Josse (02 226 12 11, reservations 02 218 37 32, www.botanique.be). Métro Botanique. **Open** 10am-6pm daily.
The main corridor of 'Le Bota' is lined with luxuriant foliage and ponds, a reminder of when the building was the centre of a vast botanical garden before the war. Audiences here revel in indie rock, with the likes of Josh Ritter and the Divine Comedy appearing on stage. The best of its three separate venues is the mid-sized La Rotonde, where the audience stands on steep steps and everyone gets a great view of the band.

Halles de Schaerbeek

22 rue Royale Ste-Marie, Schaerbeek (02 218 21 07, www.halles.be). Tram 92, 94 or bus 65, 66.
The Halles began life as a covered market in 1865, and is now a multi-use French cultural centre. It promotes both avant-garde and mainstream culture, running from rock and folk music to theatre and dance. Smaller concerts take place in the downstairs club, but bigger acts appear in the main hall. It looks gorgeous, and there's an awesome view from the balcony, but the sound can be a little muddy.

Jazz Station

193-195 chaussée de Louvain, St-Josse (02 733 13 78, www.jazzstation.be). Bus 29, 63. **Open** *Bar* 11am-10pm Wed-Sat. *Concerts/rehearsals* vary. No credit cards.
As well as jazz concerts, this place offers an experimental space for new and emerging bands; in the daytime, jazz outfits hold open rehearsals so that serious fans can see how it's all put together. With low entry fees, a swinging bar and an exhibition space, this is a superbly creative venue.

Arts & leisure

Théâtre 140

140 avenue Plasky, Schaerbeek (02 733 97 08, www.theatre140.be). Pré-métro Diamant or bus 29, 63.
Jo Dekmine and Renée Paduwat run the 140, as they have done for decades; the 2010 season was the theatre's 47th. The fresh, exciting programme includes physical and innovative theatre from home and abroad.

Blistering barnacles!

Explore Tintin's world at a playful new museum.

Belgium is the home of the comic strip or *bande dessinée*, and Tintin is the country's most easily identifiable popular icon. The cub reporter and his chums – including his faithful white fox terrier Snowy and the gruff Captain Haddock (known for his extravagant curses and 'blistering barnacles!' catchphrase) – shift more T-shirts, postcards and books than anything else Belgian.

It was about time, then, that Tintin's creator, Georges Rémi (better known as Hergé) was duly honoured – and in June 2009, the **Musée Hergé** finally opened its doors. The museum was a long time coming, with the idea first being mooted in 1979. It is largely privately financed, with Hergé's widow contributing some $20 million to ensure that her husband's work could be brought out of bank vaults and into the light.

The choice of Louvain-la-Neuve, a new university town south-east of Brussels (half an hour by train),

was an inspired one, enabling award-winning French architect Christian de Portzamparc to experiment with an urban structure in a woodland setting. The result is a playful series of colours, angles and cubes, reflecting the boxed nature of Tintin's adventures. Nothing is quite as it seems; even the central lift shaft is chequered black and white, resonant of the famous rocket. Walking through the museum is akin to embarking on one of Tintin's journeys, as odd steps and walkways lead you into the unknown. As you explore, you'll discover an impressive archive of photographs, drawings and research materials that enabled Hergé to create his meticulously accurate stories.

A restaurant and library round off the day out – along with a well-stocked shop, of course.

■ Musée Hergé, Louvain-la-Neuve (02 62 62 421, www.musee herge.com).

BRUSSELS BY AREA

1907

MARCHE Ste MARIE

Anderlecht & the West

Despite being set just across the canal from central Brussels, Anderlecht, Koekelberg, Molenbeek and Jette are unlikely to feature on most visitors' sightseeing agendas.

Ex-industrial, largely grey and uninspired for the most part, they are nevertheless home to a couple of appealingly offbeat attractions, including the **Basilique du Sacré Coeur** in Koekelberg and the **Musée Magritte**, set in the large, anonymous commune of Jette.

Beside the railway yards and factories of the Willebroek Canal in run-down, residential Molenbeek is **Tour et Taxis** – a turn-of-the-century complex of warehouses and railway sheds which has become a major events and exhibition space.

In Anderlecht, the down at heel boulevards around Gare du Midi gradually give way to green spaces and café-lined squares; the majority of sights are near St-Guidon métro station, including the beautiful **Collégiale des Sts Pierre et Guidon** and the 16th-century **Béguinage de l'Anderlecht**.

Beer and footie fans should also seek out the **Musée Bruxellois de la Gueuze** and the **Stade Constant Vanden Stock**, home to Brussels' biggest football club.

Sights & museums

Basilique du Sacré Coeur

1 parvis de la Basilique, Koekelberg (02 425 88 22). Métro Simonis. **Open** *Church* summer 8am-6pm daily; winter 10am-5pm daily. *Dome* summer 9am-5pm daily; winter 10am-4pm daily. **Admission** *Church* free. *Dome* €3. No credit cards.
Commissioned by Léopold II in 1905, this vast structure is an extraordinary mix of Gothic and art deco, with a lit-up cherry-coloured crucifix on top. It took seven decades to finish.

Béguinage de l'Anderlecht

8 rue du Chapelain, Anderlecht (02 521 13 83). Métro St-Guidon. **Open** 10am-noon, 2-5pm Tue-Sun. **Admission** €1.50. No credit cards.
Founded in 1252, this ancient convent consists of four modest 16th-century houses and a garden. The museum documents the life of the *béguinage* – a religious community of lay sisters, known for their charitable works.

Collégiale des Sts Pierre et Guidon

Place de la Vaillance, Anderlecht (02 523 02 20). Métro St-Guidon. **Open** 9am-noon, 2-5pm daily. **Admission** free.
Founded before the tenth century, the current Collegiate Church is late 15th-century Gothic. The long altar is illuminated by light filtered through the stained-glass windows; below is one of Belgium's oldest Romanesque crypts.

Maison d'Erasmus

31 rue de Chapitre, Anderlecht (02 521 13 83, www.erasmushouse.museum). Métro St-Guidon. **Open** 10am-6pm Tue-Sun. **Admission** €1.50. No credit cards.
The house where Erasmus stayed is a small, red-brick seat of learning, set in a shady garden. Now a museum, it contains first editions of his *In Praise of Folly* and *Adages*, letters from Charles V and Francis I and portraits of the great man by Dürer and Holbein.

Musée Bruxellois de la Gueuze

56 rue Gheude, Anderlecht (02 521 49 28, www.cantillon.be). Métro Clemenceau or pré-métro Lemonnier. **Open** 8.30am-5pm Mon-Fri; 10am-5pm Sat. **Admission** €5. No credit cards.
Enjoy a tasting tour around Brussels' last working brewer of gueuze (see box p94), the unusual beer fermented naturally in Anderlecht's gloomy climate. The entrance price to the museum includes a glass of beer.

Musée Magritte

135 rue Esseghem, Jette (02 428 26 26, www.magrittemuseum.be). Métro Belgica or tram 51, 94. **Open** 10am-6pm Wed-Sun. **Admission** €7; €6 reductions. No credit cards.

Magritte's unassuming suburban residence is a fittingly bizarre monument to the artist. The window and fireplace in the front room appear in numerous Magritte paintings, but perhaps the most surprising discovery is the modest back room in which he painted.

Musée de la Résistance

14 rue van Lint, Anderlecht (02 522 40 41). Métro Clemenceau. **Open** 9am-noon, 1-4pm Mon, Tue, Thur, Fri. **Admission** free.

Members of Belgium's resistance put together this striking collection of original documents relating to their struggle in the war years.

Nightlife

Libertine/Supersport

1 avenue du Port, Molenbeek (no phone, http://libertinesupersport.be). Métro Yser. No credit cards.

This is the place for some serious partying. The hedonistic crowd is a workable mix of preppy types and total alternatives, all melded together in one glorious party night. Belgian and international DJs play guest spots, starting with housey funk and moving on to thumping progressive sounds.

Magasin 4

NEW *51b avenue du Port, Molenbeek (02 223 34 74, www.magasin4.be). Métro Yser.* No credit cards.

The old Magasin 4 was dilapidated, sweaty and graffiti-ridden. In 2010, the new M4 opened its doors just across the canal in an old industrial building. It's not so dilapidated, but it is sweaty and the graffiti makes way for neon. It remains one of the city's wilder venues, with rock and indie bands alternated with dubstep and drum 'n' bass.

Tour et Taxis

3 rue Picard, Molenbeek (02 420 60 69, www.tourtaxis.be). Métro Ribaucourt or Belgica or bus 14. No credit cards.

This vast former customs warehouse now houses offices, restaurants and a handful of design shops. It's also an important venue for events and exhibitions – among them one of the biggest world music festivals in Europe, Couleur Café (www.couleurcafe.be). Held in late June, Couleur also incorporates a crafts village, workshops and some 50 food stalls.

VK Club

76 rue de l'Ecole, Molenbeek (02 414 29 07, www.vaartkapoen.be). Métro Comte de Flandre. No credit cards.

Just as the nominally francophone Botanique has its Flemish counterpart in the Ancienne Belgique, Magasin 4 has a Flemish twin in the Vaartkapoen or VK Club. The place itself is great, with a lively line-up of bands, but the area can be rough. The venue runs buses from the Gare Centrale, though; phone for details.

Arts & leisure

Stade Constant Vanden Stock

2 avenue Théo Verbeeck, Anderlecht (02 522 1539, tickets 02 529 40 67, www.rsca.be). Métro St-Guidon. No credit cards.

RSC Anderlecht are still by far the biggest football club in the land, with the team's regular appearances in the Champions League harking back to European triumphs decades ago. On match days the football-oriented bars stretching all the way along avenue Théo Verbeeck, by the impressive stadium, are packed out with enthusiastic fans clad in club colours. The atmosphere here is usually friendly, but bear in mind that the home end, stand four, can be raucous, and heavy if Bruges are in town.

DECEMBRE 1945 AU 15 JANVIER 19

URRÉALISME

de Tableaux, Dessins, Objets, Photos et Texte

BATTISTINI, BOTT, BOUMEESTER, BOUVET, BRAUNER, BRYEN, BURY,
E, CHIRICO, DOMINGUEZ, DUHAMEL, DUMONT, DUMOUCHEL, ERNST,
IRE, GOETZ, HAVRENNE, HEROLD, JEAN, LABISSE, LEFRANCQ,
TTE, MALET, MARIEN, NOUGE, NOVARINA, SANDERS, SAVINIO,
AIRE, SENECAUT, SIMON, UBAC, VANDESPIEGELE, WERGIFOSSE, WITZ

I 22 DÉC. A 21 H., CONFÉRENCE DE M. MARI

E SURRÉALISME EN 1945

I 5 JANV. A 21 H., CONFÉRENCE d'Ach. CHAV

POINTS DE REPÈRE

Musée Magritte

Grote Markt

Antwerp

Flanders' largest metropolis,
Antwerp effortlessly fuses
history with red-hot fashion and
cutting-edge culture. Its nightlife is
among the best in northern Europe
and attracts clubbers from far and
wide. Another big draw is the lively
summer arts festival, Zomer van
Antwerpen (see p36).

The city developed as a trading
port in the 12th century. As the
rival port of Bruges slowly silted
up and the Flemish textile industry
flourished, so Antwerp boomed.
By the mid 16th century, it was the
leading trading centre in Europe,
with a population of 100,000 and
a glittering diamond industry.
Ambitious new buildings went
up, reflecting the city's new status,
and a raft of artists made it their
home, Peter Paul Rubens and
Anthony van Dyck among them.

Antwerp's historical centre
clusters around the **Grote Markt**,
with its fine guildhouses and 16th-
century **Stadhuis** (Town Hall).
Just off the square is the cathedral,
Onze Lieve Vrouwekathedraal,
home to four of Rubens' works.

A minute's walk west from
the Stadhuis brings you to the
river Scheldt and the **Steen**, a
fine medieval syronghold whose
name translates as 'the Stone'.

North-east of the Grote Markt,
the narrow streets behind the
cathedral emerge at the pretty
square of Hendrik Conscienceplein,
home to the exuberant, early 17th-
century Baroque church of St
Carolus Borromeuskerk. Close by is
the lovely **Rockoxhuis Museum**,
with its small but exquisite art
collection. East of here you'll find
St Jacobskerk, where Rubens is
buried; his home, the **Rubenshuis**,
is a few streets away.

The southern side of the city,
't Zuid, is scattered with galleries,
restaurants, bars and clubs – and
many of Antwerp's best museums.

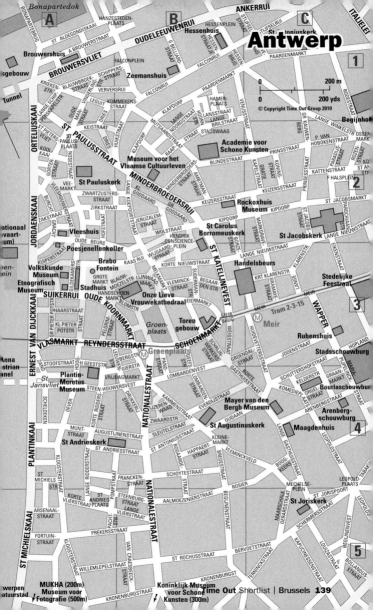

Onze Lieve Vrouwekathedraal p142

Among them are the idiosyncratic **Mayer van den Bergh Museum**; the **Koninklijk Museum voor Schone Kunsten** (Royal Museum of Fine Arts); contemporary arts museum **MUKHA**; design museum **MoMu**; and the splendid **Museum voor Fotografie**.

To the north of the city centre, the 19th-century **Bonaparte** dock area has an urban, bohemian air, especially in the 't Eilandje quarter. This is to be the site of the **Museum Aan de Stroom** (www.mas.be), which will explore the city and the world from an ethonological, maritime and artistic perspective. It's due to open in spring 2011; until then, you'll have to make do with admiring the dramatic, ultra-modern building.

Sights & museums

Koninklijk Museum voor Schone Kunsten

1-9 Leopold de Waelplaats (03 238 78 09, www.kmska.be). **Open** 10am-5pm Tue-Sat; 10am-6pm Sun. **Admission** €6; free-€4 reductions. No credit cards. Devoted to Flemish painting from 1350 to the present day, this outstanding museum is best known for its collection of Flemish Primitives and works from Antwerp's Golden Age. The remarkable 17th-century section has paintings by Rubens, Jordaens and Van Dyck. The Rubens works are mostly religious, with *Venus Frigida* the only notable exception, while Jordaens' subjects are more varied. Van Dyck's work is the least flamboyant, as evinced by *Portrait of the Painter Marten Pepyn*. The museum also has a large collection of paintings by James Ensor, the surrealists and the CoBrA artists.

Mayer van den Bergh Museum

19 Lange Gasthuisstraat (03 232 42 37, http://museum.antwerpen.be/mayervandenbergh). **Open** 10am-5pm

SHORTLIST

Best for art
- Koninklijk Museum voor Schone Kunsten (see left)
- Onze Lieve Vrouwekathedraal (see p142)
- Openlucht Museum voor Beeldhouwkun Middelheim (see p142)
- Rubenshuis (see p145)

Best for fashion mavens
- Ann Demeulemeester (see p150)
- Het Modepaleis (see p153)
- MoMu (see p142)
- Verso (see p153)

Best for a sugar rush
- Chocolatier Goossens (see p152)
- Désiré de Lille (see p148)
- Philip's Biscuits (see p153)

Best eating
- Izumi (see p148)
- De Kleine Zavel (see p148)
- Het Nieuwe Palinghuis (see p149)
- Het Pomphuis (see p149)

Best clubs
- Café d'Anvers (see p155)
- Red & Blue (see p155)

Best boozing
- Bar Tabac (see p146)
- Den Engel (see p148)
- De Pelikaan (see p149)

Best for quaffing genevers
- De Vagant (see p150)

Best for a cultural fix
- deSingel (see p155)

Best for gifts
- Mekanik Strip (see p153)
- Vervloet Kaashandel (see p153)

Tue-Sun. **Admission** €4; free-€2 reductions. **Map** p139 C4.

Five minutes' walk south-east from the centre, this engaging museum displays the private art collection of Fritz Mayer van den Bergh. Purpose-built in 1904 by Mayer van den Bergh's mother after his early death, it is an immensely charming place. Its prize exhibit is Pieter Bruegel the Elder's astonishing *Dulle Griet* ('Mad Meg'), a Bosch-like allegory of a world turned upside down. Look out, too, for a powerful crucifixion triptych by Quentin Matsys, works by Bouts, Van Orley and Cranach, and some lovely 15th-century carved wooden angels.

MoMu

28 Nationalestraat (03 470 27 70, www.momu.be). **Open** 10am-6pm Tue-Sun. **Admission** €6; free-€4 reductions. No credit cards. **Map** p139 B4.

Fashion followers will adore MoMu, the design museum, located in the beautiful late 19th-century ModeNatie complex – also home to the Flanders Fashion Institute and the fashion department of the Royal Academy of Fine Arts, as well as a trendy café-restaurant. Contemporary fashion and a historic costume and lace collection are the highlights, and there are some stunning temporary exhibitions – in 2010, British milliner Stephen Jones was the subject of a major retrospective.

MUHKA

16-30 Leuvenstraat (03 260 99 99, www.muhka.be). **Open** 11am-6pm Tue, Wed, Fri-Sun; 11am-9pm Thur. **Admission** €5; free-€4 reductions.

Antwerp takes a proactive approach towards encouraging new artistic talent. A high-profile contemporary art museum, MUHKA (the Museum voor Hedendaagse Kunst van Antwerpen, to give it its full name) showcases works from the 1970s onwards. The focus is firmly on temporary – often challenging – exhibitions, displayed in inviting, light-flooded rooms.

Museum voor Fotografie

47 Waalsekaai (03 242 93 00, www.fotomuseum.be). **Open** 10am-5pm Tue-Sun. **Admission** free. No credit cards.

The museum houses one of Europe's most important collections of photography, including works by the likes of Man Ray, Henri Cartier-Bresson, Irving Penn, Lee Friedlander and Robert Adams. Workshops, temporary exhibitions, film screenings and lectures add to the appeal – along with a great café. The latest addition, a wing designed by architect Georges Baines, contains large exhibition halls and also accommodates Antwerp Film Museum.

Onze Lieve Vrouwekathedraal

Handschoenmarkt (03 213 99 51, www.dekathedraal.be). **Open** 10am-5pm Mon-Fri; 10am-3pm Sat; 1-4pm Sun. **Admission** €5; free under-12s. No credit cards. **Map** p139 B3.

Built in the 14th century, Onze Lieve Vrouwekathedraal (Our Lady's Cathedral) is the largest Gothic church in Belgium. Although fires, iconoclastic fury and damage at the time of the French Revolution destroyed many of its original features, a 25-year renovation restored much of its splendour, and the white, light-filled interior now gleams. Among its paintings and sculptures are four of Rubens' works: *The Raising of the Cross*; *The Descent from the Cross*; *The Resurrection*; and *The Assumption*, over the altar.

Openlucht Museum voor Beeldhouwkunst Middelheim

61 Middelheimlaan (03 828 13 50, www.middelheimmuseum.be). **Open** *May, Aug* 10am-8pm Tue-Sun. *June, July* 10am-9pm Tue-Sun. *Sept, Apr* 10am-7pm Tue-Sun. *Oct-Mar* 10am-5pm Tue-Sun. **Admission** free. No credit cards.

This impressive, open-air sculpture museum is about five kilometres from the city centre: city trams 7 and 15 stop

City of couture

Why six is the magic number.

MoMu

To fashion ignoramuses, the Antwerp Six may sound like a notorious gang of bank robbers. In fact, as anyone with even a passing interest in clothes will know, it's the nickname of the group of Belgian designers that took the 1988 London Fashion Week by storm.

All six still live or work in the city. Ann Demeulemeester, one of the best-known of the sextet, runs a shop by the **Fine Arts Museum** (see p150), while Dries van Noten sells his designs at **Het Modepaleis** (see p153); his A-list accolytes run from Maggie Gyllenhaal to Jane Birkin.

Elsewhere, bald and bearded Walter van Beirendonck now looks more like a member of ZZ Top than an *enfant terrible* of the Six. A lecturer at the Royal Academy, he showcases his sartorial creations at **Walter** (see p153).

Then there's the honourary seventh member of the group, Martin Margiela, who graduated a year after the others. Media-shy but always daring, Margiela left the label that bears his name in December 2009; it's now run by his design team.

All seven designers are well documented in the **MoMu** (see left) fashion museum. But while they have earned their place in fashion history, a new wave of talent is on the make.

Already well on the ascendant are Veronique Branquinho, who graduated in fashion from Antwerp Royal Academy in 1995, and Bruno Pieters, one of the star graduates of 1999.

Looking to the future, one hotly-tipped name is Six Lee, who wowed with a conceptual menswear range in 2009. Another is Alexandra Verschueren, who won the Antwerp Academy's Grand Jury prize for her exquisite, origami-like paper designs. Meanwhile, Mariel Manuel is a fabulously talented designer and illustrator, who has already produced a capsule collection for Swedish brand Weekday. One thing's for sure: Antwerp is still turning out the catwalk stars of the future.

MoMu p142

a 15-minute walk short of it. Buses 18 and 32 go closer, or it may be easier to take a taxi. However you get there, it's worth the trip. The collection is magnificent, with works by the likes of Rodin and Henry Moore along with modern talents such as Belgian artists Panamarenko and Vermeiren. The biennial summer exhibition of international sculpture is not to be missed.

Provinciaal Diamantmuseum

19-23 Koningin Astridplein (03 202 48 90, www.diamantmuseum.be). **Open** 10am-5.30pm Mon, Tue, Thur-Sun. **Admission** €6; free-€4 reductions. West of Antwerp's striking Centraal Station is the diamond district, with a visible police presence keeping the sparklers safe. The Diamantmuseum, on a square facing the station, has three floors of treasures. Visitors are taken on an interactive tour showing how rough diamonds are turned into the polished final product, and can ogle some spectacular stones and jewellery.

Rockoxhuis Museum

12 Keizerstraat (03 201 92 50, www. rockoxhuis.be). **Open** 10am-5pm Tue-Sun. **Admission** €2.50; free-€1.25 reductions. No credit cards. **Map** p139 B2.
The Rockoxhuis Museum occupies the lovely 17th-century townhouse of Mayor Nicolaas Rockox, best known for his friendship with Rubens. Although the house is filled with period furnishings, it's more a gallery than a re-created home, and the main attraction is the small but perfectly formed art collection. Key pieces include works by Matsys, Van Dyck and local boys Joachim Beuckelaer and Frans Snyders.

Rubenshuis

9-11 Wapper (03 201 15 55, www. rubenshuis.be). **Open** 10am-5pm Tue-Sun. **Admission** €6; free-€4 reductions. No credit cards. **Map** p139 C3.

Home to the artist for most of his life, the Rubenshuis has become a major tourist draw. It is one of the most notable Baroque buildings in Antwerp; inside, highlights include the semi circular gallery (based on the Pantheon in Rome) and Rubens' spacious studio. The only disappointment is that there aren't more of Rubens' paintings on display. Look out, though, for an endearing self-portrait (c1630) and a later, more anxious-looking one of him in the studio. It's wise to come early to avoid the large tour parties.

St Jacobskerk

73 Lange Nieuwstraat (03 232 10 32, www.topa.be/sint-jacobskerk). **Open** *Apr-Oct* 2-5pm Mon, Wed-Sun. *Nov-Mar* 9am-noon Mon-Sat. **Admission** €2; free-€1.50 reductions. No credit cards. **Map** p139 C2.
From a distance, St Jacobs looks most impressive – though the closer you get, the more it seems to diminish. Little houses completely surround it, only just leaving room for the entrances. The interior is decorated in a heavy Baroque style; this was a wealthy district, and its parishioners made sure the church reflected their status. Rubens is buried here, and painted the work that hangs over his tomb, *Our Lady Surrounded by Saints*, specifically for the purpose. St George is believed to be a self-portrait, and the Virgin a portrait of Isabella Brant, Rubens' first wife. Mary Magdalene, meanwhile, is Hélène Fourment, his second wife.

Steen (Nationaal Scheepvaartmuseum)

1 Steenplein (03 201 93 40). **Open** 10am-5pm Tue-Sun. **Admission** €4; free-€3 reductions. No credit cards. **Map** p139 A3.
Almost as old as Antwerp itself, the castle that once guarded the river has become a symbol of the city. Built in 1200, the Steen was part of the fortifications; it later served as a prison, then as a sawmill, before being turned into

the National Maritime Museum. Today it houses an endearingly old-fashioned collection of maps, nautical objects, model ships and old photos of Antwerp dock life, though this will all move to the new MAS museum (see p141) in 2011. Real ships can be found in the outdoor section, while the spacious terraces by the castle allow for a quiet drink and a stroll by the Scheldt.

Vleeshuis

38-40 Vleeshouwersstraat (03 233 64 04, http://museum.antwerpen.be/vleeshuis). **Open** 10am-5pm Tue-Sun. **Admission** €5; free-€3 reductions. No credit cards. **Map** p139 A2.

The Vleeshuis (Butcher's Hall) was built as a guildhouse and meat market by the Butchers' Guild in 1503. It's a puzzling construction, in late Gothic style with little turrets and walls that alternate red brick with white stone. Today the hall is used as a museum of musical instruments, representing 600 years of Antwerp's musical history. It also holds early music concerts.

Eating & drinking

Amadeus

20 Sint-Paulusstraat (03 232 25 87, www.amadeusspareribrestaurant.be). **Open** 6.30-11pm Mon-Thur; 6-11pm Fri-Sun. **€€**. **American**. **Map** p139 A2.

This spare-rib restaurant, set in an old art nouveau glass factory, has a USP. A litre of house red sits unceremoniously on the table – drink as much or as little as you like, and you'll be charged for the amount you quaff. Then there are the ribs: as many as you can eat, with the accompaniment of your choice. No cutlery is required.

Bar Tabac

43 Waalsekaai (03 238 19 37, www.bartabac.be). **Open** 9pm-late Wed-Sun. No credit cards. **Bar**.

BT doesn't really start to shake its tail feather until gone midnight, when a superb soundtrack (from Madonna to Serge Gainsbourg) complements an atmosphere rarely more than a couple of notches from cool. If you've had an evening of indistinct drinking in designer bars and were wondering exactly why Antwerp is hyped to the nines, breeze into the Bar Tabac, particularly on a Sunday night, and all will suddenly become clear.

Berlin

2 Kleine Markt (03 227 11 01). **Open** 8am-late Mon-Fri; 10am-late Sat, Sun. **Bar**. **Map** p139 B4.

Dark and broody, but run with impeccable taste, Berlin has become something of an institution with singles, couples and families alike (there's a big play area at the back for small fry). Food is served throughout the day, but be warned: evenings and weekend afternoons can be a bit of a scrum.

De Broers van Julienne

45-47 Kasteelpleinstraat (03 232 02 03, www.debroersvanjulienne.be). **Open** noon-10pm Mon-Sat; 5.30-9pm Sun. **€**. **Vegetarian**. **Map** p139 C5.

There's a certain hush about this charming meat-free restaurant, with its calm colonial style interior decor and pretty, tree-shaded garden for alfresco dining in summer. The food is prepared using natural and organic ingredients, while the shop and bakery at the front are equally classy.

Café Beveren

2 Vlasmarkt (03 231 22 25). **Open** noon-late Mon, Thur-Sun. No credit cards. **Bar**. **Map** p139 A3.

This is dockside Antwerp – and the kind of spot you might find in Rotterdam or Hamburg, where age-mellowed regulars fumble with their reading glasses before commencing another round of cards. The red-lined banquettes encase the café in a lost era. Note the fully working De Cap fairground organ and old Rowe Ami jukebox, and watch out for spontaneous outbreaks of old-time dancing.

Het Pomphuis p149

Ciro's

6 Amerikalei (03 238 11 47, www. ciros.be). **Open** 11am-11pm daily. €€.
Belgian.

Ciro's was last decorated in 1962, and as such seems to have gone full circle in its own retro way. The crowds come for the steak and chips, regarded as the best in Antwerp. New ownership has changed nothing – which is just how the regulars like it.

Désiré de Lille

14-18 Schrijnwerkerstraat (03 232 62 26, www.desiredelille.be). **Open** 9am-10pm daily. €. No credit cards. **Café.**
Map p139 B3.

Désiré started off as a funfair stand, selling freshly made waffles, fruit-filled doughnuts and *laquemants* (a kind of baked pancake). These days, it trades in a genteel 1930s restaurant, its interior filled with banquettes and railway carriage lights. A glass pergola at the back gives a conservatory feel and leads to a magnificent garden.

Den Engel

5 Grote Markt (03 233 12 52, www. cafedenengel.be). **Open** 9am-late daily. No credit cards. **Bar. Map** p139 A3.

Antwerp's bar of all bars. It isn't fabulous or fashionable, and whatever edges it once cut blunted long ago; it is simply an institution, providing ramshackle relief from the official goings-on next door at the Town Hall. Councillors clink glasses, journalists accept drinks and gossip from politicians, while locals of all ages provide a cheery backdrop. Next door's Den Bengel (the Miscreant) copes with the overflow from Den Engel (the Angel).

Entrepôt du Congo

42 Vlaamsekaai (03 257 16 48, www. entrepotducongo.com). **Open** 8am-3am Mon-Fri; 8am-4am Sat, Sun. No credit cards. **Bar.**

This pioneering enterprise began the regeneration of the southern quaysides into the trendy quarter of galleries and designer bars it is today. A century ago, boats from the Congo would dock here, unloading crates of colonial plunder into this grand corner edifice. These days, it sports a classy, bare wood-and-tile interior and remains popular, despite a plethora of competition a mere anchor's toss away; perhaps it's the excellent bar food.

Hippodroom

10 Leopold de Waelplaats (03 248 52 52, www.hippodroom.be). **Open** noon-2.30pm, 6-11pm Mon-Fri; 6-11pm Sat.
€€-€€€. **Modern European.**

Hippodroom's long and slender dining room – complete with massive works of art and minimally set tables – contrasts perfectly with its turn-of-the-century exterior. Its confident aesthetic style extends to the menu, which might run from sushi to French-inspired fillet of lamb with truffle risotto.

Izumi

14 Beeldhouwersstraat (03 216 13 79, http://www2.resto.be/izumi). **Open** noon-2pm, 6.30-10.30pm Tue-Sat.
€€. **Japanese.**

Nestled in its old Antwerp townhouse since 1978, Izumi enjoys an unassailable reputation as the city's best Japanese restaurant. Expect classic, well-executed belly of tuna, fried eel with cucumber, squid, octopus, urchin and marinated seaweed, plus ample spreads of sushi, sashimi and teriyaki.

De Kleine Zavel

2 Stoofstraat (03 231 96 91, www. kleinezavel.be). **Open** noon-2.30pm, 6-10.30pm Mon-Thur; noon-2pm, 6.30-11.30pm Fri; 6.30-11.30pm Sat; noon-2pm, 6-10.30pm Sun. €€€.
Modern European. Map p139 A3.

The KZ is one of Antwerp's dining hotspots, with chef-owner Carlo Didden serving up imaginative French- and Med-inspired food to a discerning yet unpretentious crowd. Mains might run from grilled baby lobster with green herb oil and summer salad to lamb with sweetbreads, pak choi, glasswort and tomato confit. If you're on a budget, there's a set lunch menu.

Lucy Chang

16-17 Marnixplaats (03 248 95 60, www.lucychang.be). **Open** noon-midnight daily. **€**. No credit cards. **Asian**.

The first thing you see in here is a market stall, to the right of which is a long, low bar. This is designed for those who want to pop in for a small plate of dim sum or a bowl of noodle soup. The food is from Laos, Vietnam, Thailand, Malaysia and China; everything comes at once, and is perfect for sharing.

Maritime

4 Suikerrui (03 233 07 58, www. maritime.be). **Open** noon-2.30pm, 6-9.30pm Mon, Tue, Fri-Sun. **€€€**. **Seafood**. **Map** p139 A3.

Maritime has a classically Belgian feel, with its wooden beams, chi-chi chairs and red tablecloths. The food is similarly classic, with a heavy leaning to eels and mussels. And not just eels in green sauce – try them in cream or fried in butter, or have a go at mussels in a Madras curry sauce. Lobster is popular too. All in all, the perfect spot for a fishy treat.

Het Nieuwe Palinghuis

14 Sint-Jansvliet (03 231 74 45, www. hetnieuwepalinghuis.be). **Open** noon-3pm, 6-10pm Wed-Sun. **€€-€€€**. **Seafood**. **Map** p139 A4.

There's no missing the maritime theme here: the walls are hung with prints of 19th-century Antwerpenaars fishing their cotton smocks off, and even the loo seats are embedded with shells. Fish is, unsurprisingly, the order of the day – eel, scallops with truffles and mussels in cream with garlic. It's pricey, but worth every penny.

'T Oerwoud

2 Suikerrui (03 233 14 12). **Open** noon-late daily. **€**. **Café/Bar**. **Map** p139 A3.

A step back from the quayside, two steps from the brazen tourism of the town centre and opposite the medieval fortress of the Steen, 'T Oerwoud (the Jungle) is a relaxed eaterie (salads, soups and pastas) that also operates as a busy pre-club livener. Spotlights blaze over the curved bar, speakers boom with dance tunes, and the nachos machine and upholstered leather seating of the chill-and-chat back area soon become buried in a fug of Bastos.

De Pelikaan

14 Melkmarkt (03 227 23 51). **Open** 9am-late daily. No credit cards. **Bar**. **Map** p139 B3.

The downtown and ever downbeat Pelican has been dragging writers, designers and musicians through its doors and keeping them glued to its bar counter for longer than most care to remember. Set in the shadow of the cathedral, it makes no effort to appeal to curious passers-by, leaving the dressing up to tackier venues nearby. It isn't even dressed down: it's just got out of bed and put on whatever it could find on the bedroom floor. Drink, swap stories, get drunk, go home. Perfect.

Het Pomphuis

Droogdok, 7 Siberiastraat (03 770 86 25, www.hetpomphuis.be). **Open** 11am-2.30pm; 6-11pm Mon-Fri; 11am-11pm Sat, Sun. **€€€**. **Modern European**.

This magnificent old building, once the pumphouse for the dry dock, was converted into a restaurant back in 2003. Massive arched windows and lofty ceilings surround crisply laid tables. The menu is unusual for Antwerp, with dishes such as goats' cheese salad with dates, apples and beetroot syrup or grilled tuna with soy shoots, sugar snaps and *lomo de pata negra*.

Sombat Thai Cuisine

1 Vleeshuisstraat (03 226 21 90, www.sombat.be). **Open** noon-2.30pm, 6-10.30pm Tue-Fri; 6-11pm Sat, Sun. **€€€**. **Thai**. **Map** p139 A2/3.

This expansive restaurant, regarded as Antwerp's finest Thai, sits in the shadow of the Gothic Butcher's Hall. Mixed dishes are popular here, so spring rolls turn up with minced pork in a banana leaf, crispy noodles and assorted tasty dipping sauces.

De Vagant

25 Reyndersstraat (03 233 15 38, www.devagant.be). **Open** 11am-late Mon-Sat; noon-late Sun. No credit cards. **Bar**. Map p139 A3.
Genever was to Antwerp what gin was to London, the opiate of historic port cities drowned in a sea of cheap booze. Prohibition arrived in 1919 and wasn't repealed until 1984. This bar opened a year later, offering 200 types of once-forbidden genever in myriad strengths and flavours, accompanied by small chunks of meat and cheese. Sipped and not slammed, genever boasts a proud history, detailed on the menu and celebrated in an exquisite interior of pre-prohibition posters and old flagons.

Het Zand

9 Sint-Jansvliet (03 232 56 67). **Open** 11am-late daily. No credit cards. **Bar**. Map p139 A4.
Located by the grand entrance of the St Anna foot tunnel, Het Zand displays the calculating hand of the Celtic fraternity. Yet, despite the fading promise of a peeling Guinness gift shop sign, this is essentially a boozy hostelry in the classic Antwerp tradition. Wooden tables heave under heavy lunches, old geezers prop up the bar, while the unusual local tradition of displaying death masks of former regulars is upheld overhead.

Zuiderterras

37 Ernest van Dijckkaai (03 234 12 75). **Open** 9am-midnight Mon-Thur; 9am-1am Fri-Sun & June-Aug. €€€. **Modern European**. Map p139 A3.
It's worth walking along the quay just to get a look at this sleek, shiny building. The Bob van Reeth creation has a

circular bar and a terrace looking over the river. The modern European menu (bouillabaisse served with grilled focaccia, say) may be on the expensive side, but it's a wonderful place to be at sunset nonetheless.

Shopping

A clothes shopper's paradise, Antwerp also has a well-deserved reputation for its fine antiques and delightful bric-a-brac shops, most of which are in the St Andries district: head for Steenhouwersvest, Lombardenvest and Kloosterstraat.

Stretching between the station and the city centre, traffic-free Meir is the main shopping drag, with a mix of international chains and smaller boutiques. For an overview of the city's shopping zones, see http://visit.antwerpen.be

Ann Demeulemeester

Leopold de Waelplaats (03 216 01 33, www.anndemeulemeester.be). **Open** 11am-7pm Mon-Sat.
Ann Demeulemeester, the star member of the Antwerp Six, designs clothes that are slick yet sensual: her pieces are often subtly androgynous, and in monochrome hues. Fittingly, her minimalist shop is located opposite the city's Fine Arts Museum.

Avant-Scène

33 Leopoldstraat (03 231 88 26). **Open** 11am-6pm Tue-Sat. Map p139 C4.
You'll find pieces from Belgium's foremost furniture designers at Avant-Scène, including the Van Severen brothers and Xavier Lust.

Bilbo

Oude Korenmarkt 12 (03 226 8480). **Open** 10am-6pm Mon-Fri; 10am-6.30pm Sat. Map p139 A3.
Packed with new and used vinyl and CDs, Bilbo offers rock, indie, techno, house – anything, really. Have a rootle through and see what gems you find.

XSO p153

Chocolatier Goossens

6 Isabellalei (03 239 13 10, www. goossens-chocolatier.com). **Open** 9am-6pm Mon-Sat. No credit cards. Founded in 1955, this is probably the finest chocolatiers in Antwerp. Teddy bears, chocolate lips and even Kama Sutra reliefs made from 100% cocoa butter make scrumptious gifts.

Christa Reniers

22 Drukkerijstraat (03 233 26 02, www.christareniers.com). **Open** 11am-1pm, 2-6pm Thur-Sat. **Map** p139 B4. Brussels-based Reniers is one of Belgium's top jewellery designers, creating sleekly modern rings, chokers and bracelets in silver and gold, dotted with candy-hued stones.

Closing Date

15 Korte Gasthuisstraat (03 232 87 22). **Open** 11am-6.30pm Mon-Sat. **Map** p139 B4. Clubbers with cash and eccentrics with panache come here to pore over racks of clothes by the likes of Dsquared2, Vivienne Westwood and Owen Gaster.

Coccodrillo

9A/B Schuttershofstraat (03 233 20 93, www.coccodrillo.be). **Open** 10am-6pm Mon-Sat. **Map** p139 C4. Prada, Patrick Cox, Jil Sander, Ann Demeulemeester, Dries van Noten and Helmut Lang are among the fashion heavyweights represented at this full-on footwear mecca.

Donum

47 Hopland (03 231 39 18, www. donum.be). **Open** 10am-6pm Mon-Fri; 10am-6.30pm Sat. **Map** p139 C3. Set in an old school, this cool interior design shop stocks pieces from big hitters such as B&B Italia, Vitra, Moooi and Flos.

Erotische Verbeelding

165 Kloosterstraat (03 226 89 50, www.erotischeverbeelding.com). **Open** 11am-6pm Mon-Sat. **Map** p139 A5.

This women-only store sells sex aids, tasteful-looking dildos, a smattering of S&M and assorted slinky lingerie.

Fish & Chips

36-38 Kammenstraat (03 227 08 24, www.fishandchips.be). **Open** 10am-6.30pm Mon-Sat. **Map** p139 B4. Antwerp's chaotic temple to cool. On Saturdays, DJs spin tunes in a booth overhanging the ground floor, whose streetwear and clubbing labels include Wesc, Etnies, Adidas and Fred Perry.

Goossens

31 Korte Gasthuisstraat (03 226 07 91). **Open** 7am-7pm Tue-Sat. No credit cards. **Map** p139 C4. Founded in 1884, this small and popular traditional bakery offers a good choice of pastries and cakes, all displayed on metal racks.

Huis A Boon

4 Lombardenvest (03 232 33 87, www.glovesboon.be). **Open** 10am-6pm Mon-Sat. This glove shop is a wonderfully evocative time capsule, with hundreds of different pairs of gloves for men and women displayed on dark shelves or stowed away in little drawers.

'T Koetshuis (Chelsea)

10 Kloosterstraat (03 248 33 42, www.antiek-koetshuis.be). **Open** noon-6pm Tue-Sat; 1-6pm Sun. No credit cards. **Map** p139 A4. Its official name is Chelsea, but 'T Koetshuis (the coachhouse) is what you'll find written over the door. The art deco and art nouveau antiques are selected and displayed with care, so don't expect any bargains.

Louis

2 Lombardenstraat (03 232 98 72). **Open** 10am-6pm Mon-Sat. **Map** p139 B4. One of the first boutiques to champion Belgian fashion, Louis remains a shrine for fashion-forward shoppers of both sexes. Martin Margiela, Rick Owens Veronique Branquinho and Raf Simons are among the staple labels.

Mekanik Strip

73 St Jacobsmarkt (03 234 23 47, www.mekanik-strip.be). **Open** 10am-6.30pm Mon-Fri; 10am-6pm Sat. **Map** p139 C2.

Mekanik carries a huge selection of English, French and Dutch comics, plus books, videos, posters and Tintin collectibles. It also a gallery space too.

Het Modepaleis

16 Nationalestraat (03 470 25 10, www.driesvannoten.be). **Open** 10am-6.30pm Mon-Sat. **Map** p139 B4.

Belgian superstar designer Dries van Noten showcases his mens' and womenswear collections in this landmark building, dating from 1881.

Nadine Wijnants

26 Kloosterstraat (mobile 0484 643 303, www.nadinewijnants.be). **Open** 11am-6pm Fri, Sat. **Map** p139 A4.

One of the top jewellery designers in Belgium, Wijnants creates charming, affordable pieces with semi-precious stones, silver, bronze and gold plate.

Philip's Biscuits

11 Korte Gasthuisstraat (03 231 26 60). **Open** 10am-6pm Mon-Sat. No credit cards. **Map** p139 B4.

Call in at this delightful old-timer for macaroons, *speculoos* (ginger biscuits) and hand-shaped butter biscuits.

Soap

13 Plantinkaai (03 232 73 72). **Open** 9am-6.30pm Mon-Thur; 9am-8pm Fri; 9am-6pm Sat. **Map** p139 A4.

Soap is the salon where the city's more stylish folk come to get their hair coiffed to perfection.

SN3

46-48 Frankrijklei (03 231 08 20, www.sn3.be). **Open** noon-6.30pm Mon; 10am-6.30pm Tue-Sat.

Housed in a former cinema, this spacious, slightly snobby designer boutique carries collections by the likes of Marni, Balenciaga, Dior, Lanvin, Galliano and Prada.

Verso

11 Lange Gasthuisstraat (03 226 92 92, www.verso.be). **Open** 11am-7pm Mon-Thur; 11am-9pm Fri, Sat. **Map** p139 C4.

Fashionistas glide around this temple to cutting-edge design, fingering pieces from the likes of Helmut Lang, Miu Miu, YSL, Armani and Versace. So exclusive it hurts.

Vervloet Kaashandel

28 Wiegstraat (03 233 37 29). **Open** 8am-6pm Mon-Sat. No credit cards. **Map** p139 B3.

Luc Wouters specialises in fine cheeses from across Belgium, including his own hard goat's cheese variety.

Walter

12 St Antoniusstraat (03 213 26 44, www.walt.de). **Open** 1-6pm Mon; 11am-6.30pm Tue-Sat. **Map** p139 B4.

Walter van Beirendonck (see box p143) and Dirk van Saene's shop feels more like a gallery; among the labels are van B's own collection.

XSO

13-15 Eiermarkt (03 231 87 49). **Open** 10am-6pm Mon-Fri; 10am-6pm Sat. **Map** p139 B3.

Set in a quiet courtyard in the centre of town, this sizeable shop mixes Japanese purity (white walls, slate floors) with international fashion flair. Labels include Issey Miyake, Kenzo and Giorgio Armani.

Nightlife

To get the lowdown on what's on where, visit www.noctis.com or pick up flyers at shops like Fish & Chips (see p152). Annoyingly, only the more underground clubs will

Café d'Anvers

welcome scruffy trainers and baggy jeans; it's always best to dress to impress.

Café d'Anvers
15 Verversrui (03 226 38 70, www. cafe-d-anvers.com).
This legendary venue was a church and cinema before its transformation into a kicking club in the early 1990s. Expect progressive house from Thursday to Saturday, with DJs running from local luminaries to international stars like Sasha.

Hessenhuis
53 Falconrui (03 231 13 56, www. hessenhuis.com). **Open** 10.30am-late daily. No credit cards. **Map** p139 B1.
By day, Hessenhuis acts as a museum and art gallery, but at night it transforms itself into a popular pre-club destination, attracting townie gays and their female friends. The interior is a combination of modern and rustic, though the clientele is full-on chic, ready to party and enjoy the live entertainment or theme nights. Breakfast is served on Sundays.

Petrol
21 d'Herbouvillekaai (03 226 49 63, www.petrolclub.be).
Petrol is a laid-back place where funky house alternates with electronica, drum 'n' bass, reggae and plenty more besides – and where clubbers can be (and wear) whatever they want.

Popi
12 Plantinkaai (03 238 15 30, www. popi.be). **Open** 2pm-late Mon-Fri; 11am-late Sat, Sun. No credit cards. **Map** p139 A4.
Brash, cheeky (its name refers to the Russian for backside) and impossibly pink, Popi doesn't take itself in the least bit seriously. Abba, Eurotrash and drag sum up the free-fall entertainment. Popi is ten years old now, but it still doesn't know – or care – what it wants to be when it grows up.

Pure
AEC Building, 10 Indiestraat (03 234 09 92, www.pure-antwerp.be). **Open** 11pm-late Sat.
Pure is held in a beautiful old factory space in the docks – one of Antwerp's more sparkling sin bins. The musical focus is progressive house and funky soul, but be aware that the club closes for the summer, re-opening in September with a big bash.

Red & Blue
11-13 Lange Schipperskapelstraat (03 213 05 55, www.redandblue.be). **Open** 11pm-7am Sat & special nights. **Map** p139 A1.
The name comes from the club's location in the old red-light district. The girls may have moved on, but the boys have arrived and plan to stay. Along with Brussels' La Démence (see p81), Saturday's men-only night is regarded as Belgium's best, with Dutch dance divas pouring across the border (Fridays are mixed). R&B is a real event; Grace Jones once drove through the sweaty dancers in a stretch limo.

Arts & Leisure

deSingel
25 Desguinlei (03 248 28 28, www.desingel.be).
South of the centre, this is Antwerp's modern equivalent to Brussels' Bozar, with a cutting-edge programme of dance, theatre music and architectural exhibitions, presented in a massive, 1960s building. You'll spot some cultural big-hitters amid the line-up: choreographer Sidi Larbi Cherkaoui, say, or film-maker Patrice Chéreau.

Vlaamse Opera
8 Van Ertbornstraat (03 202 10 11, www.vlaamseopera.be). Box office: 3 Frankrijklei (070 22 02 02).
Flemish Opera productions are divided between the opera house in Ghent and the old but acoustically splendid Antwerp Hall.

Markt

Bruges

BRUGES BY AREA

With its modest population of 116,000, Bruges is mobbed by about three million tourists every year, many of them from Britain, making it the most popular destination in Belgium for foreign visitors. Yet despite the crowds, it remains a romantic, atmospheric city that invites gentle wandering through its historic squares, alleyways and quays.

The city's golden age came during the 15th century, when it was a thriving port. Merchants came here from all over Europe to trade in wool, lace and diamonds, building Gothic brick houses along the canals and narrow lanes in the northern quarter. This age of plenty is also reflected in the rich collections of art in the city's museums and churches.

By far the easiest and most enjoyable way to visit Bruges is on foot – it's compact, largely traffic-free and easy to get around.

The traditional starting point for any visit is the main square, the **Markt**, near which you'll find another beautiful square, the **Burg** – home to the 14th-century **Stadhuis** (Town Hall). South of here is the **Vismarkt** (Fish Market), still held every morning from Tuesday to Saturday, while to the east is the charming **Groenerei** canal, with its trees and gabled houses. West of Vismarkt, Huidevettersplaats (Tanners' Square) leads to the **Rozenhoedkaai**; the view of the canal from here is an eternal favourite with photographers. The quay leads to another picturesque canal, the **Dijver**, where the big attractions are the **Groeninge Museum** and the **Brangwyn Museum-Arentshuis**.

Further south still is the serenely lovely **Begijnhof**, founded in 1245. Its rows of modest whitewashed houses are set around an inner lawn, covered in daffodils in spring.

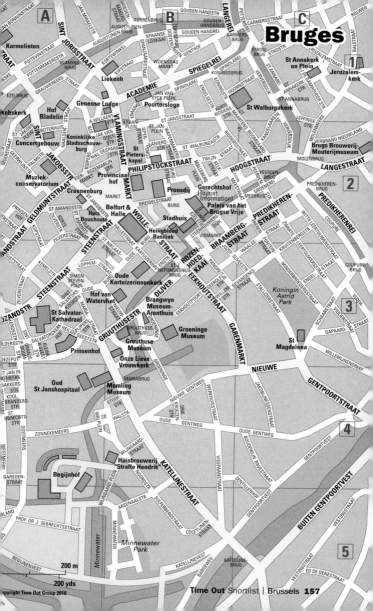

Bruges

200 m

200 yds

Sights & museums

Belfort

Markt. **Open** 9.30am-5pm daily.
Last entry 4.15pm. **Admission** €8;
free-€6 reductions. No credit cards.
Map p157 B2.

You can't miss the Belfort: it's one of
the main square's most impressive
buildings. The view from the top of the
80-metre (263-foot) belfry makes the
climb – all 366 steps of it – worth the
effort. The city's *carilloneur* climbs up
every Sunday to play at 2.15pm, also
giving ringings on the stroke of 9pm
on Mondays, Wednesdays and
Saturdays in summer.

Brangwyn Museum-Arentshuis

16 Dijver (050 44 87 63). **Open**
9.30am-5pm Tue-Sun. **Admission**
€2; free-€1 reductions. **Map** p157 B3.
Set in the intimate Arentspark, this
small museum is named after the
Bruges-born British painter and
engraver Frank Brangwyn, whose
works are on display inside.

Groeninge Museum

12 Dijver (050 44 87 43). **Open**
9.30am-5pm Tue-Sun. **Admission**
€8; free-€6 reductions. **Map** p157 B3.
Over the canal from the Memling, the
Groeninge is the most prestigious
museum in Bruges, covering 600 years
of Belgian painting. Pride of place goes
to its outstanding collection of Flemish
primitives, in particular works by Jan
van Eyck. Look out, too, for pieces by
the likes of Memling, Rogier van der
Weyden, Hieronymus Bosch and
Gerard David. There are also some fine
works by Belgian surrealists, including Ensor, Magritte and Delvaux.

Gruuthuse Museum

17 Dijver (050 44 87 62). **Open**
9.30am-5pm Tue-Sun. **Admission**
€6; free-€5 reductions. Ticket includes
entry to Onze Lieve Vrouwerk.
Map p157 B3.

The Gruuthuse Museum is set inside a
15th-century mansion that originally
belonged to the powerful Gruuthuse
family, who had a monopoly on *gruut*,
a mix of dried flowers and plants used
in the brewing process. Lodewijk van
Gruuthuse was a diplomat, patron of
the arts and friend of Edward IV of
England; he also invented a rather nas-
tier version of the cannonball. The furniture in the grand reception hall dates
from the 16th, 17th and 18th centuries,
as do the silverware and ceramics. The
bust of Charles V, showing a young
and candid emperor, is one of the most
important pieces in the collection.
Many of the other exhibits are objects
from daily life, including the ancient
musical instruments in the music cab-
inet and a large collection of lace.

Heiligbloed Basiliek

13 Burg. **Open** *Apr-Sept* 9.30am-noon,
2-6pm Tue-Sun. *Oct-Mar* 10am-noon,
2-4pm Tue, Thur-Sun; 10am-noon Wed.
Admission *Chapel* free. *Treasury*
€1.50. No credit cards. **Map** p157 B2.
The Basilica of the Holy Blood is the
oldest building on the Burg, tucked
away in a corner next to the Stadhuis.
Its bizarre interior is well worth a look.
In the Upper Chapel is a crystal phial
containing two drops of holy blood,
which is exhibited every Friday. The
phial is supposed to have been given to
Thierry d'Alsace by the Patri of
Jerusalem during the second Crusade,
and is one of the holiest relics of
medieval Europe.

Jeruzalemkerk

*3A Peperstraat (050 33 00 72,
www.kantcentrum.com).* **Open**
10am-5pm Mon-Sat. **Admission**
Combined ticket with Kantcentrum
€2.50; €1.50 reductions. No credit
cards. **Map** p157 C1.
The Jeruzalemkerk was built by a
wealthy family of Italian merchants;
indeed, the church still belongs to their
descendants. It's a curious, three-level
building, supposedly constructed

according to the model of the Holy Sepulchre in Jerusalem. Inside, highlights include a crucifix decorated with bones and skulls over the altar, a copy of the tomb of Christ in the crypt and some fine stained glass.

Kantcentrum

3A Peperstraat (050 33 00 72, www.kantcentrum.com). **Open** 10am-5pm Mon-Sat. **Admission** Combined ticket with Jeruzalemkerk €2.50; €1.50 reductions. No credit cards.

At the Kantcentrum, or Lace Museum, women demonstrate the intricate skills of lace-making, which has been a speciality of the low countries since the 15th century. Exquisite, gossamer-fine antique lace is also displayed.

Memling Museum

38 Mariastraat (050 44 87 70). **Open** 9.30am-5pm Tue-Sun. **Admission** €8; free-€6 reductions. **Map** p157 A/B4.

Within the hospital's ancient chapel is the renovated Memling Museum, dedicated to the 15th-century painter Hans Memling, who lived and studied in Bruges. Memling undertook numerous commissions for the English aristocrat John Donne and the Italian banker Portinari. His talent as a portrait artist and his hunger for detail are quite astonishing; this is a small but remarkable collection of his work.

Onze Lieve Vrouwkerk

Mariastraat. **Open** 9.30am-5pm Tue-Fri; 9.30am-4.45pm Sat; 1.30-5pm Sun. **Admission** *Church* free. *Choir* €2; free-€1 reductions. No credit cards. **Map** p157 B4.

A small stone bridge and a cobbled lane lead from Arentspark to the Church of Our Lady – an imposing brick structure with a massive tower, best seen from the garden. The church is famed for its works of art, which include Michelangelo's *Madonna and Child*, while in the choir are the burial tombs of Charles the Bold and his daughter, Mary of Burgundy.

S H O R T L I S T

Best views in town
- Belfort (see left)
- Rozenhoedkaai (see p156)

Best for art-lovers
- Brangwyn Museum-Arentshuis (see left)
- Groeninge Museum (see left)
- Memling Museum (see left)
- Onze Lieve Vrouwkerk (see left)

Best restaurants
- Bistro Refter (see p161)
- In Den Wittekop (see p162)
- De Karmeliet (see p162)
- Parkrestaurant (see p162)

Best coffee stop
- Bean Around the World (see p161)

Best terraces
- B-Café (see p162)
- Joey's Café (see p162)

Best bars
- Brugs Beertje (see p162)
- 'T Estaminet (see p162)
- De Garre (see p162)
- De Republiek (see p166)
- The Top (see p164)

Best for clothes
- L'Héroine (see p166)
- Joaquim Jofre (see p166)
- Olivier Strelli (see p166)

Best for present-buying
- 'T Apostelientje (see p164)
- Diksmuids Boterhuis (see p164)
- Tintin Shop (see p166)

Best for chocoholics
- Dumon (see p166)
- De Proeverij (see p164)
- Sukerbuyc (see p166)

BRUGES BY AREA

Stadhuis

Craenenburg p162

Groeninge Museum p158

St Salvator-kathedraal

St Salvatorskerkhof (www.sintsalvator.be). **Open** 2-6pm Mon; 8.30am-noon, 2-6pm Tue-Fri; 8.30am-noon, 2-3.30pm Sat; 9-10.15am, 2-5pm Sun. **Admission** free. *Treasury* €3. **Map** p157 A3.

Work on this huge cathedral began in the tenth century. After four fires and the Iconoclastic Riots, however, nothing of that period has survived save the base of the tower. There are several paintings by Bernard van Orley in the right transept, but unfortunately the lighting is bad and they are quite difficult to see. However, the treasury has now been restored and relit, allowing visitors to admire a spectacular painting by Dirk Bouts known as the *Hippolytus Altarpiece.*

Stadhuis

12 Burg (050 44 81 13). **Open** 9.30am-5pm daily. **Admission** Combined ticket with Paleis van het Brugse Vrije €2; free-€1 reductions. No credit cards. **Map** p157 B2.

The main square's Stadhuis (Town Hall) was built in splendid Gothic style in the 14th century, and is worth checking out for its lavish Gothic Hall on the first floor, which boasts a spectacular vaulted ceiling. The walls, meanwhile, are painted with scenes relating the history of the city – often with more verve than accuracy. The paintings date from the early 20th century.

St Walburgakerk

Koningstraat & Hoornstraat. **Open** Apr-Sept 10am-noon, 2-5pm, 8-10pm Mon-Sat; 2-5pm Sun. **Admission** free. **Map** p157 C1.

Follow Hoogstraat east of the Burg and turn left on Verversdijk canal, lined with impressive 18th-century houses. Down the little lane on the left, the Jesuit church of St Walburga, built between 1619 and 1641, is decorated with tall, Tuscan-style columns. The style is Baroque and the dominant colours gold and white, yet the interior is more harmonious than overbearing.

Eating & drinking

B-Café

25 Wollestraat (050 33 42 29, www.b-online.be). **Open** noon-6.30pm Mon, Tue, Thur-Sat; 3-6pm Sun. **€**. **Café**. **Map** p157 B2.

This stylish café is set above design store B (see p164). Its decked terrace offers unexpected views of the city spires, and it serves excellent pasta, bruschetta and coffee.

Bean Around the World

NEW *5 Genthof (050 70 35 32).* **Open** 10am-7pm Mon, Thur-Sat; 11.30am-7pm Wed. **€**. **Café**. **Map** p157 B1.

A relaxing coffee shop run by a Californian, this place offers free international newspapers, an internet terminal and Wi-Fi. A perfect spot to come and surf with a great cuppa.

Bistro Refter

NEW *2 Molenmeers (050 44 99 00).* **Open** noon-2pm, 7-10pm Tue-Sat. **€€**. **Bistro**. **Map** p157 C2.

A new bistro opening from Geert van Heck of De Karmeliet (see p162). It's called Refter because it's set in the refectory of an old Carmelite building, although the decor is ultra sleek and modern. This place is much more affordable than its three-star sister; it's a set menu-only affair, which makes everything that little bit easier.

Bistro de Schaar

2 Hooistraat (050 33 59 79, www.bistrodeschaar.be). **Open** noon-2.30pm, 6-11pm Mon-Wed, Fri-Sun. **€€**. **Bistro**.

Located out of the tourist centre, just off Predikherenrei, this cracking little bistro offers a modern take on cosy rusticity. Grills are popular, as are less traditional dishes such as prawns in garlic or cheese-filled ravioli.

Brugs Beertje

5 Kemelstraat (050 33 96 16, www.brugsbeertje.be). **Open** 4pm-1am Mon,

Thur, Sun; 4pm-2am Fri, Sat. **Bar**.
Map p157 A3.
Drinkers rave about this dark brown pub, which sells no less than 300 different beers. Set up by 'beer professor' Jan De Bruyne, it's now mainly run by his wife Daisy, who takes a more lenient line when asked for 'a lager'.

Craenenburg

16 Markt (050 33 34 02, www. craenenburg.be). **Open** 7am-midnight daily. No credit cards. **Bar**. Map p157 A2.
Set on the site of the house where Maximilian of Austria was held captive, this is a typical Bruges tavern with yellowed walls, wooden tables and elaborate stained glass.

Eetcafé de Vuyst

15 Simon Stevinplein (050 34 22 31, www.eetcafedevuyst.be). **Open** 10am-6pm Mon, Wed-Fri; 10am-9.30pm Sat, Sun. **€€**. **Café-bar**. Map p157 A3.
A cheery café-bar, with glass-topped tables containing original paintings. There are various *moules* options, as well as salads, crêpes and a good-value three-course lunch.

Est Wijnbar

7 Braambergstraat (050 33 38 39, www.wijnbarest.be). **Open** 4pm-late daily. No credit cards. **Wine bar**. Map p157 B2.
You can choose from some 90 different wines at this airy, inviting wine bar, which also hosts intimate jazz and blues gigs every Sunday from 8pm; entry is free.

'T Estaminet

5 Park (050 33 09 16). **Open** 11.30am-3am Mon-Wed, Sun; 4pm-3am Thur; 11.30am-6am, Fri, Sat. **Bar**. Map p157 C3.
This old tavern is by Astrid Park, in a quarter seldom reached by tourists. The owner has built up a superb jazz collection, attracting writers, politicians and women with dogs.

De Garre

1 De Garre (050 34 10 29). **Open** noon-midnight Mon-Thur; noon-1am Fri; 11am-1am Sat; 11am-midnight Sun. No credit cards. **Bar**. Map p157 B2.
Found at the end of the shortest blind alley in Bruges, just off Breidelstraat, this bar sells 130 different beers. It's set in a 16th-century house with wooden beams and bags of atmosphere.

In Den Wittekop

14 St Jacobsstraat (050 33 20 59, www.indenwittenkop.be). **Open** noon-2pm, 6-10pm Tue-Sat. **€€**. **Café**. Map p157 A2.
Despite being close to the tourist centre of the city, this ageing café offers an authentic Bruges experience, along with classic *steak frites* and eels cooked in a variety of ways.

Joey's Café

16a Zuidzandstraat (050 34 12 64). **Open** 11.30am-late Mon-Sat. No credit cards. **Bar**. Map p157 A3.
Located in the Zilversteeg shopping centre, this tiny, candlelit bar is run by a local musician. The relaxed mood and sounds draw a lively crowd, with a summer terrace for alfresco drinks.

De Karmeliet

19 Langestraat (050 33 82 59, www.dekarmeliet.be). **Open** noon-2pm, 7-10pm Tue-Sat. **€€€€**. **Belgian**. Map p157 C2.
At the three Michelin-starred De Karmeliet, staples include rabbit, local breeds of chicken, truffles and scallops. The decor is airy and modern, and you can see the chef at work. This is a cathedral to fine dining, but expect to pay for the privilege.

Parkrestaurant

1 Minderbroedersstraat (050 34 64 42, www.parkrestaurant.be). **Open** 11.30am-10pm Tue-Sun. **€€€**. **Modern European**. Map p157 C3.
This elegant restaurant occupies a patrician mansion facing the park. The

Off the tourist trail

Cultural and cool, Ghent makes for a great day trip.

Could Ghent be Belgium's best-kept secret? Along with an exquisite, traffic-free medieval centre, cut through with romantic canals and little bridges, it offers a heady mix of art galleries, bars, boutiques and restaurants; in July, don't miss the raucous festival (09 210 10 10, www.gentse feesten.be). It makes for a great day trip from Bruges (a mere half an hour by train). Alternatively, book into one of the myriad hip B&Bs and make a night of it.

Not-to-be-missed sights include the 13th-century St Niklaaskerk, whose soaring towers dominate the wide Korenmarkt (Cornmarket), and St Baafskathedraal (St Baafsplein, 09 225 49 85) – home to Van Eyck's stunning *The Adoration of the Mystic Lamb*. Then there's the imposing medieval Gravensteen castle (St Veerleplein, 09 225 93 06) on the north-west edge of the centre, surrounded by water.

Modern art aficionados should make a beeline for the Museum of Contemporary Art, SMAK (09 240 76 01, www.smak.be), which boasts works by the likes of Bacon, Warhol and Hockney. It's south of the centre, in the leafy Citadelpark – a ten-minute walk from Sint-Pieters station. Here, too, is the Museum voor Schone Kunsten (Museum of Fine Arts, 1 Fernand Scribedreef, 09 240 07 00, www.mskgent.be), with a heady array of artistic greats – Bosch, Magritte, Brueghel and Rubens among them.

Save some energy for the city's vibrant nightlife, though. A sizeable student population means there's always plenty going on, and there are cafés and bars galore around the Korenmarkt. Patershol, north of the historic centre, is awash with bars and elegant restaurants too; with its canals and medieval streets, it can be magical of an evening.

■ City of Ghent Tourist Office (Belfort, 17A Botermarkt, 09 266 56 60, www.visitgent.be).

chefs produce some wonderful dishes using Ardennes beef, Ostend sole and Sisteron lamb, and the garden is an idyllic spot for summer dining.

De Proeverij
6 Katelijnestraat (050 33 08 87, www. deproeverie.be). **Open** 9.30am-6.30pm daily. **€**. **Café**. No credit cards. **Map** p157 B4.
Coffee at this stylish café comes with a saucer of whipped cream and chocolates from Sukerbuyc (see p166), just opposite. Order hot chocolate and you get a dish of pure melted chocolate to mix with a mug of steaming milk.

De Stove
4 Kleine St Amandstraat (050 33 78 35, www.restaurantdestove.be). **Open** 7-10pm Mon, Tue, Fri; noon-2pm, 7-10pm Sat, Sun. **€€€**. **Modern European**. Map p157 A2.
This beguiling little restaurant serves artfully simple, accomplished dishes; red perch with salsa, quinoa and olive oil, say, or wild duck with pearl onions and red wine sauce.

Tanuki
1 Oude Gentweg (050 34 75 12, www. tanuki.be). **Open** noon-2pm, 6.30-9.30pm Wed-Sun. **€€**. **Japanese**. Map p157 B4.
Tanuki's oriental minimalism offers a striking contrast to the Flemish restaurants in the neighbourhood. Sushi and sashimi are always fresh.

The Top
5 St Salvatorskerkhof (050 33 03 51, www.cafethetop.be). **Open** 6pm-2am daily. No credit cards. **Bar**. Map p157 A3.
This lively bar attracts a mixed crowd, ranging from young locals looking for a wild night out to tourists hunting for a decent dance.

De Versteende Nacht
11 Langestraat (050 34 32 93). **Open** 5pm-late Mon-Sat. **Bar**. Map p157 C2.

This bar is filled with comic books, and its walls covered with cartoons. Weekly live jazz sessions draw the crowds on Wednesday nights.

Shopping

'T Apostelientje
11 Balstraat (050 33 78 60, www. apostelientje.be). **Open** 1-5pm Tue; 9.30am-12.15pm, 1.15-5pm Wed-Sat; 9.30am-1pm Sun. **Map** p157 C1.
A lot of machine-made, imported lace in town is passed off as authentic Bruges handiwork, but you'll find the genuine article here; its owner has been in the business for over 20 years.

B
25 Wollestraat (050 49 09 32, www. b-online.be). **Open** 10am-1pm, 2-6pm Mon-Sat. **Map** p157 B2.
There's plenty to covet in Katrien van Hulle's contemporary design shop. Its offers the cream of the crop of Belgian design, from elegant ceramics to sculptural lights and gorgeous textiles.

Bottle Shop
13 Wollestraat (050 34 99 80). **Open** *Summer* 9am-11pm daily. *Winter* 9am-7pm daily. **Map** p157 B2.
The Bottle Shop's astonishing range of local beers and spirits runs from Trappist brews and hard-to-find gueuze beers to genevers.

Callebert
25 Wollestraat (050 33 50 61, www.callebert.be). **Open** 3-6pm Mon, Sun; 10am-noon, 2-6pm Tue-Sat. **Map** p157 B2.
This contemporary design store is a stylish affair, stocking international names. Check out ceramics by Pieter Stockman and Bob van Reeth, or furniture by the Van Severens brothers.

Diksmuids Boterhuis
23 Geldmuntstraat (050 33 32 43). **Open** 9am-12.30pm, 1.30-6.30pm Mon-Sat. No credit cards. **Map** p157 A2.

Rozenhoedkaai

Drop by this rustic, friendly shop to buy butter, cheese and smoked ham fresh from the Flemish polders.

Dumon

6 Eiermarkt (050 34 62 82, www. chocolatierdumon.be). **Open** 10am-6pm Mon, Tue, Thur-Sat; 10am-5pm Sun. **Map** p157 A2.

This tiny basement shop stocks a huge range of artisan chocolates.

L'Héroine

32 Noordzandstraat (050 33 56 57, http://users.skynet.be/fb143674). **Open** 10am-6.30pm Mon-Sat. **Map** p157 A2.

Héroine's offerings include dresses by Belgian designers Mieke Cosyn and Ann Huybens, as well as menswear by Dries van Noten and jewellery by Antwerp's Wouters & Hendrix.

Joaquim Jofre

7 Vlaamingstraat (050 33 39 60). **Open** 9.30am-6.30pm Mon-Sat. **Map** p157 B2.

Joaquim Joffe is worth checking out just to marvel at the art deco interior. The women's clothes are classic, well cut and beautifully finished.

Olivier Strelli

3 Eiermarkt (050 34 38 37, www. strelli.be). **Open** 10am-6.30pm Mon-Sat. **Map** p157 A2.

This Brussels designer has established a loyal following in West Flanders with his sober fashions for men and women.

De Patience

2 Spinolarei (050 34 21 89, www.bnart. be). **Open** 2-6pm Thur-Sat. No credit cards. **Map** p157 B1.

Calligrapher Brody Neuenschwander, who worked on Peter Greenaway's *Prospero's Books* and *The Pillow Book* runs this gallery and shop. His postcards make eccentric souvenirs.

De Reyghere

12-13 Markt (050 33 34 03, www.de reyghere.be). **Open** 8.30am-6.15pm Mon-Sat. **Map** p157 B2.

Established in 1888, De Reyghere specialises in international newspapers, books on Bruges, and fiction – including a small section of English novels.

Sukerbuyc

5 Katelijnestraat (050 33 08 87, www. sukerbuyc.be). **Open** 8.30am-6.30pm daily. No credit cards. **Map** p157 B4.

A family-run chocolate shop that sells rich, dark chocolates made with 100% cocoa butter and sugar-coated sweets for Catholic christenings.

Tintin Shop

3 Steenstraat (050 33 42 92, www. tintinshopbrugge.be). **Open** 9.30am-6pm Mon-Sat; 11am-6pm Sun. **Map** p157 A2.

Cartoon books, T-shirts and toys featuring the Belgian boy reporter.

Nightlife

De Republiek

36 St Jacobsstraat (050 34 02 29, www.derepubliek.be/index2.html). **Open** 11am-late daily. No credit cards. **Map** p157 A2.

This candlelit café, attached to an arts complex, is a good place to pick up tips on jazz, films and dance events. It's also home to the late-night Cactus Club (www.cactusmusic.be).

Arts & Leisure

Concertgebouw

34 't Zand (070 22 33 02, www. concertgebouw.be).

The brutally modern design of this concert hall, opened in 2002, was a striking (and controversial) departure from the city's Gothic aesthetic. Its programme takes in concerts, dance, chamber music and more.

De Werf

Werfstraat 108 (050 33 05 29, www.dewerf.be).

North of the city centre, this arts centre is best known for its jazz line-ups.

Essentials

WHEREVER CRIMES AGAINST HUMANITY ARE PERPETRATED.

Across borders and above politics.
Against the most heinous abuses
and the most dangerous oppressors.
From conduct in wartime
to economic, social, and cultural rights.
Everywhere we go,
we build an unimpeachable case
for change and advocate action
at the highest levels.

HUMAN RIGHTS WATCH TYRANNY HAS A WITNESS

WWW.HRW.ORG

HUMA
RIGHT
WATC

Métropole p172

Hotels

Thanks to the presence of the EU and the institutions that serve it, Brussels punches above its weight when it comes to hotels, with a myriad of great options.

For those with sufficient funds, grand period hotels such as the **Métropole** (see p172) and **Le Plaza** (see p172) come adorned with swanky chandeliers, art nouveau flourishes and a whiff of fin de siècle decadence.

These, days, though, they're vying for trade with new upstarts: boutique townhouse hotels and upmarket guesthouses, with sleek interiors that wouldn't look out of place in Manhattan or Berlin. The new **Pantone Hotel** (see p177) is a paean to minimalist modern design, while **Sweet Brussels** (see p174) is an effortlessly cool – and refreshingly affordable – option.

For those that favour a less stripped-down aesthetic, kitsch is

something of a forte in the capital: knick-knacks abound in the likes of **Les Bluets** (see p176) and **Noga** (see p173).

Other townhouse hotels stick to an elegantly classical style, from the romantic **Le Dixseptième** (see p171) to the exquisite **Manos Premier** (see p177), where polished antiques and glittering chandeliers exude a timeless charm.

This being Brussels, there is no shortage of chain hotels, beloved of Eurocrats. They may not be the most exciting choice for style-conscious travellers, but rates can be very tempting at the weekend and during the summer holidays, when the politicians are gone and rooms need to be filled.

If you're after peace and quiet, do a little research before booking a central hotel, particularly in Lower Town. The buzz won't necessarily quieten down once

ESSENTIALS

you do, and Belgian drivers are notoriously fond of honking their horns. If in doubt, reserve a room at the back or ask about double glazing.

Antwerp

Hotels are plentiful in Antwerp, but it's still a good idea to book ahead in summer.

The options range from sleek, large-scale establishments like the **Radisson Blu Astrid** (see p178) to the smaller, quirkier likes of **Room National** (see p178). If your budget allows, the **De Witte Lelie** (see p179) is a luxurious retreat, with 11 sumptuous suites.

Bruges

Bruges' abundance of hotels are being seriously challenged by an ever growing number of small B&Bs (*gastenkamers*), often located in lovingly restored houses in the old quarters of the city. Shining examples of their kind include

Number 11 (see p181), **Charming Brugge** (see p181) and **Coté Canal** (see p181).

There are some glorious hotels, too, including the canalside **Hotel De Orangerie** (see p181) and **Hotel Die Swaene** (see p181); it would take a heart of stone to resist the romance.

Classification & booking

We have divided the hotels by area, then divided them into four price categories (not including seasonal offers and discounts) for one night in a double room. For deluxe hotels (€€€€), you can expect to pay more than €350; for properties in the expensive bracket (€€€), €210-€349; and for moderate (€€) €120-€209. Budget rooms (€) go for less than €120.

Resotel (02 779 39 39, www. belgiumhospitality.com) is a free booking service for hotels across Belgium, which can negotiate up to 50 per cent off the rack rates.

Dominican

Lower Town

Grand Place & Around

Atlanta
7 boulevard Adolphe Max, 1000 Brussels (02 217 01 20, www.nh-hotels.com). Métro/pré-métro De Brouckère. €€.
The Spanish NH Hoteles chain has five properties scattered across the city, but the Atlanta is its flagship. Housed in an elegant early 20th-century building, it has modern, cheerful decor, and a terrace with great rooftop views. The highlight of any stay at an NH hotel is the attention to detail: you can even choose the type of pillow you want.

Le Dixseptième
25 rue de la Madeleine, 1000 Brussels (02 517 17 17, www.ledixseptieme.be). Métro Gare Centrale. €€.
Le Dixseptième is a real gem: a boutique hotel with 24 rooms, located not far from the Grand'Place. Popular with business folk looking for a hotel with a more personal touch, the 17th is also ideal for a romantic weekend away. Twelve of the rooms are housed in the 17th-century building (once the home of the Spanish ambassador); the rest, equally spacious but more prosaic, are in a new block to the rear. There's a bar and a lovely period salon overlooking an inner courtyard where breakfast is served each morning.

Dominican
9 rue Léopold, 1000 Brussels (02 203 08 08, www.thedominican.be). Métro Gare Centrale. €€€.
This was originally a 15th-century abbey, and its high ceilings, stone floors and tranquil cloisters remain. Most rooms face on to the courtyard, adding to the calm atmosphere of the place. The pleasant bedrooms are decorated in stylishly muted but warm tones; each has a small seating area, a plasma TV, free WI-Fi and a Nespresso coffee machine.

Floris Arlequin Grand'Place
17-19 rue de la Fourche, 1000 Brussels (02 514 16 15, www.florishotels.com). Métro/pré-métro De Brouckère. €€.
The contrast between this modern, 92-room hotel and the little cobbled street on which it stands couldn't be more stark. Rooms vary in size, but are comfortable, bright and clean; three offer panoramic views over the rooftops, as does the top-floor breakfast room.

A la Grande Cloche
10-12 place Rouppe, 1000 Brussels (02 512 61 40, www.hotelgrandecloche.com). Pré-métro Anneessens. €.
This family-run hotel is located in a quiet square, equidistant from Midi station and the Grand'Place. The

ESSENTIALS

Hotel Amigo

rooms are neat and fairly comfy – though the queen sized beds are a bit of a squeeze for two (the twin rooms avoid the problem, and are usually pretty spacious). Cheaper rooms tend to have a small shower room rather than a full bathroom.

Hotel Amigo
1-3 rue de l'Amigo, 1000 Brussels (02 547 47 47, www.hotelamigo.com). Métro Gare Centrale or pré-métro Bourse. €€€€.
Steeped in history and luxuriously kitted out, the Amigo accommodates pop stars and politicians alike. It exudes tastefully modern luxury, with sleek decor, tactile fabrics and a smattering of local colour: an image of Tintin here, a Magritte print there. The seriously wealthy check into the top floor Blaton Suite, then take in the views over town from its vast private terrace.

Métropole
31 place de Brouckère, 1000 Brussels (02 217 23 00, www.metropolehotel. com). Métro/pré-métro De Brouckère. €€€.
This grande dame opened in 1895, and its public areas – including the café (see p60) – are exquisite. The entrance leads into an Empire-style reception hall,

with columns, gilt flourishes and stained-glass windows, while an original cage lift conveys guests up to their rooms in the main building. These can be slightly disappointing by comparison and a little staid for some, though decor varies from room to room (and depending on how much you spend).

Le Plaza
118 boulevard Adolphe Max, 1000 Brussels (02 278 01 00, www.leplaza-brussels.be). Métro/pré-métro Rogier or De Brouckère. €€€.
Owned by a prominent Belgian family, Le Plaza dates from 1930. The headquarters of the Nazis and later the Allied Forces in the war, it was largely spared the bombing. The winter garden, which did suffer, was rebuilt and now houses the restaurant. Original fittings run from crystal chandeliers to marble bas-reliefs, while the sumptuous rooms are decorated in shades of cream and ochre. The only drawback is the surrounds – the boulevard has more than its fair share of sex shops.

Radisson SAS Royal Hotel
47 rue du Fossé aux Loups, 1000 Brussels (02 219 28 28, www.royal. brussels.radissonsas.com). Métro/pré-métro De Brouckère. €€€.

Behind the elaborate art deco façade of the Radisson SAS lies a top-class business hotel with good leisure facilities and the superb Sea Grill, where executive chef Yves Mattagne has won two Michelin stars. Rooms are divided into four types: all come with luxury trappings and Wi-Fi, but little flourishes set each style apart.

Saint-Michel

15 Grand'Place, 1000 Brussels (02 511 09 56, http://atgp.be). Métro Gare Centrale or pré-métro Bourse. €€.
If you want to wake up to a view over one of Europe's most beautiful squares, stay at the Saint-Michel. Just be aware that if there's an event on in the Grand'Place you might not get the earliest night. Situated behind a picturesque façade on the south-eastern side of the square, the late 17th-century building once belonged to the Tanners' Guild.

St-Géry & Ste-Catherine

Hotel Orts

38-40 rue Auguste Orts, 1000 Brussels (02 517 07 07, www.hotelorts.com). Pré-métro Bourse. €€.

The Orts opened its doors in 2006, injecting some style into this formerly lacklustre area. The architecture is grand fin-de-siècle Brussels and looks particularly stunning at night, thanks to theatrical lighting. The individually colour-themed rooms are spacious and finished to a high standard; corner rooms are more modest in size, but benefit from a double vista. It's a perfect location for sightseeing and nightlife.

Marriott

1-7 rue Auguste Orts, 1000 Brussels (02 516 90 90, www.marriott.com/ brudt). Pré-métro Bourse. €€€.
While the Marriott's façade is a beautifully restored remnant of the 19th century, its interior is comfortably modern. Rooms are kitted out to a high standard with large beds, Wi-Fi and bright decor; bathrooms, in muted shades of beige, are more relaxing.

Noga

38 rue du Béguinage, 1000 Brussels (02 218 67 63, www.nogahotel.com). Métro Ste-Catherine. €€.
Noga means star in Hebrew, and this lovely hotel, located on a tranquil street

Hotel Orts

ESSENTIALS

in Ste-Catherine, lives up to its name. It's friendly and delightfully kitsch, with nautical-themed knick-knacks in the airy public areas jostling for space with pictures of royals and bric-a-brac. The rooms, which have showers but no baths, are bright and spacious.

Welcome
23 quai au Bois à Brûler, 1000 Brussels (02 219 95 46, www.hotel welcome.com). Métro Ste-Catherine. **€€**.

Each of the guest rooms here is unique, decorated with antiques and artefacts to represent a different destination (Bali, India, Japan and Morocco among them). Other options include the Tibet room, which has a small terrace and is decorated in dramatic shades of red and black, or the Jules Verne room, which follows a round-the-world theme and has a large balcony. The exotic interior, paired with the friendliness of the owners, makes this a great spot.

The Marolles

Galia
15-16 place du Jeu de Balle, 1000 Brussels (02 502 42 43, www.hotel galia.com). Métro/pré-métro Porte de Hal or Gare du Midi. **€**.

This simple, family-run hotel offers good-value accommodation overlooking the square where the flea market is held, making it an ideal roost for bargain hunters. It's decorated with images of Belgian comic strips, while the rooms are basic but cheery, with triples and quads available. The brighter front rooms are triple-glazed to block out the noise from the square.

Sweet Brussels
NEW *78 avenue de Stalingrad, 1000 Brussels (0486 259 137 mobile, www.sweetbrussels.be). Métro Gare du Midi.* **€**.

The owners of this 19th-century townhouse have done a fine job of converting it into a stylish B&B. Stripped-back wooden floors, boxspring beds, old-fashioned cast-iron radiators, fresh flowers and some glorious freestanding baths give an idea of the decorative ethos and attention to detail.

Upper Town

Du Congrès
42-44 rue du Congrès, 1000 Brussels (02 217 18 90, www.hotelducongres. be). Métro Madou. **€€**.

Four elegant townhouses have been beautifully renovated to create a sleek, modern hotel with original fin-de-siècle features. Some of the rooms have wonderful fireplaces and cornicing; others may not boast as many authentic features, but make up for it in terms of space and tranquillity – particularly the rooms overlooking the garden.

Eurostars Sablon
2-8 rue de la Paille, 1000 Brussels (02 513 60 40, www.eurostarssablon.com). Tram 92, 93, 94 or bus 95. **€€€**.

In the heart of the Sablon antiques area, five minutes' walk from the Grand'Place, this intimate hotel is tucked away on a quiet cobbled street. Don't be put off by the modern façade; inside you'll find an inviting little hotel with 32 understated rooms and suites.

NH Hotel du Grand Sablon
2 rue Bodenbroek, 1000 Brussels (02 518 11 00, www.nh-hotels.com). Tram 92, 93, 94 or bus 95. **€€**.

Antiques hunters will enjoy a stay at the NH. It's enviably located by the pretty place du Grand Sablon, site of the weekly antiques market. The building itself is handsome, and the rooms comfortable and well-proportioned.

Stanhope Hotel
9 rue du Commerce, 1000 Brussels (02 506 91 11, www.thonhotels.be). Métro Trône. **€€€**.

The Stanhope has almost doubled in size in recent years, but that hasn't changed its calm, intimate atmosphere.

Boutique B&Bs

Chic townhouses turned bed and breakfast.

Chambres en Ville

As the EU continues to expand, and the Eurostar brings in ever-increasing numbers of visitors to Brussels, so the need for more bedrooms grows.

There's bags of room in Brussels' classic, stately-looking townhouses – something that their enterprising owners are keen to turn to their advantage. With so much available space in such big properties and no tax on rental income, a brace of upmarket, beautifully styled B&Bs have been launched, following the example set in Bruges (see p156).

The large and lofty rooms offer space that traditional hotels would die for. Consider, if you will, the spacious **Chambres en Ville** (see p176). Run by Philippe Guilmin, and set in a magnificent 19th-century house, it offers five charming rooms, furnished with an artist's eye for detail. Quirky, individual touches abound, from burnished brass bedsteads and antique pillars to individually chosen artworks.

Not only rooms but sometimes whole floors are given over to the B&B experience. At the recently launched **Contemporary House** (42 rue Général Capiaumont, 1040 Brussels, no phone, www.contemporaryhouse.be), just beyond the EU Quarter in Etterbeek, you get a whole suite of three rooms for your bucks, occupying the second floor of an imposing red-brick house.

Other Brussels properties are blurring the line between B&B and hotel, with entire houses being converted into rooms, studios and apartments. It's more akin to staying in a small-scale boutique hotel than a traditional, meet-the-owner B&B experience. Two fine examples are the stylish, downtown **Sweet Brussels** (see p174), whose rooms are double the size of standard hotel offerings, and the immaculately styled, architect designed **Urban Rooms** (see p177) – every bit as cool as many a boutique hotel, and a fraction of the price.

ESSENTIALS

Pantone Hotel

The original rooms, carved out of a row of elegant townhouses, evoke a mannered English country house, while the newer rooms combine antique-style furnishings with modern wood floors and swanky bathrooms.

EU Quarter

Silken Berlaymont
11-19 boulevard Charlemagne, 1000 Brussels (02 231 09 09, www.hoteles-silken.com). Métro Schuman. **€€€**.
The hotel's EU Quarter location and carefully-appointed rooms (each with a desk and internet connection) mark it out as a business hotel, though the modern architecture, spa and extensive photography collection add character. The in-house restaurant, with its artful modern cuisine and garden views, is a bonus, while the spa incorporates a sauna, steam room and Turkish bath.

Ixelles

Les Bluets
124 rue Berckmans, 1060 Brussels (02 534 39 83, www.bluets.be). Métro Hôtel des Monnaies. **€**.

Set in a building dating from 1864, Les Bluets has been a hotel for over 30 years and has acquired a fair amount of decorative features in that time. Every room is crammed with antiques and kitsch souvenirs, while plants and flowers spill out from balconies and bathrooms. Nothing is standard – the decor, the room sizes or the amenities. Smokers are not welcome as guests.

Chambres en Ville
19 rue de Londres, 1050 Brussels (02 512 92 90, www.chambresenville.be). Métro Trône. **€**.
The proprietor of this delightful B&B, Philippe Guilmin, is hospitality itself, offering a handful of individually decorated rooms with spacious en suite bathrooms. The rooms have stone and wooden floors, high ceilings, wall hangings and homely touches such as fresh flowers, while the large breakfast table is often shared with Guilmin's cosmopolitan, friendly clientele.

Conrad Brussels
71 avenue Louise, 1050 Brussels (02 542 42 42, www.conradhotels.com). Métro Louise. **€€€€**.

ESSENTIALS

It's hard to fault the quality of the Conrad's decor, even if it's not to everyone's taste. Service is impeccable, with rooms tidied almost too frequently, and room service is tailor-made: you can choose exactly which ingredients go into your sarnie or salad. Given all the swank (flunkies in top hats, a vast chandeliered reception area) it's no surprise that the Conrad is set on the smartest shopping street in town.

Manos Premier

100-106 chaussée de Charleroi, 1060 Brussels (02 537 96 82, www.manos hotel.com). Métro Louise. €€€-€€€€.
With its ivy-clad front, dotted with fairy lights, there's something very romantic about this converted townhouse. Its 50 rooms are elegantly appointed with antiques and Louis XVI-style decor, while the gorgeous public spaces include the Kolya restaurant, with its lovely conservatory, an opulent, African-themed bar with curvy velvet armchairs and a peaceful garden. The icing on the cake is the magnificent Moorish-style hammam.

Rembrandt

42 rue de la Concorde, 1050 Brussels (02 512 71 39, http://rembrandt. dommel.be). Métro Louise then tram 94 or bus 71. €.
There's something rather quaint about this one-star hotel, with its reception that closes at 10pm and a breakfast room filled with china ornaments and gilt-framed still lifes. The rooms are similarly homely, with high ceilings, flowery wallpaper, old dark wood furniture and framed prints on the wall. It's clean, quirky and great value.

Thon Hotel Bristol Stéphanie

91-93 avenue Louise, 1050 Brussels (02 543 33 11, www.thonhotels.be/ bristolstephanie). Métro Louise. €€€.
The lobby here is strangely old-fashioned, with its swagged curtains and over-the-top sofas. Once you get

beyond that, though, things rapidly improve. Thon claims to have the biggest hotel rooms in Brussels; they certainly are spacious, with room for a desk. Superior rooms have a sofa, while Club rooms can sleep up to four people.

Urban Rooms

NEW *10 rue Alsace Lorraine, 1050 Brussels (www.urbanrooms.be). Métro/pré-métro Porte de Hal.* €-€€.
Two young architects are behind this slick, inexpensive little B&B – and it shows. The three ensuite rooms are coolly modern and contemporary, with white linen, flatscreen TVs, modern art on the walls and sleek bathrooms. There's also a modish breakfast room, and a terrace overlooking the garden. At the time of writing, its owners were charging special launch rates: get in there quick, before prices shoot up.

Warwick Barsey

381 avenue Louise, 1050 Brussels (02 649 98 00, www.warwickbarsey.com). Métro Louise then tram 94. €€€.
The interior of this luxurious boutique hotel is the work of French design maestro Jacques Garcia, who created an opulent reception area in his signature rich red with Napoleon III-style furnishings. The restaurant and rooms are similar in style, exuding a warmth and intimacy that make the Barsey a perfect winter hotel – though there's also a courtyard for summer lounging. Set at the leafier end of avenue Louise, it's a bit of a hike from the centre.

St-Gilles

Pantone Hotel

NEW *1 place Loix, 1060 Brussels (02 541 48 98, www.pantonehotel.com). Métro Hôtel des Monnaies.* €€.
Design buffs will adore the new Pantone Hotel. It's part of the colour matching group's design-driven arm, Pantone Universe, and – as you might expect – rooms come in a vivid palette of hues; it's not too overpowering,

ESSENTIALS

though, thanks to the white walls and linen. Feeling daring, fiery or tranquil? Choose a room depending on your mood.

Beyond the Centre

Crowne Plaza Brussels City Centre – Le Palace

3 rue Gineste, 1210 Brussels (02 203 62 00, www.crowneplaza.com). Métro/pré-métro Rogier. **€€€**.

The Crowne Plaza dates back to 1908, and is one of the city's landmark hotels. Major refurbishment has seen the faded 1930s updates replaced with a linear art nouveau look, in keeping with the building's age. There's no stinting on modernity, though, with all the comforts you'd expect from a contemporary hotel.

Hilton Brussels City

20 place Rogier, 1210 Brussels (02 203 31 25, www.brussels-city.hilton.com). Métro/pré-métro Rogier. **€€-€€€**.

If you want a standard five-star Hilton, go to the Hilton Brussels on boulevard de Waterloo. If you prefer smaller hotels (and lower prices), head for the four-star Hilton Brussels City. Housed in three 1930s buildings, it retains some art deco features, and offers a more personalised service with the help of some of the best hotel staff in town. The rooms in the different buildings offer various configurations, but the unfussy decor remains the same.

Sheraton Brussels Hotel & Towers

Manhattan Center, 3 place Rogier, 1210 Brussels (02 224 31 11, www.sheraton.be). Métro/pré-métro Rogier. **€€€€**.

This is Brussels' biggest hotel, with 30 floors of spacious, elegant rooms and all the comforts and services you'd expect. Constant modernisation has resulted in a newly renovated lounge bar and 'smart rooms', an added perk for high-powered business types, on the exclusive top five floors. Further

draws include the panoramic views of the city from the upper storey rooms and the top-floor heated indoor pool.

Antwerp

Boulevard Leopold

Belgëilei 135, 2018 Antwerp (486 67 5838 mobile, www.boulevard-leopold. be). **€-€€**. No credit cards.

This small B&B is in an initially unprepossessing neighbourhood, devoid of life at night; when the shutters open in the day, though, it reveals itself to be Antwerp's traditional, thriving Jewish quarter. With its exquisite original features, the 19th-century house works well as a backdrop for the owners' take on shabby chic: not so shabby but very chic, with flatscreen TVs, an espresso machine and impressive baths in two of the rooms.

Molenaars Droom B&B

35 Molenstraat, 2018 Antwerp (03 259 15 90, www.bedandbreakfastdream. com). **€**.

Run by Greta Stevens, 'Miller's Dream' occupies a 19th-century colonial-style mansion near the park, south of Britselei. There are three spacious en suite rooms, decorated with modern art and idiosyncratic antiques.

Radisson Blu Astrid

7 Koningin Astridplein, 2018 Antwerp (03 203 12 34, www.parkplaza.com). **€€€**.

It may appear to be made from Lego, but the Astrid's interior is much easier on the eye. Bedrooms are plushly comfortable, with desks and free Wi-Fi even in the standard rooms, while facilities include a pool, sauna, jacuzzi and fitness centre. It's just across stately Astrid Square from Centraal Station, close to the Diamond District and Meir.

Room National

NEW *Nationalestraat 24, 2000 Antwerp (04 75 234 703, www.roomnational.be).* **€€**.

Room National's three rooms are beautifully appointed, and perfect for a romantic getaway: no surprise that one of the owners is a fashion designer, the other a stylist. Studio one is a chic, airy all-white suite with a kitchenette and bathroom; studio two is similarly proportioned, but with more colour. The other room is a cosy, inviting ensuite; note it doesn't have kitchen facilities.

Vandepitte B&B
49 Britselei, 2000 Antwerp (03 288 66 95). **€**.

Its south Antwerp location is somewhat uninspiring, and two of the three rooms are small (although one does have a bathroom to die for). Nonetheless, Vandepitte makes up for it all with its show-stealing penthouse: black stone floors, views over Antwerp, ethnic art and bags of space. Breakfast is equally impressive and delicious.

De Witte Lelie
16-18 Keizerstraat, 2000 Antwerp (03 226 19 66, www.dewittelelie.be). **€€€-€€€€**.

The building that houses this opulent hotel may be 17th-century, but the interior is utterly contemporary. There are 11 good-sized rooms and suites: expect low-key luxury (crisp linen, polished decor, Wi-Fi and a free minibar) – and,

Room National

ESSENTIALS

Number 11

ESSENTIALS

if you're in the grand Presidential Suite, acres of polished parquet, a resplendant chandelier and sofas to curl up on.

Bruges

Baert Gastenkamer

28 Westmeers, 8000 Bruges (050 33 05 30, www.baert-gastenkamer.be). €.
Run by the delightful Huub Baert and Jeannine Robberecht, this charming B&B is set in a restored coach house that once belonged to a convent. There are two bright, snug rooms, with leafy little private canalside terraces.

Charming Brugge

Komvest 13, 8000 Bruges (04 95 20 16 02, www.charmingbrugge.be). €-€€.
This fabulously stylish three-bedroom B&B is set in an olde-worlde townhouse. Its glossy decor is worthy of *Architectural Digest*, with dramatic colour schemes of chocolate brown, black and white, bold damask cushions and arty light fixtures. Bikes are available for hire for €6 a day, and the city centre is ten minutes' walk away.

Coté Canal

Hertsbergestraat 10, 8000 Bruges (04 75 45 77 07, www.bruges-bedand breakfast.be). €€.
This 18th-century guesthouse overlooks the Groene Rei canal. The muted hues in the two ensuite bedrooms give a design-magazine feel, but the high ceilings, dainty antiques and soft damask fabrics and wallpapers are pleasingly old-school. Modern comforts such as Wi-Fi and sumptuous linens bring it back to the 21st century.

Hotel Adornes

26 St Annarei, 8000 Bruges (050 34 13 36, www.adornes.be). €€.
This friendly family hotel in a canalside location near St Annakerk is ideal for exploring the historic centre and the quiet Guido Gezelle quarter to the east. Rooms here are comfortable and simple, and the hotel offers its guests free parking spaces and bicycles too.

Hotel De Orangerie

10 Kartuizerinnenstraat, 8000 Bruges (050 34 16 49, www.martins-hotels. com).
This canalside 15th-century convent has a wonderfully central location and timeless charm. Think sweetly old-fashioned rather than slickly modern: exquisite wallpapers, marble bathrooms and polished antiques. That's not to say you'll lack modern comforts, mind, with air-conditioning, Wi-Fi and DVD players among the little extras.

Hotel Die Swaene

1 Steenhouwersdijk, 8000 Bruges (050 34 27 984, www.dieswaene-hotel.com). €€.
Right in the centre of the city, and set next to a canal, this 15th-century mansion has a wonderfully romantic feel. The hotel's 22 rooms are individually decorated – some with four-poster beds, if you're out to impress. There's also a candlelit restaurant looking over the water, and an indoor pool.

iRoom

Verversdijk 1, 8000 Bruges (050 33 73 53, www.iroom.be). €.
Though not as achingly fashionable as some of the city's more expensive guesthouses, this handsome B&B is certainly up to date: rooms come with Wi-Fi, flatscreen TVs, DVD players and rain showers in the bathrooms. The decor is clean and stylish.

Number 11

Peerdenstraat 11, 8000 Bruges (050 33 06 75, www.number11.be). €€.
Inside this lovely 17th-century guesthouse, the aesthetic is textbook modern-classic: stripped down wooden floors and vintage chandeliers, the odd freestanding bath, swathes of statement wallpaper and white-painted beams. Formerly an artist's house, it is dotted with paintings and sculptures

Getting Around

Airport

0900 700 00, www.brussels airport.be.
Brussels' main airport is at Zaventem, 14 kilometres (nine miles) north-east of the capital, and has good road and rail connections into the city centre. You'll find the information desk (open 7am-10pm daily) in the check-in area. Hotel information and a phone link for reservations are in the arrivals section. Hotel shuttle buses run from level 0.

A train service, **Airport City Express** (02 528 28 28, www.b-rail.be), runs to Gare du Midi, Gare Centrale and Gare du Nord. Tickets cost €5.10. There are four trains an hour from 6am to midnight; the journey time is 20mins. Women travelling alone at night are safest alighting at Gare Centrale.

The **Airport Line** bus no.12 (070 23 2000, www.stib.be) leaves the airport three times an hour between 6am and 7pm Mon-Fri, making five stops on its way to the EU Quarter; it costs €3 (or €5 from the driver). Outside of these times you need to take the no.21, which makes more than 20 stops.

De Lijn bus 471 (070 220 200, www.delijn.be) also travels between Brussels Gare du Nord and the airport; a single ticket costs €2 (or €3 from the driver). A **Brussels Airlines Express** bus (052 33 40 00) runs hourly to Antwerp from 5am (7am Sun) to midnight and costs €10 for a single ticket.

Taxis wait by the arrivals building and should display a yellow and blue licence. The fare to central Brussels is around €40 – many accept credit cards but check first. Wheelchair users can book a taxi from **Taxi Hendriks** (02 752 98 00, www.hendriks.be).

The car rental desks in the arrivals hall are open from 6.30am to 11pm daily.

Ryanair (www.ryanair.com) serves what it calls 'Brussels South', situated 55 kilometres (34 miles) away in Charleroi (07 125 12 11, www.charleroi-airport.com). Bus A connects with arrivals and runs the 20-minute journey to Charleroi train station, where a half-hourly train takes 50 minutes to reach Brussels (combined ticket with city transport €11.30).

Brussels City Shuttle (no phone, www.voyages-lelan.be) runs a bus (€13 one-way) from Charleroi airport to Brussels Gare du Midi. Journey time is about an hour. Taxis from Charleroi to central Brussels cost about €95.

Arriving by car

If you're driving to Brussels from the UK, **Eurotunnel** (UK 08443 353535, www.eurotunnel.com) can transport you and your vehicle from the M20 near Folkestone to Coquelles near Calais in 35 minutes. There are motorway connections to Brussels from there. It's a 24-hour service with up to three trains an hour 7am-midnight and one every two hours during the night. There are facilities for the disabled. Hertz and Eurotunnel have a Le Swap rental system for a left-hand and right-hand drive rental car in France and the UK.

Arriving by coach

Eurolines (UK)
08717 818 818, www.eurolines.co.uk.

Eurolines (Brussels)
02 274 13 50, www.eurolines.be.
Métro/pré-métro Gare du Nord.
Open 8.30am-8.30pm daily.
Eurolines buses depart from CCN Gare
du Nord (80 rue du Progrès). The journey to London Victoria takes around
seven hours.

Arriving by rail

There are up to ten Eurostar
trains a day between Brussels and
London, with a journey time of one
hour 50 minutes. Check in at least
30 minutes before departure.

Eurostar St Pancras
08432 186186, www.eurostar.com.
Eurostar Gare du Midi
02 528 28 28, www.eurostar.com.

Public transport

Brussels' cheap, integrated public
transport system is made up of
métro, rail, buses and trams, with
tickets allowing for any changes
en route for up to an hour. A map is
invaluable, as stations are not well
signposted. Maps and timetables
are available from information
centres at **Gare du Midi**, **Porte
de Namur** and **Rogier**.

Métro, trams & buses

Public transport in the capital is
run by **STIB/MIVB** (0900 10 310,
www.stib.be). **De Lijn** (070 220
200, www.delijn.be) runs suburban
buses from its main Gare du Midi
terminal. Public transport operates
from around 5.30am to midnight.

Tickets, lines & passes

Tickets are sold at métro and
rail stations, on buses and trams,
at STIB info centres and at
newsagents. Points of sale for
monthly passes are métro **Porte**

de Namur, **Gare du Midi**,
Rogier and **Merode**, SNCB
stations and online. Tickets must
be validated, by using the machines
at métro stations and at the start of
the journey on trams and buses.
They are then valid for one hour
on all forms of transport and with
unlimited changes, though you
need to revalidate each time.

A new electronic system of
ticketing is being gradually
introduced across the STIB
network, so there are currently
two types of ticket. **Jump** is a card
system offering single (€1.70), five
or ten (€12.40) journeys as well as
one or three day passes (€9.50)
– validate these in the orange
machines. **MOBIB** is the new
electronic system – touch the card
on the red reader to validate the
fare. A MOBIB card requires a €5
refundable deposit and a passport
photograph. Fares for MOBIB are
slightly cheaper than Jump (€1.60
for a single, €11.30 for ten journeys
or €9.20 for three days).

The **Brussels Card** for
tourists offers unlimited public
transport for one, two or three
days, plus admission to 30
museums, for €24, €34 or €40
respectively. Children under six
travel free if accompanied by
an adult with a valid ticket.

A night bus service, **NOCTIS**,
was introduced in 2007. The 11
routes run on Friday and Saturday
only, and services stop at 3am.
A single journey costs €1.70 with
Jump, €1.60 with MOBIB or €2
from the driver.

Métro stations are indicated
by a white letter 'M' on a blue
background, while red and white
signs mark tram and bus stops.
Brussels is served by four métro
lines (1, 2, 5, 6) and two pré-métro
underground tram lines (3, 4)
running north–south through town,
linking Gare du Nord and Midi.

Rail travel

SNCB (02 528 28 28, www.b-rail.be) runs an efficient, cheap national rail system. Its website is extremely user friendly, and available in a choice of languages, including English. Tickets can be bought online and printed at home, or purchased at the station – though leave plenty of time in case of queues.

Brussels has three linked mainline railway stations: the **Gare Centrale** (1km from the Grand'Place), **Gare du Midi** (South Station) and **Gare du Nord** (North Station). All three stations have baggage facilities. Midi's left luggage office is by the Eurostar terminal.

Taxis

Taxi ranks are found by mainline stations and at strategic points like **Porte de Namur**, **place d'Espagne**, the **Bourse** and **De Brouckère**.

Taxis can accommodate up to four people, and the tip is included in the meter fare. If you have a complaint to make against a driver, or you've lost an item in a taxi, record the registration number of the vehicle and contact the taxi service of the Ministry of Brussels Capital Region on 0800 147 95 or online at www.brusselstaxi.be.

The clock starts at €2.40 (€4.40 after 10pm) and is then charged at €1.23 per kilometre, provided the journey is inside the 19 communes – if not, then it's double.

Autolux
02 411 41 42, www.autolux.be.
Taxis Bleus
02 268 00 00,
www.taxisbleus.be.
Taxis Verts
02 349 49 49, www.taxisverts.be.

Driving

It's not easy driving around Brussels. You're better off taking public transport or walking. Dents on the right side of many cars show the damage caused by the '*priorité à droite*' rule, the reason for so many accidents. Cars must give way to any vehicle from the right, even on a major road, unless marked otherwise. A white sign with a yellow diamond on the road means cars from the right must stop for you.

A comprehensive tunnel system links major points in the city, making it possible to traverse Brussels without seeing the light of day. The inner ring is a pentagon of boulevards (marked with signs showing a blue ring on which the yellow dot is your current location). The outer ring is a pear shape, divided into an east and west motorway ring.

The speed limit on motorways is 120kph (75mph), on main roads 90kph (56mph), and in built-up areas 50kph (31mph). There are no tolls on Belgian roads. The wearing of seat belts is compulsory in the front and rear of the car. The legal maximum blood alcohol level is 0.5g/l (approx one glass of wine). A driving licence from your home country is acceptable if you are staying in Belgium for less than 90 days.

If your car is towed, go to the nearest police station to obtain a document releasing it. Police may give you the document free of charge or demand a nominal fee, depending on the area of town. They will then give the address of the garage holding your car. Present the police letter there and pay another fee – the sum can vary – to get your car back. Be warned: on-the-spot fines are common for speeding.

It takes around 40 minutes to reach Antwerp, 50 minutes to get to Ghent, and 90 minutes for Liège and Bruges. Calais and Amsterdam are two-and-a-half hours away, Paris three hours.

Places are signposted in two languages (except in Flanders), so Antwerp is given as Anvers/Antwerpen, Ghent is Gand/Gent, and Bruges is Bruges/Brugge.

Cycling

Cycling on the main roads in central Brussels can be a daunting prospect. Lanes are shown by two broken white lines and are less secure than the cycle tracks, which are separated from the traffic. Some city lanes go against the flow of traffic.

A map of local cycle lanes and tracks can be found at the Pro-Vélo bike shop. In Brussels city, the rent-a-bike scheme Villo! allows you to rent a bike from 180 bike stations.

Pro-Vélo
15 rue de Londres, Ixelles (02 502 73 55, www.provelo.org).
Pro-Vélo offers bike hire and guided tours in Dutch and French.
Villo!
078 05 11 10, www.villo.be.
Villo! is an urban cycling scheme that allows you to hire a city bike for any period. For visitors there is an option of a one or seven-day basic registration (€1.50 or €7) bought from any of the stations using your bank debit card. You are then able to use the bikes when you like using a PIN number.

The first 30 minutes are free; after that, rates start from 5c for the next 30 minutes and €1 for the next hour. Bikes can be picked up and dropped off at any of the Villo! stations – maps are on the stations or there are apps available for WAP and iPhones. Check the website for further details of the scheme.

Walking

The centre of town, although uneven in places, is easy to navigate, with plenty of traffic-free streets around the **Grand'Place**. The only real challenge is the uphill slog to the Upper Town.

The Institut Geographique National (02 629 82 82, www.ngi.be) has maps of walking trails outside the centre.

Antwerp

Three to four trains an hour shuttle between Brussels and Antwerp, a 40-minute journey.

Antwerp isn't large, and the city centre is entirely walkable. The bars and restaurants around of Waalsekaai and Vlaamsekaai are a longish though enjoyable stroll from the centre: after the first time, though, you might want to make use of the good bus and tram links.

Transport is relatively cheap, especially if you buy your ticket or pass in advance (from shops, kiosks and the tourist office). A tour of the docks to the north of the city (try Flandria on 03 231 31 00, www.flandria.nu) is essential to understand its maritime contexts, both past and present.

Bruges

From Brussels, there are two trains an hour (50 minutes). It's a 15-minute walk to the centre, or you can take a taxi or bus from outside the station.

There are two main ways to get around Bruges: foot and canal boat – and the latter is the best way to experience the city from the medium it was designed for. Plenty of tour boats ply the waters from clearly marked stops. Fortunately, the station is enjoyably walkable from all points.

ESSENTIALS

Resources A-Z

For information on travelling to Belgium from within the European Union, including details of visa regulations and healthcare provision, see the EU's travel website: http://europa.eu/travel.

Accident & emergency

The general standardised emergency number to call throughout Europe is **112**.

If you need to telephone the fire brigade or an ambulance, call **100**; call **105** for a 24hr ambulance service provided by the Red Cross. For the police, the number is **101**.

For advice on doctors, mental-health issues and theft or loss of possessions, call the Community Help Service helpline (02 648 40 14).

Credit card loss

American Express
02 676 21 21,
www.americanexpress.com.
Diners Club
02 626 50 24, www.dinersclub.be.
Mastercard
toll free 0800 150 96,
www.mastercard.com/be.
Visa International
toll free 0800 183 97,
www.visaeurope.com.

Customs

For customs allowances, see http://fiscus.fgov.be/interfdanl/downloads/voyagers.pdf.

Dental emergency

The Health Unit at Brussels' American Embassy (02 508 22 25) can provide a list of English-speaking dentists, as can the Community Help Service helpline (02 648 40 14). Call 02 426 10 26 for a current list of dentists on duty after-hours.

Hospitals also offer emergency dental treatment. Try Brussels' Saint-Luc University Hospital (02 764 16 02, www.saintluc.be), St Jan Hospital in Bruges (050 45 21 11, www.azsintjan.be) and Antwerp University Hospital (03 821 3000, www.ua.ac.be).

Disabled

New buildings are wheelchair-friendly; older ones, unfortunately, are less so. Bear in mind, too, that the cobbled streets in Brussels, Antwerp and – in particular – Bruges can be tricky to negotiate in a wheelchair.

Public transport in Brussels is mostly accessible for less mobile people: trams and buses have low platforms and new buses have retractable ramps. Many métro stations are wheelchair accessible, and there are braille/tactile guides in all métro stations. A minibus service (02 515 23 65, www.stib.be) can transport disabled travellers door to door from 6.30am-11pm. In Antwerp, most buses and trams now have wheelchair boarding access.

Electricity

The current used in Belgium is 220V AC. It works fine with British appliances (which run on 240V), but you'll need an adaptor. American appliances run on 110V and you'll need to buy a converter. Good hotels should normally be able to supply these.

Embassies

For embassies not listed, check
the Yellow Pages or www.brussels.
info/embassies.

American Embassy
*27 boulevard du Régent, 1000 Brussels
(02 811 40 00, www.usembassy.be).*

Australian Embassy
*6-8 rue Guimard, 1040 Brussels
(02 286 05 00, www.belgium.
embassy.gov.au).*

British Embassy
*10 avenue d'Auderghem, 1040
Brussels (02 287 62 11, http://
ukinbelgium.fco.gov.uk).*

Canadian Embassy
*2 avenue de Tervuren,
1040 Brussels (02 741 06 11,
www.ambassade-canada.be).*

Irish Embassy
*180 chaussée d'Etterbeek,
1040 Brussels (02 282 34 00,
www.embassyofireland.be).*

New Zealand Embassy
*Level 7, 9-31 avenue des Nerviens,
1040 Brussels (02 512 10 40,
www.nzembassy.com/belgium).*

Internet

In Brussels, Fnac (see p67) also
has a cybercafé.

Cyber City
*Avenue Georges Henri 484-486, 1200
Woluwe-St-Lambert, Brussels (02 733
46 30).*

Mie Katoen
*Kleine Kraaiwijk 10, 2000 Antwerp
(03 231 13 09, www.miekatoen.com).*

Bean Around the World
*Genthof 5, 8000 Bruges (50 70 35 72,
www.beanaroundtheworld.com).*

Opening hours

Most shops open from 9am to 6pm,
often closing on Sunday.
Department stores open until 9pm
on one day a week, often Friday.

Most museums open 9am to 5pm
Tuesday to Saturday, and often on
Sunday. Many close on Monday,
and during the winter months. It's
always worth checking before
making a special journey.

Pharmacies

Pharmacie Van Damme
*Rue de Louvain 22, 1000 Brussels
(32 2 511 32 93).*

City Pharma
*Kammenstraat 61, 2000 Antwerp
(03 232 77 55).*

Multipharma
Park 7, 8000 Bruges (50 33 64 69).

Police stations

For the police, call **101**.

Brussels Central Police Station
*30 rue du Marché au Charbon (02 279
79 79, www.polbru.be).*

Antwerp Police Headquarters
*Oudaan 5, 2000 Antwerpen (03 338
55 11, http://politie.antwerpen.be).*

Bruges Police Station
*Lodewijk Coiseaukaai 2, 8000
Bruges (32 50 44 88 44, www.
politiebrugge.be).*

Post

Post offices are generally open
9am to 5pm Monday to Friday.
    For postal information and to
find your nearest post office, visit
www.post.be.

Brussels Central Post Office
*1 boulevard Anspach, Lower Town
(02 226 21 11). Métro/pré-métro
De Brouckère.*

Antwerp De Post
*Groenplaats 43, 2000 Antwerp
(22 012345, www.depost.be).*

Bruges De Post
*Markt 5, 8000 Bruges
(22 012345
www.depost.be).*

ESSENTIALS

Smoking

Smoking in confined public places is illegal. This includes train stations (except open-air platforms) and restaurants (unless an eaterie has a separate smoking area).

Telephones

From within Belgium, dial the city code and number (Antwerp 03, Bruges 050, Brussels 02, Ghent 09), even when in the city itself.

To call Belgium from abroad, dial the international access code, then 32, then drop the 0 from each city code. See www.goldenpages.be or http://whitepages.truvo.be for phone numbers. As mobile phones now dominate, like elsewhere, public telephone booths are a rarity, but look in stations, post offices and close to the Grand'Place. Telephone cards are sold at newsstands, post offices, train stations and supermarkets.

Operator assistance
1324 all languages.
Directory enquiries
1405 (English enquiries for numbers).

Time

Belgium is on Central European Time, one hour ahead of GMT, six hours ahead of US Eastern Standard Time.

Tipping & VAT

Service and VAT are included in hotel and restaurant prices, though people often throw in a few extra euros if the service has been exceptional. Tips are also included in metered taxi fares, although taxi drivers expect extra tips from foreigners. At cinemas and theatres, tipping the attendant 20c to 50c for a programme is expected.

Tourist information

See www.belgiumtheplaceto.be, www.visitflanders.co.uk and www.visitbelgium.com.

Brussels Info Point (BIP)
2-4 rue Royale, Upper Town (02 513 89 40, www.biponline.be). **Open** 9am-6pm daily.
There is also a small tourist office in the Hôtel de Ville on the Grand' Place, same contact details as above.
Toerisme Antwerpen
Grote Markt 13, 2000 Antwerpen (03 232 01 03, www.antwerpen.be). **Open** 9am-5.45pm Mon-Sat; 9am-4.45pm Sun.
Toerisme Brugge
Stationsplein 5, 8000 Bruges (50 44 46 46, www.brugge.be). **Open** 10am-5pm Mon-Fri; 10am-2pm Sun.

What's on

The Bulletin
www.ackroyd.be
Brussels' English-language weekly, with listings.
Kiosque
www.kiosque.be
Pocket-sized, French-language monthly listings mag with English section.
The Ticket
www.theticket.be
Pocket-sized listings magazine in French and Dutch.

Visas

EU nationals and citizens of Iceland, Monaco, Norway, Liechtenstein and Switzerland can enter Belgium without a visa. EU nationals only need to show a valid national ID card. Citizens of Australia, Canada, New Zealand, Japan and the United States can enter Belgium for three months without a visa. For longer stays, apply to your Belgian consulate.

Vocabulary

Although it is officially bilingual (Flemish and French), Brussels is largely French-speaking. For this reason, we have usually referred to Brussels' streets and sights by their French name. In town, all street signs are given in both languages, as they are on our maps.

French is also the language of Wallonia (the south), while Flemish, a dialect of Dutch, is the language of Flanders (the north), where Antwerp and Bruges are found. Note that Belgians say *septante*, *huitante* and *nonante* instead of the the French *soixante-dix*, *quatre-vingt* and *quatre-vingt-dix*.

English is widely spoken in Brussels and Flanders, but attempts to speak French in Flanders will fall on deaf ears at best. It's a politically vexed issue; if you can't speak Dutch, use English.

Words and phrases are listed in English, then French, then Dutch (with pronunciation for Dutch given in brackets).

General expressions

Good morning/hello bonjour *hallo* ('hullo'), *dag* ('daarg'); **good evening** bonsoir *goedenavond* ('hoo-dun-aav-ond'); **goodbye** au revoir *tot ziens* ('tot zeens'), *dag* ('daarg'); **how are you?** comment allez-vous? *hoe maakt u het?* ('hoo markt oo hut'); **OK** d'accord *okay, in orde* ('in order'), *goed* ('hoot'); **yes** oui *ja* ('yah'); **no** non *nee* ('nay'); **please** s'il vous plaît *alstublieft* ('als-too-bleeft'); **thank you** merci *dank u* ('dank oo'), *bedankt* (bur-dankt'); **how much?/how many?** combien? *hoeveel, wat kosthet?* ('hoofail' 'vot cost hut'); **I would like** je voudrais *ik wil graag* ('ick will hraak'); **toilet** WC *toilet* ('twalet'); **do you know the way to?** est-ce que vous savez où se trouve? *weet u de weg naar?* ('vait oo de veg nar'); **left/right** gauche/droite *links/rechts* ('links'/'reckts'); **do you speak English?** parlez-vous anglais? *spreekt u Engels?* ('spraykt oo engels?'); **I don't understand** je ne comprends pas *ik begrijp het niet* ('ick be-gripe hut neet'); **open/closed** ouvert/fermé *open/gesloten* ('open'/'he-slo-tun').

Accommodation

Do you have a room? avez-vous une chambre? *heeft u een kamer* ('hay-ft oo an kam-er'); **for two people?** pour deux personnes? *voor twee personen?* ('vor tway per-sone-an'); **double bed** un grand lit *een tweepersoonsbed* ('an tway per-sones-bed'); **with bathroom/shower** avec salle de bain/douche *met badkamer/douche* ('mat bat camer/doosh'); **expensive/cheap** cher/pas cher *duur/goedkoop* ('doer/hoot-cope').

At the restaurant

I'd like to reserve a table je voudrais réserver un table *ik zou graag een tafel reserveren* ('ick zoo hraak an ta-full ray-sir-va-run'); **for two people/at eight o'clock** pour deux personnes/a vingt heures *voor twee personen/om acht uur* ('for tway per-sone-an/om acht oor'); **the bill, please** l'addition, s'il vous plaît *mag ik de rekening, alstublieft?* ('mach ick de ray-cun-ing, als-too-bleeft'); **two beers, please** deux bières, s'il vous plaît *twee bieren/pilsjes/pintjes, alstublieft* ('tway beer-an/pils-yes/pint-yes, als-too-bleeft').

ESSENTIALS

Index

Sights & Areas

Eating & Drinking

ESSENTIALS

ESSENTIALS

The travel apps city lovers have been waiting for…

Apps and maps work offline with no roaming charges

Search for 'Time Out Guides' in the app store

timeout.com/iphonecityguides